Successful Kitchen Operation
and Staff Management Handbook

Successful Kitchen Operation and Staff Management Handbook

J. A. Van Duyn

Management Consultant
on human and material resources

Contributor to restaurant
and food service industry journals

Prentice-Hall, Inc.
Englewood Cliffs, New Jersey

Prentice-Hall International, Inc., *London*
Prentice-Hall of Australia, Pty. Ltd., *Sydney*
Prentice-Hall of Canada, Ltd., *Toronto*
Prentice-Hall of India Private Ltd., *New Delhi*
Prentice-Hall of Japan, Inc., *Tokyo*
Prentice-Hall of Southeast Asia Pte. Ltd., *Singapore*
Whitehall Books, Ltd., *Wellington, New Zealand*

© 1979 by
Prentice-Hall, Inc.
Englewood Cliffs, N.J.

Library of Congress Cataloging in Publication Data

Van Duyn, J   A
    Successful kitchen operation and staff management
handbook.

    Bibliography: p.
    Includes index.
    1. Restaurant management.   2. Food service
management.   I. Title.
TX911.3.M27V36   658'.91'64795   79-4340
ISBN 0-13-863027-5

Printed in the United States of America

How This Book Will Help You Profit

Here's an easy-to-read, easy-to-adapt, practical guide to successful kitchen management. This handy book is written for the profit-oriented kitchen operator who wants to become more efficient and more successful. The tested and proven ways in this one-stop source show you how to plug all kitchen operation gaps and boost your bottom line results to increments of hundreds of thousands of dollars. More, this book gives you the "secret" success formulas of the country's most profitable restaurants, both single and chain operations.

Successful Kitchen Operation and Staff Management Handbook was written in response to a very real need in the Restaurant and Food Services industry for a clear, concise and, above all, easy-to-read *practical* guide for field-tested successful kitchen operations and staff management. To emphasize the pertinence of the book, I have interviewed highly successful operators of both one-store units and restaurant chains, as well as top people in the marketing and produce fields. These interviews—included in the appropriate sections—are empirical illustrations of the text. The systems and procedures apply equally to restaurant or food service enterprises.

Naturally, a particular method or procedure that works well for one restaurateur or one institutional food service operator may not work for another. Each must adapt to individual situations. Nevertheless, this book offers something never before published anywhere: insight into the *actual* procedures and operations of a large variety of successful kitchen operators/restaurateurs.

This helpful book offers you ready-to-use working tools for profitable managerial planning and control. The step-by-step instructions will enable you to achieve a highly satisfactory Profit and Loss (P&L) Statement at the end of your accounting period, whether you're operating a small, medium, or large restaurant, a fast-food chain store, or an institutional food service unit. In addition, the illustrations include a catalog of the actual forms used by highly successful restaurants. These sample forms include Daily Forecasting (the most important form for effective kitchen operations control), Food Order, Food Inventory, Steak Count, Top Cutting Summary, and Beverage Inventory; while the appendix contains a sampling of a financial overview of the restaurant business, generated by one of the best known CPA firms, Laventhol and Horwath.

It's a well-known fact that the key to any profitable business is planning and control, but in kitchen management, control is the very lifeblood of profitable operations. Even a temporary relaxing of controls in any part of kitchen operation can be very expensive. Continuous neglect of controls can result in death, i.e., bankruptcy of the restaurant or food service operation. Consequently, you must establish a simple but effective control system that alerts you *immediately* to any problem or potential problem. In a single operation, a control system can be manual, but in a chain restaurant operation, because of the widespread units, it is advisable to run the controls via an economical mini-computer system. Whether using manual or data processing methods, you, the manager, must have a detailed report every ten days, or three times a month, so that you can stay on top of every transaction in your kitchen operation.

In sum, this book brings you fresh, new, but field-tested methods in kitchen management. The techniques offered can be used immediately for complete control over your operations and subsequent increase in your restaurant or food service unit productivity and sales.

98 WAYS THIS BOOK WILL HELP YOU BOOST PROFITS IN YOUR KITCHEN OPERATIONS

5 Key Ingredients to Successful Kitchen Staff Management

A large number of profitable restaurants maximize the individual contributions of their people by applying the philosophy that a "home-grown" management staff, well versed in operational procedures, can best contribute to the establishment and achievement of their goals.

See Chapter 11 for tested, modern approaches in this field that will significantly increase your staff's contributions as well as your profits.

12 Tested Ways to Control Prime Cost

The largest expense item in a kitchen operation is prime cost, which is comprised of food, beverage, and payroll. "Typically, 65¢ out of every dollar in restaurant sales consists of prime cost."* Consequently, the prime cost *must* be both cost controlled and quality controlled.

You start to control the cost of food and beverages with the forecasting step, and you continue right through with purchasing, ordering, receiving, storing, preparing (such as standard portions in food), and serving meals and drinks. You do quality control parallel to the above procedures by inspecting, checking (sometimes double checking), and measuring all food and beverages. This is an on-going, daily process which is as necessary in a kitchen operation as controlling the raw material that goes into the manufacturing of any product.

See Chapter 1 for a detailed description of ways to control prime cost—also, for pros and cons on manual and data processing report systems that keep you

Profitable Restaurant Management, by K.I. Solomon & N. Katz, Prentice-Hall, 1974, p. 33.

up to date on everything in your operation, thus enabling you to control prime cost.

7 Ways to Pick Lean, Charged-Up Line Managers and Staff

Since the essence of any service organization, such as a restaurant, is its people, it is critical that the people who staff your operations meet *your* requirements insofar as performing their tasks and responsibilities goes. To ensure this, *before* you hire anybody, identify and define the knowledge, skills, and personal characteristics that *you* feel are needed for each job in your operation. Next, draw up policies and procedures for evaluating individual productivity, recognizing merit, and rewarding accomplishments.

See Chapter 12 for a detailed description of how to write meaningful job descriptions, evaluation sheets, and all the other necessary forms. Sample forms accompany the text.

10 Ways to Overcome the Most Common Kitchen Crises

There isn't a kitchen manager in the world who hasn't been faced, at the most inappropriate time (Secretaries Week or Mother's Day, among others), with discoveries such as these: the chef, or the bartender, or one of the waiters or waitresses has a drinking problem; the meat cutter enjoys verbal confrontations; the dishwasher, icemaker, or some other essential machine broke down; the temperamental cashier walked out.

See Chapter 13 for case histories of how kitchen operators across the country have handled the human side of restaurant management; from the problem drinker to an argumentative employee, from the kitchen prima donna to the indolent worker, this key section gives answers. In addition, this chapter offers you a fail-safe method for ensuring yourself against relying on any one machine.

5 Ways to Control Administrative and Occupation Costs

Unless strictly controlled, administrative expenses can skyrocket. And, while occupation costs are more or less fixed items, they too need close policing.

See Chapter 5 for proven ways you can control administrative/overhead costs such as printing, stationery and office supplies, telephone, professional fees, protection and bank pick-up, credit card commissions, and bad debts. The chapter also provides ways to slash occupation costs which include rent, property taxes, interest and insurance, all illustrated with examples of substantial savings.

9 Ways of Increasing Productivity and Sales with a Motivated Kitchen Staff

By positively motivating your employees, you increase their productivity and your sales. But this can only be done when the climate you set is right.

See Chapter 12 for what is a "proper" environment, and how, through sound personnel policy covering wages, benefits, and appropriate training, you can have enthusiastic, dedicated employees, who take pride in their job and their place of work.

6 Ways to Select and Handle Purveyors/Vendors

A large restaurant chain may not have problems with purveyors, since vendors will vie with each other to get a large account. However, such is not the case with small and even medium size single restaurants, as managers of such kitchen operations know too well.

See Chapter 6 for selection criteria of purveyors, and for a fail-safe way to ensure that your vendors compete with each other in pleasing you as to both price and quality. The method works whether your monthly order to any particular vendor is $2,000 or $200,000.

7 Ways to Maximize "Customer Satisfaction" and Build Your Reputation

Maximizing your customers' satisfaction is another way of increasing volume with *no* increase in personnel.

See Chapter 7 for the "small" details that you might overlook, but which, nevertheless, affect customer satisfaction. One example: see to it that the person who takes reservations for lunch or dinner has a pleasant manner, a warm voice, and a good vocabulary. And, especially important, that he or she is courteous. Managers would be surprised to learn how many customers they lose by a brusque "Make it fast," "Don't bother me," "Too busy," "Yeah, sure" type of person on the telephone taking reservations.

This chapter also shows you that the big *plus* is not *always* expensive entrees. While the specialty of the nationally known and highly successful restaurant chain, Victoria Station, is prime rib, the famous Perry's of San Francisco specializes in eggs benedict, burgers, and London broil. Moreover, Perry's high profit items are the egg dishes. Then also, other restaurants are famous for their corned-beef sandwich, matzoball soup, sauerbraten, etc. In sum, many successful restaurants built their reputation for good food on simple dishes.

5 Ways to Stay Within Your Budget

When you operate a small or medium size restaurant, though you may not have an accounting background, you must—if you want to stay in business and *even* prosper—have a smattering of the basic accounting techniques.

See Chapter 4 for a guaranteed system that shows you not only how to stay within your budget, but also how to get your daily percentage of profit. It gives you precise accounting procedures that enable you to know to a penny your overhead, or as auditors call it, your administrative and occupation costs.

In addition, this chapter gives you a functional, simple accounts payable system which shows you how to divide your journal into three separate sections. These are: (1) who is to be paid—the Purveyor/Vendor Section; (2) what is to be paid—the Voucher Section, and (3) when—the Date Section. Thus, at all times you have complete control over the vendor payments, discounts, and cash commitments. In addition, the chapter shows you step by step how to set up your sales journal and general ledger. All information is accompanied by examples and forms.

5 Secrets of Inventory Control Through Forecasting

Many successful restaurants no longer use the "traditional" inventory control. Instead, they implement the much more accurate and timely "Forecasting" method, which involves purchasing, ordering, receiving, and storing.

See Chapter 2 for the tested and proven method of restaurant operation forecasting. The chapter also gives you tested techniques for establishing quality control in your receiving procedures. The technique will insure not only accurate quantity, size and weight, but perhaps most important, that the quality of the merchandise adheres to your order qualifications. In addition, the easy-to-apply first-in-first-out inventory system ensures that no food is wasted in either dry or refrigerated products.

6 Ways to Boost Your Cash Flow via the Most Up-to-Date Methods

A business, just like a person, cannot stand still; it needs to grow. But growth requires money. In a kitchen operation this money for growth has to come from retained earnings and cash flow. *See Chapter 15* for a money-saving tool: low-cost, small business computers.

See Chapter 3 for tested and proven methods for systemizing your kitchen operations and organizing all tasks via an activity chart; for reducing direct operating expenses such as laundry, linen and/or linen rental, china, glassware and silver, cleaning and cleaning supplies, all of which contribute to a dramatic boost in your cash flow. *See Chapter 15* for a money-saving tool: low-cost, small business computers.

4 Ways to Get the Most Out of Your Marketing/Advertising Dollars

Some successful restaurants engage in aggressive marketing without any traditional advertising or promotion. However, such restaurants usually have an outstanding public relations person on their payroll full time. No matter which media you use for promoting your place of operations, it should be in accord not only with the type of food and beverages you serve, but also with the style and decor and climate of your place.

See Chapter 10 for advice from top restaurateurs on how to get the most out of your dollars spent on advertising and marketing. This applies whether you're using radio, television, newspapers, magazines, promotion and entertainment, outdoor, direct mail, or whatever.

See Chapter 4 for a simple, legible audit checklist to show you the present status of your kitchen operation down to the last detail, highlighting your productivity index to show day-by-day progress.

17 Ways to Avoid the Most Common Pitfalls in Kitchen Staff Management

No matter how capable a manager is, he cannot possibly supervise everything everywhere in his business. And the most common pitfall in kitchen staff management is not delegating tasks and responsibilities. If you have hired the right people and set the right climate, you can delegate responsibilities with confidence. They will be galvanized to live up to your expectations. *See Chapter 14* for pointing out how to avoid these common pitfalls in kitchen staff management. *See Chapter 8* for dealing with the country-wide major problem of the FDA interpretation of the sanitation codes. *See Chapter 9* for a explanation of who, what, and where about OSHA and the OSHA recordkeeping; also, the latest forms, OSHA No. 200 and No. 101.

Scientific management of the kitchen and staff is what this handbook is all about. The systematic approach to high level profits is set forth in the following pages, offering clear-cut practical procedures for meeting the increasingly tough challenge of escalating the restaurant and food service organization's bottom line.

J. A. Van Duyn

ACKNOWLEDGMENTS

The author is deeply grateful to the individuals listed below for allowing themselves to be interviewed, and for sharing their experiences, knowledge, and successful methods with the readers.

Bruno Andrighetto—Vice President, Lee Ray-Trantino Co.
Arnold Ertola—Owner/Manager, Shenanigans Restaurant
J. Edward Fleishell—Owner, Le Club Restaurant
Jon Larrick—Vice President of Marketing, Velvet Turtle
Al Levie—President, Gulliver's Restaurant Chain
George McCullagh—Director of Support Services, Victoria Station
Jack Rowe—Owner/Manager, Midway
Doug Scott—Director of Food Purchasing, Victoria Station
Jim Thomson—Owner/Manager, Pacific Cafe Restaurants
Ismael Venegas—Director of Food standards, Tia Maria and Red
    Onion
Lou Vincent—Owner/Manager, Vincent's Tavern
Mike Walsh—Owner, The Holding Company Restaurant

Table of Contents

chain of command ● Establish top authority; establish standards ● Enforce quality control

Chapter 12: Setting the Right Climate to Boost Your Kitchen Productivity

Chapter Highlights ● 133
Utilizing Human Resources ● 133
The Ten-Point Kitchen Productivity Booster Checklist ● 134
Job Profile ● 135
Periodic Restaurant Evaluation Report ● 138

Chapter Highlights ● 149

Mediate little personal grievances quickly; don't let them grow into big problems ● Restaurant business is teamwork ● How to deal with an employee's drinking problem ● Dealing with closet cases ● The employer-employee relationship ● Enforce your set of rules ● Crisis management ● You have to plan ahead ● $$$-saving idea ● Don't get caught short-handed ● When there is spur-of-the-moment termination ● Rule of thumb in employee relationship ● Employees should know where they stand with raises ● Keep communication lines open between you and your staff ● Earn your staff's respect ● Two different kinds of drinking problems ● Should an employer counsel an employee? ● When an employee's life style causes problems ● Proper relationship with your employees ● A professional cannot afford to be temperamental ● Every drinking problem is different ● How to handle closet cases ● Try working out problems with employees ● Whan a guy deserves a break ● Good management is prepared for employees ● The handy back-up list

Chapter Highlights ● 159

Ensure that your staff is aware of your cost of doing business ● Check often quality control in your kitchen ● The manager should supervise the work, not do the work ● Manager must communicate and delegate ● Effective management ideas ● Your restaurant is a reflection of your personality ● If you have a problem in your restaurant, you are responsible for it ● When managers don't know good food ● One man's reason for going into the restaurant business ● A restaurant is only as good as its chef ● Catering to your target customers ● How to keep up high standards ● How to solve the "favoritism" problem ● Staff discipline themselves ●

Quality makes a restaurant • Friendly relationships make a kitchen operation • Don't ever forget: people work for the money, but the big plus is congenial job atmosphere • Take interest in employees' problems • Staff-motivating idea • Ways to encourage your chef's creativeness • An extra incentive: year-end bonus • A common pitfall: the fallacy of "hard selling" • The usual effect of "hard-sell" technique • Trick in selling: be helpful but not pushy in selecting food and wine • Selling is a question of degree • When you hire a chef

Kitchen Staff • 165

A chef should pick his own staff

Manager's role • 165

Lighting and music—critical for creating appropriate atmosphere • Importance of staff's clean hands and nails • Pros and cons of the family-like relationship • Quality restaurants vs. show places • Teaching a manager to delegate • Develop potential of subordinates

**Successful Kitchen Operation
and Staff Management Handbook**

PART ONE
Kitchen Operation

1

How to Control Prime Cost
for Successful Restaurant
and Food Service Management

CHAPTER HIGHLIGHTS

The difference of opinion among established restauranteurs as to what constitutes "prime cost" is well known in the industry. Some restaurant operators claim that prime cost is comprised of food and liquor alone; while others hold firmly that in today's world of union wages (or pay rates competitive with union wages), labor is a definite cost factor. Thus, according to the latter group it is a combination of food, liquor, *and* labor that makes up prime cost. Both groups, however, agree that controlling and monitoring prime cost are prerequisites for operating a profitable restaurant. The consensus, in fact, extends further. They concur that to *effect* food cost control, a realistic determination of the cost of all food items on the menu, including the "give-away" items such as bread, butter, and salad, is a MUST. Moreover, this calculation of cost on the pro forma—i.e., the forecasting of the amount—and the forecasting of the *actual* amount and the *actual* cost percentage on a formal or informal form must be done *before* each new restaurant or branch opens. Then after the restaurant begins to operate, by checking the figures, the actual operating figures against the projected costs at regular, short intervals, the restaurateur exercises firm control over the food cost as well as quality.

As you know, liquor cost requires even stricter control than food cost. Consequently, whether there is a separate bar in the restaurant or not, experienced restaurateurs check daily or twice a week the liquor sale against the stock as well as against the original pro-forma liquor percentage. And it goes without saying that a restaurant owner cannot stay in business unless the cost of labor is monitored as stringently as food and liquor. Thus, all restaurant operators are in accord about the tedious albeit necessary work that has to be done *before* each restaurant or branch opens, and about the continuous, close checking *after* each restaurant opens. The reason is simple: this method provides a steady control of prime cost, which in turn effects a well-run, successful business.

Mechanics of Controlling Food Cost

While different restaurateurs have different ways of projecting food cost, here's a very basic, simple technique that you might use to ascertain what your primary cost is going to be *prior* to the opening of a restaurant. The most important factor in this method is defining realistically the cost of all food items on the menu. This, as you know, is an exacting but mandatory task for setting up a profitable business.

Within this matrix you apply control over your food cost:

- Prior to the opening of each restaurant or branch
- Three weeks or so after the restaurant starts operating
- Regularly every two weeks or ten days for the duration of your business.

Prior to the Opening of Each Restaurant or Branch

Food Cost

Whether your restaurant is your first, third or thirtieth enterprise, it's a mistake to believe that your food cost will run at 38%—the theoretical median of the industry. Such a concept can handicap you from the start, because when the restaurant opens, the odds are that your food cost is not going to run 38%. Depending on the location, it may run 39 or even 40, or it may run only 36%. And if it runs higher than you expected, it may cause you to fire the chef or do some other irrational acts which subsequently could possibly lead you to bankruptcy. The many failures of both experienced and inexperienced operators in the restaurant field attest to this fact. Yet, by projecting the cost through a simple forecasting method *prior* to the printing of the menu, *prior* to the opening of the restaurant, the restaurateur can assess exactly the percentage his food cost will run.

In using this technique you cost out *every* single entree on your menu. Before you do that, however, you determine the exact weight/measure of your serving portions. Since meat and fish are the costliest items, you "portion-control" these items first. But vegetables, potatoes, and salads would have to be portion-controlled also.

Once you have decided on the serving portions, you check what the merchandise—meat, fish, and vegetables—sold at for a whole year, and base your costing on the average of the entire period. If you are costing zucchini, for example, you don't want to take that day's market price. You contact your produce man. If he tells you that zucchini has sold from a low of $2.00 a crate up to a high of $8.00 a crate the past year, the average will be $5.00 a crate—the amount you base your costing on.

As you know, some recipes—that is, some entrees—may require separate costing. For instance, if it is stuffed meat, fish, avocado, or whatever, you need to take into account the cost of the stuffing as well as the cost of the meat, fish, avocado, or tomato. Next, let's assume that you have ten items on the menu (whether your new unit will be a limited menu restaurant specializing in specific entrees, or a general restaurant), and you are forecasting your prime cost for 100 meals on the pro forma. You cost each one of the ten items, based on the average market price and the measure/yield of the portion. With certain items, however, you cannot take yields the usual way. To illustrate: you or your chef prepare a sauce to go over a meat or fish entree, and it costs $10.00. You cannot just add the weight of the ingredients and take your yield. It wouldn't be accurate. A much better way is to prepare the sauce, portion it out, and base your cost on how many portions you can get. As you probably know, you are always going to have less than the total weight of your recipe because some of the sauce goes off in steam, some of it gets stuck on the side of the pot, and some of it is just plain wasted.

There are other costs that are rather difficult to define prior to the opening of a restaurant because you cannot accurately estimate how much the customer will consume of certain give-away items.

a. The Give-Away Items

Even though bread, butter, salad, or a cup of soup and all of the condiments are not expensive items, their costs are significant enough to warrant your spending a few minutes to try to estimate them properly *prior* to the opening of each new restaurant. In other words, since the give-away items are part of the total cost of each entree on the menu, their costs have to be computed also. Take bread, for example. If your new branch or restaurant is in an unfamiliar location, you can arrive at an approximate cost by calling other restaurants or people you know in the industry, or your bread company. Actually, the bread company would be able to give you the most accurate figures to work with.

CASE IN POINT

"Before we open a restaurant," says Jim Thomson, part-owner and manager of the successful California chain, Pacific Cafe restaurants, well known for excellent seafood at reasonable prices, "we determine the cost of all sale items *and* the cost of the give-away items such as salad. We know exactly what we put into the salad; what the break is going to be on the salad dressings; how many people are going to order blue cheese as opposed to the less expensive Italian dressing; and we try to arrive at a cost figure. We believe that the time spent on computing the cost of give-away items is worth our effort, because so far we've never been off more than a cent or two. For example, in our latest store on Ghirardelli Square in San Francisco, we estimated the cost of give-away items on each entree at 45¢. And in fact, it runs 46¢."

b. Sales/Product Mix

Once you have compiled your forecast amount for each item on your list, sales/product mix is the next factor to be taken into consideration. Sales/ product mix gives you the number of various items sold on any given day. Actually the sales/product mix at this juncture is hypothetical, since there is no way of knowing the true sales/product mix until the restaurant has been open for a month or so. Nevertheless, if you plan to open another restaurant that will specialize in seafood, or prime rib, or any other specific entree, you *know* that the sale of that item is going to be high. So you lean in your projected sales/

product mix toward the items you are going to feature, as well as the favorites that are known sellers. Consequently, in the sales/product mix column, after each item note your estimated figure of how well that particular item is going to sell.

If the sales/product mix adds up to more or less than 100—the previously defined number of meals—simply add or subtract from the items you have over- or under-estimated. Then take a long hard look at your estimate. Does it look accurate? For example, you may say, "Come to think of it, I don't believe we'll sell as many New York steaks as London broils." And so you reduce the number of New York steaks and increase the number of London broils on your pro forma.

c. How to Calculate the Actual Food Cost

When you use this simple technique, you take your forecast amount and multiply it by the sales/product mix figures. To illustrate: if you estimated that you're going to sell ten of your #1 entree, and your food cost on that item is $3.50 *plus* 45¢ (the estimated cost of your give-away items on each entree), the total cost of this particular entree is ten x $3.95, or $39.50. Thus, you take one item after another on your list of ten entrees, and apply to each the same calculation.

THE ½% GENERAL
EFFICIENCY FACTOR

Next, in order to get the true actual food cost of each of your entrees, as well as the actual food cost percentage, you must also allow for the *general efficiency factor:* the unavoidable waste element. This amount usually runs ½, or at the most ¾, of a percent of each item. The general efficiency factor's percentage depends on what type of food you are going to serve, and what will have to be thrown out at the end of the evening. For example, certain vegetables, sauces, and other items cannot be used to the last ounce. Consequently, some of these will have to be "86."

When you have multiplied your forecast amounts by your sales/product mix figures, take a look at the next column—the sell price. In this column write your previously determined sell price of each of the ten listed entrees. Next, you multiply the sell price of #1 entree by ten (the sales/product mix for this entree), and repeat the same procedure for all your entrees. Thus, your actual food cost for #1 entree will be: $3.50 plus 45¢ plus 2¢ (general efficiency factor) times 10 = $39.70; while in the sell price column you have #1 entree—$11.50 x 10 = $115.00

d. How to Calculate the Actual Food Cost Percentage

You simply divide the actual food cost by the sell price, then multiply the resulting figure by 100 (or move the decimal point to the right by two) and you get the actual food cost percentage. For example, your #1 entree's food cost is $3.50 plus 45¢ (give-away item), plus 2¢ (efficiency factor) totaling $3.97. If you are going to sell #1 entree at $11.50, then your actual food cost percentage on that particular item is 34.5%. That is, you divide the $3.97 by $11.50, resulting in 0.3452, which multiplying by 100 (or moving the decimal point to the right by two) comes out to 34.5%. Subsequently you calculate the actual food cost percentage of each one of your listed entrees, thus completing your food cost pro forma. Some of your items of course will run higher, while some will run lower. But it should average out to your predetermined actual food cost percentage. (A sample food cost pro forma is shown in Figure 1-1.)

NOTE: In case it slipped your mind, generally, the more expensive an item, the higher your food cost is going to be. For example, the breakfast cookery runs a low food cost, while a steak house runs a high food cost. Also, if your actual food cost figures come out too high on the pro forma in comparison to the sell price, you have to make some adjustments. Perhaps the sell price is too low; perhaps the food cost is too high. If you have done a thorough market research for your new restaurant or branch, and you are convinced that your sell price is in line with other restaurants offering similar quality items at similar locations, then it is your food cost that is too high. And you will have to reduce your food cost one way or another.

PRIME COST PRO FORMA

Item	Forecast Amt.	Sell Price	Act. Amt.	Act. %
#1	$3.50 + 45¢ + 2¢ x 10 = $39.70	$11.50 x 10 = $115.00	$39.70	34.5%
#2	$4.35 + 45¢ + 2¢ x 8 = $38.56	$12.50 x 8 = $100.00	$38.56	38.5%
#3	$1.25 + 45¢ + 2¢ x 15 = $25.80	$ 5.50 x 15 = $ 82.50	$25.80	31.2%
#4				
#5				
#6				
#7				
#8				
#9				
#10				

FIGURE 1-1

Conversely, Al Levie, president of the highly successful two-state Gulliver's Restaurant chain, says:

A FORMULA FOR SUCCESS

I think that the restaurateurs who are using the historical concept of pricing their menus based on food cost are essentially missing a marketing opportunity. Let me give you an actual case history. A number of years ago a phenomenon happened in the restaurant business: Chuck's Steak House opened. Chuck Rolls, the owner, a bright young man and a graduate of Cornell's hotel school, didn't pay any attention to food cost. Basing his price on market research, he was selling his steaks for about $3.75. (That's probably what he sold it for in those days.) Anyway, he ran a very, very high food cost: 50% or more. But his combined food, labor, and liquor was probably under 70%, giving him at least a 30% for overhead and profit. He made a lot of money. In essence, he was blocking himself in with quality by buying meat from a quality company. Consequently, he had a quality product which he sold at competitive price, resulting in a tremendous volume. This in turn caused his cost of occupancy, labor cost, and his overhead cost percentages to drop, so that even though his food cost percentage was around 50, he was able to work with a prime cost below the 70% mark.

Our criterion for prime cost on food, liquor, and labor is 65% in our stores. That's what we shoot for. When we opened the first Gulliver's restaurant, we threw out the old-fashioned idea of pricing our menu on food cost. If we did, we'd be charging $10.00 for prime rib today. And, instead of doing $2 million in this Burlingame, California, restaurant, for example, we'd be lucky if we did a million and a quarter dollars. When our prime cost goes up, or when our gross profit margin diminishes, we know it's time to make some adjustments. Since we do not change our product quality, nor the size of our portions, we do our cost effectiveness through the use of the "management by exception" method. In our restaurants management by exception is a strong basis.

In the last three weeks, for example, the onion market went from like $4.50 a sack to $19.50 a sack. Since a sack contains fifty pounds of onions, that's like going from 9¢ a pound to 39¢ a pound. Well, we happen to use an awful lot of onions in one of our dishes. It's our spinach on the dinner menu. Why, we probably use 700 pounds of prepared onions a week. So, when our cost on onions rose dramatically in a three-week period, we did some adjusting. We started buying what is called "pieces" from the people who slice onions for firms who sell onion rings. We are able to buy onion pieces at 15¢ a pound, which means that we went from a cost of 39¢ a pound on onions down to 15¢ a pound simply by using an alternative that, nevertheless, does not lower the quality of our product. Of course, we don't buy pieces unless the onion market is out of line. But this is one example of what can be done when the food cost rises; of how to save $$$$ via management cost effectiveness.

In summary: to insure yourself against any unexpected high food cost, do your homework *before* you open a new restaurant or branch. In fact, if you have done a thorough preliminary job, your food cost percentage is not going to go higher than a point or two from your estimated figure, and you are not going to go broke.

e. Liquor Cost Percentage and How to Control It

While, as you probably know, the liquor cost is calculated the same way as the food cost, i.e., the estimated cost multiplied by the number of drinks sold, and divided by the selling price, the actual liquor cost percentage should run anywhere from 20 to 25% in order to realize profit. But again, the bar cost depends on the type of store you operate.

Insofar as the control of liquor is concerned, it depends on the size and type of restaurant, as well as the management policy. Arnold Ertola, partner and manager of Shenanigans in San Mateo, California, keeps stringent inventory control over his small but profitable restaurant. Mr. Ertola says:

I've got an inventory system where my liquor is always on par. It's the amount of liquor stock both in the liquor room and behind the bar that is controlled all the time. For example, I know at the beginning of every day that there are 16 bottles of vodka downstairs in the liquor room after I restock them the night before. My control system is simple but effective: there must be 16 bottles of vodka downstairs, whether full or empty. I can go there any time and check it. My fulls and my empties must add up to a given number.

In the same way, my pouring costs I keep within 1/10th%. In other words, I know my liquor costs, and I know my percentages. If you know the percentages going in, and you've determined what your working percentage is, *and* you stay within that percentage, that's all the control you need. At least that's what works for me.

Mr. Levie manages liquor control quite differently.

> We provide our bartenders price lists, recipes, and written procedures that detail our pouring policy, our operating and control policies, as well as other important factors. We provide our bartenders the best equipment, first class liquor—all top brands—and we pour a liberal drink. We use a ¾-ounce jigger with a ¾ ounce over-pour. Our control method is simple: we are structured for profit; we run on a cash basis. We present our bartenders with a weekly profit and lost statement. They know our policy, and they know exactly where they stand, down to the smallest detail.

A PROFIT-ORIENTED LIQUOR CONTROL METHOD

Labor Cost Percentages

All restaurateurs agree on this issue: labor is luxury. Yet its cost should be in direct relation to the food and liquor cost percentages, and the three combined should not go above 60 or 65%.

After the Restaurant Opens

Being an astute business person, after your new branch or restaurant is open for three weeks or a month, you re-examine your daily meal counts, and determine what is your actual operating sales/product mix. When you know those percentages, you check it against your forecasting figures. If it has to be modified, you repeat the same procedures you used prior to the opening of the restaurant, and you get your new, adjusted actual operating food cost percentages. Subsequently, every week, or every two weeks, or every month, you take your inventory and again compute your actual food cost, always checking it against the percentage you have established to ensure that your food cost stays within limits.

Your forecast amount on your give-away items such as, for example, the salad, is also re-computed, based on what the ingredients are costing you in actual operation, and on the number of salads served to customers. In other words, to get the actual operating cost on the salad, you calculate the dressings, the lettuce, and whatever else goes into your salad. The same adjusting process applies to your bread and butter. Then you add them up, and divide by the full number of meals served during the month, or whatever period you decided upon. Of course, catsup, mustard, and all the other condiments are estimated too.

The cost of these is taken off the invoices, added, and divided by the total number of guests served. The figure you arrive at will show your actual operating cost per person for your give-away items. If your actual operating food cost has to be adjusted by a few pennies only, you have no problem. But if your food cost is way above your previously estimated figure, you have to investigate its cause.

It may also happen that your estimated food cost percentage prior to the opening of the restaurant came to 38%, for example. And when you calculate it at the end of the first month of operation, it comes out to 36%. This is possible if the prices during that particular time happen to be lower than the rest of the year. Either way, if you keep a tight control over your prime cost, you are prepared for any fluctuation of costs, and you have a line of pre-planned action all ready.

a. Forms and Their Use

Meal count forms, inventory control forms, and prime cost forms, as all seasoned restaurateurs know, have to be set up carefully, so that they are functional and can be used at a later date to include changes and modifications. (For examples, see Figures 1-2 to 1-5 at the end of this chapter.) Prime cost form, you will agree, is very important, since it displays the cost of your entrees. Unfortunately, meat, fish, produce, and coffee can and do change in price. Consequently, it isn't unusual if you, along with many other restaurateurs, modify the prime cost form as often as four times a month to keep up with the actual food cost. Single restaurants generally use manually maintained forms, while large restaurant chains have computerized forms.

b. In Case of Problem

If your food cost goes up in the new unit, there is no reason for alarm. Everything may be running as well or even better than before. And the food cost has gone up simply because of increase in price of certain items. As long as you have taken such possibility into consideration when drawing up your original estimate and have made allowance for it, you are not going to run into any problem. You simply adjust your actual operating food cost, and continue operating the new branch or restaurant. However, if you suspect some irregularity in your kitchen operation, you don't want to let 30 days go by. That would be compounding the trouble for 30 days. You check and act quickly and decisively.

CASE IN POINT

"The restaurant industry is extremely loose in terms of purchasing," says the owner of a large East Coast quality restaurant chain. "Take, for example, dairy products. You may permit a dairy man to go into your box, see how much product you need, write an order, and deliver it to your box .... We have a rule against such things in our restaurants, but it still happens. Here, in this particular store in New York we were charged every other week for 600 pounds of butter. At least 200 pounds of that we were not getting. Our standard usage of butter in this store is between 180 to 200 pounds a week. Because we do a 'comparative' on usage every week, we were able to get down to specifics on this problem in a relatively short time. And the way I solved it was quite simple. I changed dairies. I didn't waste my time trying to get to the bottom of the situation. I believe very strongly in surveillance. I let my staff here know that I was unhappy. Then I called the dairy company and told them that I wasn't making any accusation, but I couldn't control the situation, and consequently I was changing dairies. That was all. And the problem disappeared."

WEEKLY COMPARATIVE CHECKING FOR COST-EFFICIENCY

Another possible reason for loss in the P/L statement could be misportioning, i.e., serving wrong size portions in a given area. For example, let's assume that one of your entrees is abalone, costing you anywhere from $7.50 to $8.00 or more per pound. Well, if there is a misportioning of one ounce of abalone over a month's period, it can add up to quite a high dollar figure. Thus, once you have pinpointed the problem area, you must immediately stop the misportioning of the abalone or whatever item is the problem.

NOTE: Even experienced restaurant operators sometimes underestimate the importance of having portions predetermined and of having written recipes. Yet these factors are critical. These data must be documented and kept in a book, with the chef in complete charge of it. In sum, everything in the kitchen must be prepared exactly according to the restaurant recipes, and portioned accordingly. And the same predetermined measure applies to the give-away items. For instance, if you have estimated that you are going to serve ten people per one loaf of bread, yet suddenly you find that the restaurant is serving only four people per loaf of bread, you know that you will have to do some investigative work. You may survey to check just exactly how your employees are handling the bread; what their procedure is. If bread is wasted, you know that you will have to have a talk with your staff, pointing out what's wrong. If, for example, the left-over bread is being thrown out instead of being returned for credit, that's money out of your pocket. Or if too much bread is being cut ahead of time, you know that you will have to correct that situation immediately since cut bread cannot be returned for credit. Once you have corrected the error, you determine your loss over the period in which the loss occurred, and add that to the total amount of food cost.

$$$-SAVING HINT

Simply stated, investigating even minor fluctuations in the percentage of your food cost is extremely important in controlling prime cost. If you are working in the new branch or restaurant yourself, even on a part-time basis, constant survey of the employees, insofar as their handling the products and preparing the products according to your specifications, pays off handsomely. In fact, it might make the difference between profit and loss.

CONSTANT SURVEILLANCE: DIFFERENCE BETWEEN PROFIT AND LOSS

A successful New Orleans seafood restaurant management established the control criterion of having the portion of abalone sold at 5⅓ ounces. Since the chef measures the abalone in strict accordance with the management directives and the cooking specifications book, the efficiency factor in this restaurant is a very low ¼% in the actual operating food cost percentage figure.

CASE IN POINT

HOW TO ACHIEVE A ¼% EFFICIENCY FACTOR

Responsibility of Enforcing Control of Food Cost and Quality

Most restaurant owners agree that it is the manager of the restaurant who should be in control of the kitchen operation. He or she consequently should have most of the answers, or should be able to get them within a few minutes. In other words, he should be able to answer everything that concerns the operation of the kitchen and restaurant. He should know, for example, how many customers can be expected on Mondays as compared to Saturdays. He should know how much milk the restaurant uses daily. If his immediate answer is, for example, "Five half-gallons," he knows what is going on. Or if you ask him how much half-and-half the restaurant uses a day, and he responds with "About four quarts," that's fine. However, if the person in charge of the kitchen operations cannot immediately answer such questions, he does not have control over it; ergo, the control falls upon the hourly personnel.

Since usually there are many hourly employees in a restaurant, discrepancies will happen even when the hourly staff are reliable. And one day you may find that the steak, prime rib, abalone, or other entrees served are not the established portions but at least an ounce more or less. That is why restaurateurs place so much importance on selecting the person who will be in charge. After all, it is that particular person's responsibility to know what is going on both in the kitchen and in the public area—down to the minutest detail. Not an easy job by any means.

RIB CUTTING SUMMARY
B101—0774

UNIT _____

MONTH _____

COMPLETE DAILY AND FORWARD TO SAN FRANCISCO AFTER *COB* LAST DAY OF THE MONTH.

DATE	RIB PACKER	RIB CARVER	RIB PRICE/ LB.	RIB YIELD %	RIB COST %	PORTIONS PER RIB	UNCOOKED RIBS ON HAND	RIBS RECEIVED	FRESH RIBS COOKED	UNCOOKED REMAIN	REHEATS ON HAND	REHEATS REMAIN	#RIBS USED
1													
2													
3													
4													
5													
6													
7													
8													
9													
10													
11													
12													
13													
14													
15													
16													
17													
18													
19													
20													
21													
22													
23													
24													
25													
26													
27													
28													
29													
30													
31													

COMMENTS _____

_____

_____

_____ MANAGER _____

FIGURE 1-2   Courtesy of Victoria Station, Inc.

TOP CUTTING SUMMARY
0375

UNIT _____

MONTH _____

COMPLETE DAILY AND FORWARD TO SAN FRANCISCO AFTER *COB* LAST DAY OF THE MONTH.

DATE	TOP PACKER	TOP SUPPLIER	TOP CUTTER	TOP PRICE/ LB.	STEAK YIELD %	KEBOB YIELD %	# BUTTS CUT	TOTAL RAW WEIGHT	# LUNCH STEAKS	# DINNER STEAKS	WEIGHT KEBOB & MEAT		
1													
2													
3													
4													
5													
6													
7													
8													
9													
10													
11													
12													
13													
14													
15													
16													
17													
18													
19													
20													
21													
22													
23													
24													
25													
26													
27													
28													
29													
30													
31													

COMMENTS _____

_____

_____

_____   MANAGER _____

FIGURE 1-3   Courtesy of Victoria Station, Inc.

STEAK COUNT — PRIME RIB ANALYSIS — DESSERT COUNT
0975

TOP CUTTER _____ UNIT _____ DATE _____

PRIME RIB CARVER _____ MANAGER _____

	FILET	TOP SIRLOIN				DESSERT		PRIME RIB	
ON HAND								ON HAND	
RECEIVED								RECEIVED	
TOTAL								TOTAL	
# CUT								# COOKED (+ +)	
UNCUT REMAIN								UNCOOKED REMAIN	
		L	D	L.K.	D.K.	PIE	CAKE	REHEATS AT START	
# ON HAND								# COOKED	
# CUT								TOTAL COOKED RIBS	
TOTAL								REHEATS REMAIN	
CLOSING COUNT								ACTUAL USED	
# USED									(E)
CHECK COUNT								EXPLAIN	
DIFF.									

EXPLAIN _____   EXPLAIN _____

TOP SIRLOIN YIELD — FOR STEAKS

Purveyor _____ Cost/lb. _____

Raw Wt. _____ x 16 oz./lb. = _____ oz.
                               (A)

	Steak Yield	Portion Weight (oz.)	=
L			
D			
K			

Portion Wt. _____ (B)

Steak Yield (B/A) = _____ %

TOP SIRLOIN YIELD — FOR KEBOBS

Purveyor _____ Cost/lb. _____

Raw Wt. _____ x 16 oz./lb. = _____ oz.
                               (E)

Kebob Yield (in ounces) _____
                           (F)

Kebob Yield (F/E) = _____ %
                           (G)

COST OF KEBOB MEAT

Raw Cost Per lb. _____ ÷ Kebob Yield _____ = _____ Kebob Cst./Lb.
                           (G)

RIB YIELD ANALYSIS

Rib Item	Meal Count	x	Portion Weight	=	Yield
LUNCH	_____	x	_____	=	_____
CHILD'S	_____	x	_____	=	_____
# 1	_____	x	_____	=	_____
# 2	_____	x	_____	=	_____
# 3	_____	x	_____	=	_____

PORTION WEIGHT = _____ oz.

PORTION WEIGHT TOTAL ÷ 16 = _____ LBS.
                           (B)

RIB COST ANALYSIS

Rib	Meal Count	x	Menu Price	=	Revenue
LUNCH	_____	x	_____	=	_____
CHILD'S	_____	x	_____	=	_____
# 1	_____	x	_____	=	_____
# 2	_____	x	_____	=	_____
# 1	_____	x	_____	=	_____

TOTAL PORTIONS _____ TOTAL REVENUE _____
                (F)   (D)

RIBS USED

RIBS USED _____ x AVG. WT. _____ = _____ LBS.
      (E)   (A) RAW WT. TOTAL

RIBS USED

RIBS USED _____ x AVG. WT. _____ x COST/ LB. _____ = _____
      (E)   (C) TOT. COST

RIB YIELD ANALYSIS

(B) _____ = _____ %YIELD
(A)

RIB COST ANALYSIS

(C) _____ = _____ % COST
(D) _____ = _____ PERCENTAGE
(F) _____ = _____ AVG. PORTION
(E)   PER RIB

COST PER POUND

RIB _____ SHRIMP _____ DIP _____

TOP _____ FLANK _____ KNUCKLE _____

FILET _____ BURGER _____ BACKRIB _____

FIGURE 1-4   **Courtesy of Victoria Station, Inc.**

INVENTORY TRANSMITTAL
0276

To be completed by Manager and for-
warded to San Francisco with copies of
the Food, Liquor/Beer, Wine, Guest
Supply, Merchandise/Mirror Inventory
after COB last day of the period.

TOTAL OF 50%
EMPYEE DISC.

FOOD INVENTORY		$
Prime Rib	50A11	
Top Sirloin	50A12	
Filet Mignon	50A13	
Shrimp	50A14	
Other Meat	50A15	
Beef Back Ribs	50A16	
Bread & Butter	50A21	
Salad Bar	50A22	
Dairy	50A3	
Mushrooms	50A41	
Potato	50A42	
Produce	50A43	
Beverage	50A51	
	50A52	
Miscellaneous	50A53	
Freight. Storage	50A6	
TOTAL FOOD INVENTORY		

LIQUOR/BEER INVENTORY		$
Bourbon		
Scotch		
Gin		
Vodka		
Tequila		
Rum		
Brandy		
Cognac		
Sherry/Port/Wine		
Miscellaneous		
Beer		
TOTAL LIQUOR/BEER INV	50B1	

WINE INVENTORY		$
House Wine	50B21	
Dessert	50B21	
Bar Cheese	50CC	
Bottle Wine	50B22	
TOTAL WINE INV.		

MIRROR INVENTORY		$
TOTAL SUPPLIES	50MA	

MERCHANDISE INVENTORY		$
TOTAL SUPPLIES	50MB	

GUEST SUPPLIES INVENTORY		$
TOTAL SUPPLIES	70D	

MANAGER'S SIGNATURE

FIGURE 1-5   Courtesy of Victoria Station, Inc.

2

Cost Benefits Inventory Control
Through Restaurant and Food Service
Forecasting Techniques

CHAPTER HIGHLIGHTS

The primary factors which comprise effective inventory control are: detailed record keeping; taking into consideration all the variables that can affect the number of meals served; planning according to the most current variables; counting meal tickets as each luncheon and dinner progresses; paying strict attention to "product mix," and forecasting not only the amount of products needed but the amount of cost and profit as well. Before you can take these steps, however, you must know "everything" about the products you use. This includes knowing not only the products, but also the people who manufacture or grow these products, whether it be grocery items, meat, dairy, or bakery products. In other words, for true efficacy you must establish a rapport with your distributors, manufacturers, and producers. If you fail to do this, you may employ the best inventory control and forecasting method, but unless you work *with* people and not *against* them, your operation will be neither efficient nor effective.

Principal Components of Profitable Inventory Control

One of the concerns of the restaurateur is that the kitchen should never run short of any product. However, neither does he want to tie up large sums of money in products. This is why effective inventory control through forecasting is so important.

For efficient inventory control the very first thing to do is keep accurate and detailed records by day and meal, and by the number of products served. Moreover, this careful record keeping is not a one-time chore until you set up your inventory control. It is a continual daily task to be done as long as the restaurant is operating.

The merits of this system become obvious after only a month, when just by looking at your records you will know how many hamburgers, cheeseburgers, lunch steaks, shrimp orders, and other entrees were served for lunch on a given day. The continuous use of this method should enable you to ascertain for any given day, even if it was a year ago, which day of the week it was, what the weather was, and if there were any conventions or other events in town that may have affected the volume of meals served in your store. In other words, by keeping a daily log, you will know the variables that contributed to that particular day's business profile.

Because this information is within your reach, when you are getting ready for your Tuesday night dinner, for example, all you have to do is look at your log sheets and check how many dinners you have served the last five Tuesdays that you were open. If you have served an average of 429 dinners for the last five Tuesdays, all things being considered and being equal, you would estimate that again you will serve 429 dinners this Tuesday—or very close to it. Of course, just to be safe, you might want to plan on serving 440 dinners.

Another variable to take into consideration is special events. Are there any large groups in town? Is there a well-known horse racing down at the track? Is the weather fair enough to induce people to go out for dinner? Is there a football game that evening? And the final variable: what was the "product mix" the previous five Tuesdays?

Product Mix

Product mix is the matrix that tells the restaurateur the number of orders that were served of each of the different entrees on any given day. Specifically, it displays how many orders of prime rib were served; how many orders of top sirloin steak were served; how many fillets were served; and how many shrimp orders were served in the restaurant on that day.

Based on the product mix, the restaurateur can state the exact number of prime rib orders, for example, he will have to prepare.

Next, at seven o'clock or so—after you've been open for an hour and a half—count the tickets. If your business volume is extremely slow, you may want to alter the amount of what you are going to prepare. If your business volume is extremely high, you may want to alter it just the opposite way. The main thing is this: you've got to count the tickets as the evening progresses.

For instance, let's take baked potatoes. Baked potatoes take an hour in the convection ovens to cook. If you estimate on serving 400 meals that evening, that would mean preparing 300 baked potatoes. But if halfway through the evening you see that you have already used 250 baked potatoes, then you'd better put some more potatoes in the oven. On the other hand, if you are below your average, i.e., only 100 baked potatoes were served by 7:30 p.m., then you definitely should not put any more potatoes in the oven.

In other words, you have to check constantly the flow of the traffic. Prior to dinner time you cannot cook all the meat, potatoes, and vegetables you estimated for that evening, because what do you do with it once it's cooked? If a sudden rain storm keeps customers from going out to dinner, you cannot serve the meals and all your prepared food is wasted. Nevertheless, keeping a detailed record of what you serve each day is quite valuable. For instance, you will know which day—Friday or Saturday—brings you more sales, based on the average number of meals served Friday versus Saturday night. And you also know the exact product mix for those days.

If you are not prepared, unpleasant things can happen during dinner time. For instance, suddenly the kitchen manager can call you over and say, "I've got five orders for top sirloin, but I don't have it." Then, no matter what is going on in the restaurant, you have to stop everything and run back to the kitchen and cut more steaks. Now there may be a problem at the bar. Perhaps the bartender just cut his hand, and you should be behind the bar serving customers until the bartender's hand is attended to. But you have to go and cut steaks.

Or there may be a problem elsewhere in the restaurant. The fact is, you have to leave the "floor," i.e., the public area where you're supposed to be during the shift, go to the back of the house and cut meat. And while you're doing that, you cannot be aware of what the service is like; whether the customers are happy or if they are dissatisfied; whether any employee is stealing from you. In short, you cannot possibly know what is happening in the restaurant while you're cutting meat in the back. That is why it's imperative for you to count the tickets during the meal. By counting tickets you're keeping your finger on the pulse of your store's business volume, so to speak. And if you see by the number of tickets that more products are being used than you had prepared for, you can pick a slow period, maybe a half an hour or maybe only twenty minutes, run back to the kitchen, cut additional steaks, and get right back on the floor. The main thing is to plan on that chore.

Let's take the previous example: you have been serving 429 dinners every Tuesday for the last five weeks, but this particular Tuesday there happens to be a Ladies Apparel Convention in town. This may mean that you will be serving another 40 dinners. That extra 40 dinners will not become a problem as long as you're planning for it. That is, as long as you keep yourself informed of all local coming events such as conventions and other occasions, you can insure yourself against any future panic situations.

Now when it comes to planning meals for Monday night, don't forget Monday night football. All restaurateurs agree that Monday night football is the worst thing that ever happened to the restaurant business. On the other hand, if there is an afternoon football game and the stadium is some ten miles from your restaurant, you had better plan on being hit very hard as soon as the game is out, i.e., a half an hour or so after the game.

George McCullagh, Director of Support Services, Victoria Station, Inc. (one of the more successful and highly visible restaurant chains), recalls:

> When I used to run one of our restaurants in San Francisco as the assistant manager, after every home football game that we won the place was mobbed. I mean, absolutely mobbed. People celebrated. The restaurant would fill up in ten minutes, and there would be an hour waiting line. On the other hand, if we lost, we'd get only a few people— the folks who had made commitments to meet friends, or people who were going out to dinner anyway.

CASE IN POINT

All of this points up the importance of keeping up with the latest turn of events, especially sports events, and planning for them. Now if the Bing Crosby or some other well-known golf tournament is on TV, or if the World Series is on, and you have a bar in your restaurant (especially if the bar is the main part of your restaurant) with one or two TV setups, you should plan on a big bar night. People will automatically come in, sit down, and drink all night while watching the games, tournaments, fights, or whatever the special event happens to be. Of course, if you have a dinner house, this does not apply to you. Still, you do have to know what's going on, and apply this knowledge to your forecasting.

If there is no game on Sunday, you might not fill up with the dinner crowd until seven or eight o'clock. In fact, you may never fill up. Yet, even if you are only breaking even, you may want to stay open because it's a convenience to your good customers who frequent you often, and who may have out-of-town friends visiting them for the day. Thus, even if your sales are only on an even flow, you may plan to stay open on Sundays in the hope that by getting the good will of a certain clientele, you will eventually increase the sales.

Liquor Inventory Control

To have effective inventory control of the liquor sold at your restaurant, you must figure out exactly how many drinks are to be served out of every quart of liquor. And while daily liquor inventories would be impractical, counts of used bottles should be taken daily. To arrive at how many drinks should be served, you multiply the number of bottles by the number of drinks out of each bottle.

If the potential bar cost differs from what you take in over the bar, you have a problem, and it is up to you to investigate it.

Forecasting

The smaller your product list, the tighter control you can have over your inventory, and the more accurate your forecasting will be. In other words, if you have a "limited menu" or specialty restaurant, such as a steak house, prime rib house, hamburger house or fish house, which requires only a small product list, the better chance you have of controlling not only your inventory but also the accuracy of your forecasting. (See Sample Daily Forecasting Form, Figure 2-1, and Food Order Form, Figure 2-2.)

In order to forecast on the basis of product mix your cutting percentages on the prime rib, the number of shrimp orders, the top sirloin, and the number of potatoes to be baked on any given night, you have to know the products. In fact, one of the keys to being successful in the restaurant business is to have an in-depth knowledge of the products on your product list, whether it is small or large. Without knowing extensively about the product, you cannot talk intelligently with the purveyors. And, if you do business transactions with top people, you find they really know their field. In most cases these purveyors have been in business for many years; with the majority of them it is a family business in which they grew up. In short, if you want them to respect you, you have to become familiar with their products.

One way of becoming cognizant of the products you use is to go out and take tours of different canneries. Watch them produce their merchandise; talk to the manufacturer of the products; examine their end products.

DATE_____   DAILY FORECASTING FORM
                                    0276

DAY_____   PREPARED BY: MOD_____

WEATHER_____   KS_____

LUNCH
    Forecast Amount_____ Actual Amt._____   Actual %
    ___ Item   Amount
    ___ DIP   _____; fire _____ ball tips   _____
    ___ PRIME RIB   _____   _____
    ___ BURGER   _____   _____
    ___ TOP   _____   _____
    ___ FLANK   _____   _____
    ___ SHRIMP   _____ x 4 = ____ ÷ ( ) ____lbs.____
    ___ KABOB   _____   _____
    ___ BBO   _____ x 3 = _____ bones   _____
    ___ MUSHROOMS   _____ COOK _____ lbs.
    ___ DESSERTS (CAKES)_____   _____
    ___ DESSERTS (PIES) _____   _____

DINNER   Actual Amt._____   Actual %
    Forecast Amount _____ Est. Cust. Per Dinner Rib _____
                               Actual Cust. Per Dinner Rib_____

    ___ Item   _____
    ___ PRIME RIB   _____; _____ Ramekins   _____
    ___ BBQ   _____   _____
    ___ FILLET   _____   _____
    ___ TOPS   _____   _____
    ___ SHRIMP   _____ x 7 (__) ÷ ( ) = ___ lbs.____
    ___ COMBO   _____ x 4 (__) ÷ ( ) = ___ lbs.____
    ___ KABOB   _____   _____
    ___ MUSHROOMS   _____ ÷ 2 _____ lbs. to cook   _____
    ___ POTATOES   _____ ÷ 70 = _____ bxs.   _____
    ___ DESSERTS (CAKES)_____   _____
    ___ DESSERTS (PIES) _____   _____

PRIME RIB: Ribs needed, lunch _____dinner _____total_____
           Reheats on hand _____
    Rib Firing Schedule   Employee Meal Lunch _____
fire _____at _____
fire _____at _____
fire _____at _____
fire_____a t _____   Employee Meal Dinner _____
fire _____at _____
fire _____at _____

COMMENTS: _____
          _____
          _____

FIGURE 2-1   Courtesy of Victoria Station, Inc.

FOOD ORDER FORM

DATE

DAY OF WEEK

GROCERY	ON HAND	ORDER	ORD'D.	PRICE	REC'D.	GROCERY (Cont.)	ON HAND	ORDER	ORD'D.	PRICE	REC'D.	MEAT	ON HAND	ORDER	ORD'D.	PRICE	R'D
Bleu Cheese						Ice Tea						Prime Rib					
1000 Island						Sugar Pks.						Top Butts					
French						Croutons						Filets					
Italian—Regular						Brd. Cr						Flank					
—Golden						Whl Pepper						Ball Tip					
Beets						Chives						Burger					
Garbanzos						Salad Oil						Shrimp					
Kidney Beans						Wht. Wine						Beef, Back Ribs					
Bac-O-Bits						Cheese Ck						Knuckle, Skinned					
Dill Sprs.						Sweet & lo											
Horse Rad.						Mayon.											
B.B.Q.						Peppers, Hot						BREAD					
Garlic Powder						Pickles, Swt Mix						Rye Rolls					
Au Jus						Pepperoncini						Burger Rolls					
Salt						Giardiniera						Dip Rolls					
Pepper						Apple Ring						Fr. Rolls					
Mustard						Bean Sprouts						Fr. Bread					
Lemon Ju						Beans, Green											
Teriyaki						Beans, Wax											
Catsup						Olives, Ripe						PRODUCE					
A1 Sauce						Pepper Corn						Salad					
Lea & Perrins						Red Pepr. Diced						Iceberg Lettuce					
Tobasco						Vinegar, Red Wine						Chicory					
Lg. Sli. Dill						Wine, Red Cook.						5 x 5 Toms					
Lipton Tea												Cherry Toms					
Sanka												Red Onion					
Coffee												Boiling Onion					

FIGURE 2-2   Courtesy of Victoria Station, Inc.

PRODUCE (Cont.)	ON HAND	ORDER	ORD'D.	PRICE	REC'D.	DAIRY (Cont.)	ON HAND	ORDER	ORD'D.	PRICE	REC'D.	PAPER SUPPLIES	ON HAND	ORDER	ORD'D.	PRICE	R'D
Mushrooms						Margarine						Can Liners					
Cukes						American Ch.						Foil					
Lemons						Parmesan						Film					
Potatoes						Sour Cream						T. Tissue					
Romaine Lettuce						Cottage Cheese						Paper Towels					
Red Cabbage												Seat Covers					
Avocado												Coffee Filters					
Green Onion																	
Green Peppers						**BAR ITEMS**											
Pineapple						Cherries											
						Olives											
						Onions											
CLEANING SUPPLIES						Celery											
Ajax						Oranges											
Hand Soap						Bananas											
Dish Soap						Limes											
Rinse Dry						Tomato Juice											
Silver Soak						Grpfrt. Juice											
						Orange Juice											
						Beef Broth											
						Whip Cream											
						Kaukana Ch											
DAIRY						Ritz Crackers											
Milk						Triscuits											
½ & ½						Eggs											
Buttermilk																	
Solid Butter																	
90 ct Butter																	

FIGURE 2-2   (continued)

Let these people get to know you. Establish rapport with them, and make them feel proud that their products are being served in your restaurant(s). If the manufacturer knows you and knows that his products are going to a distributor who has a one-stop program with you, chances are that he will make sure you get top quality products.

As an additional measure, you should let the manufacturer know that you are quality conscious, and that if you get the lower grade of his products, you're going to reject them and instruct your distributor to buy from a different manufacturer.

This practice can be applied to the meat industry as well. In other words, it is a good idea to take numerous tours of the meat industry to get an intimate knowledge of how they fabricate their products, and at the same time see the problems they encounter. Thus, when something goes wrong, you will have an understanding of the possible problems.

Now fresh produce is a little different "game." It is not fabricated as is the meat. It is quite seasonal. There are many different variables affecting the produce market that do not affect the rest of the trades. These variables range from weather, droughts, and other similar factors to situations that are unique to fresh produce. (For a comprehensive discussion on fresh produce, see Chapter 4.)

Again, wherever possible, establish a good relationship with your produce people; i.e., become a good account for this specific local produce man by buying 100% of your produce from him. If you do that, it will be worth it for him to give you continually quality produce. But you must understand that the buying of produce is much more on a trust basis than is the buying of any other merchandise you use. For example, it is very difficult to track the produce prices. Consequently, if you are charged what you consider a fair price, and you are getting top quality, then you should stay with that particular produce man. And if he knows that you will buy from him consistently, when he goes to the market at dawn he will buy for you first. For instance, if he knows that you use ten crates of lettuce a day, he will first pick for you ten crates of top quality lettuce.

If you wait till 8:00 a.m. and shop around for prices, the professional produce people, who have been to the market four hours earlier, have already bought all the quality merchandise. In short, you have to buy what is left. That is the reason why smart, successful restaurateurs do not shop for produce themselves.

To improve the time element of their manual inventory control system, many restaurant chains as well as one-store owners are starting to use mini- or microcomputers. The type of computer systems used in restaurants is called Point-of-Sale (POS). Specifically, via the POS systems information is transmitted to the head office instantaneously. Thus every morning management is cognizant of the total sales volume and product mix of each restaurant; i.e., how each restaurant performed the previous day.

Said a spokesman for the Victoria Station corporation:

CASE IN POINT

Prior to converting to the POS computer system, we already had all the information we needed from every one of our restaurants. In other words, the machine is not giving us any controls we did not already have. What POS is giving us is a saving in time. Time insofar as getting the information to the head office within seconds; time insofar as having the sorting, adding, and editing of data done by the computer system instead of the manager. Since it was the managers who on a pre-printed form [*see* Figure 2-1] had to give us the same data, it is the time of the manager—spent previously on this information—that we are gaining. Now the managers just key in, i.e., enter the data into the computer, and the POS system does all the work for them.

The POS systems in general consist of anywhere from one to five or six electronic "intelligent" terminals placed at strategically located "work stations" at the bar and various places in the restaurant. All terminals are connected to a mini- or microcomputer at the location, which gathers, sorts, and edits the data before transmitting these data to a large computer at the head office. If a one-store owner uses POS, then the in-house mini- or microcomputer processes all the restaurant data, and prints out all the necessary reports the restaurateur needs for inventory control, for disbursements, and for profit and loss statements. If programmed properly, the mini- or microcomputer can easily process payroll application, and print the payroll checks for the restaurant staff as well.

After he opened his second family restaurant in Dallas, Texas, the owner came to the conclusion that for complete control over inventory, purchase, goods received, and sales performance, he should switch from a manual office operation to a minicomputer system. "At the end of the day," says the pleased restaurant operator, "I get all the information to assess profits of the same day. I know exactly what's going on at both restaurants, and in addition—I think this is one of the system's major features—it points out product trends before I or my managers are aware of it. This way I can put my dollars in the high-volume product mix."

MINI SYSTEM PUTS OPERATOR'S $$$ IN RIGHT PRODUCT MIX

Considering the cost benefits that the appropriate minicomputer system can provide, restaurateurs who have efficiently run minicomputers feel that the training of current personnel to operate their computer system—once it is implemented by computer professionals—is worth the expense. The fact is that unlike the large and complex computer systems, no programmer or technician is needed for daily operating purposes of a minicomputer.

Thus, by using the described method of inventory control through forecasting—whether using a manual or a computerized system—you will be able to predict your costs much more accurately than ever before. You can project your costs and your profits at the same time. And of course, this is what business is all about. To put it simplistically, nobody is in business to exchange dollars. Everybody is in business to make money, to show profit. Just bear in mind that this principle goes not only for you but for your purveyors as well.

3

Modern Restaurant and Commercial Food Management Practices for Dramatic Boosts in Cash Flow

CHAPTER HIGHLIGHTS

There is much more involved in enlarging your cash flow than simply increasing the size of the restaurant, speeding up the food coming out of the kitchen, trying to sell more wine, offering a larger array of desserts to the guests, or even raising the prices of menu items. If you want to get your check average up, you should analyze the architecture of your organization. Is it product oriented or customer oriented? Next, define the purpose, style, goal, and technique of your total operation, and then structure your organization for profit. The structure can be very stringent or it can be loosely knit; the essential point is that it should be based on a carefully thought-out plan.

Basic Variables to Boost Your Cash Flow

a. Analysis of Your Organization

Is your organization product oriented or customer oriented? That is the very first factor you should analyze. And the question is relevant whether you are one of those restaurateurs who think that food is more important than service, or one of those who believe that service is the most important factor in a successful restaurant operation.

If your organization is product oriented, the probabilities are that you concentrate your efforts to increase cash flow by lowering the cost of your basic products. You may try to accomplish your goal by changing from one purveyor to another; that is, from one who is giving you an introductory offer on some merchandise to one who is undercutting another purveyor. Granted, this is one way of boosting your cash flow. However, the effect will prove to be

PRODUCT-ORIENTED vs. CUSTOMER-ORIENTED METHOD

temporary. If a restaurateur is product oriented, he is focusing on his own needs to sell his products. By this fact alone he is not paying sufficient attention to his customers' real needs and preferences, and no amount of clever schemes will raise his check average and thus increase his cash flow. The fact is that a large number of failures in the restaurant industry can be traced directly to product-oriented restaurateurs.

On the other hand, if your organization is customer oriented, chances are that you are deliberately creating new, value-satisfying items in an environment and at a price that is in accordance with the customer's needs, and that the customer will want to buy.

As Theodore Levitt states in his "Marketing Myopia,"* "Most important, what it [the restaurant] offers for sale is determined not by the seller but by the buyer." Using your managerial imaginativeness and boldness does not mean ignoring cost-effectiveness. It just means that in order to increase your check average you define your restaurant's style, direction, and goals based upon customer created need and *not* upon your need.

Jim Thomson, of Pacific Cafe restaurants, says:

CASE IN POINT

> We run a capacity business in all three of our stores. We believe that we have high volume because we offer good value at lower prices than other seafood restaurants. In fact, our volume in this particular store is up to the point where we can't increase it because we don't have the seating capacity. Our next logical move would have been to increase the size of our restaurant. At this location, however, because of the way the streets run, and because we have no property in the back, that alternative had to be ruled out. We could have tried to sell more wine or perhaps even more desserts by offering a larger variety of desserts. But that would have increased our check average only slightly. And because people would have lingered longer at the table, it would have actually decreased the number of covers served. So we considered the next two alternatives: (a) to increase menu prices, and (b) to supplement our standard menu with some sophisticated specialties. Now insofar as the "a" alternative was concerned, we decided against it, even though we probably could have gotten away with it. But we established our restaurants and achieved a measure of success by giving people quality seafood at reasonable prices in an informal, pleasant atmosphere. Consequently, we didn't want—to put it colloquially—to "break the faith." So we decided upon the second alternative. On an experimental basis we offered a limited number of higher priced sophisticated seafood specialties. And, I'm glad to say, it has proven to be successful. We've been increasing the check average by as much as 50¢ via the more expensive specials. Now these items are *in addition* to our regulars on the menu which have NO CHANGE IN PRICE. Thus, we're catering to two worlds: the customers who come in here because of the price, and the customers who like seafood delicacies and don't care what they pay.

A PROVEN WAY TO
INCREASE CHECK
AVERAGE

---

* **"Marketing Myopia,"** by Theodore Levitt, *Marketing Strategy*, edited by Edward C. Bursk, Editor, *Harvard Business Review*, and John F. Chapman, Executive Editor, *Harvard Business Review*, Harvard University press, Cambridge, Mass., 1964.

As stated before, being customer oriented does not mean overlooking even minor items such as salt. When you're a small one-store owner, perhaps it doesn't matter if you're paying $1.50 for a bag of salt, or $3.00 or $6.00. Such amount may not even show up in your P/L because it's too far off the right— too many decimal points away. Besides, when you're a small operator you don't have much choice. You have to pay the going price. But when you become larger, i.e., you start operating a few restaurants, you should be able to decrease your cost of that item even though it might be in line with what everybody else is paying, or what the market is. At that point, because you are using a large volume of any given item, including salt, all costs do show up in your P/L. By the same token, however, you can strike a better deal because of the sheer volume of your purchases.

Another thing—when you're customer oriented and decide to serve high quality products, you have to give serious consideration to the selection of purveyors who will give you the right quality at the right price and with the right service. Some purveyor companies offer outstanding service. But then you have to expect to pay a little more. Now you may want to organize your operation so that the purveyor's service is not as important as it might be to somebody else. For instance, some purveyors offer daily service, but if you have your operation organized so that you need daily service only in bread and dairy products, while you can keep meat, fish, and produce down to three deliveries a week, you can save the extra amount that the daily delivery would cost.

HOW TO SAVE $$$ ON DELIVERIES

If you have analyzed your organization and defined exactly your customers' preferences and needs, and based upon that you have determined your operation's direction, you can order accordingly. Moreover, you should keep your emergency orders to an absolute minimum. It costs a lot of money to have the purveyor's truck running constantly to your store.

Simply put, the purveyor is going to predicate the prices he charges you on your ordering practices—on how much you buy, and on how you pay.

Insofar as quality of products goes, you specify your quality either by brand names or by grading. When you establish the level of quality you want to serve, you have to ensure that that is exactly what you are getting from your purveyors.

Important: Purveyors appreciate good, solid customers—whether small or large—and will give these customers extra consideration. But you must be fair and honest, and most importantly, you must communicate with your purveyors.

CASE IN POINT

If you're given a better price on some item from an unknown purveyor, go with this data to your own purveyor. Ask him about the offer. And if you have a good relationship with him, he might say, "I know what that stuff is. I know where he bought it, and it's junk." But he might also say, "If you can get that product at that price, go ahead and buy it. You've got a good deal on that merchandise. It will save you money. I happen to know that he bought that stuff a while back. It didn't move, and I bet that's why he's selling it at that price. So, go ahead and buy it."

In other words, it pays to deal honestly with your purveyor. Also, small things do count. For example, when your purveyor comes to see you, offer him a cup of coffee and take some time out from your schedule to talk to him. Don't jump on him as he enters your establishment if a delivery the day before was not on time. There may have been half a dozen good reasons for being late. There may have been a bad traffic jam, a strike, or the purveyor may not have received his own products on time.

Since, in the final analysis, saving money on certain items is equivalent to increasing cash flow, here's another example of just such a case.

$$$-SAVING IDEA   Capers are very expensive at $56.00 a case—almost $5.00 a quart. Moreover, they are in short supply, and $56.00 a case is a competitive price. But if you need capers, and if you have a good working relationship with your purveyor, you can ask him if there are any other companies that may be able to sell you capers cheaper. Or you could ask him whether you should buy a different size. He then may look through his inventory and discover that he has smaller sizes—pint jars for a few dollars less. (Pint jars of capers are cheaper because most restaurateurs buy their capers in quarts.) Also, if the purveyor purchased the items at a time when the price was lower, the particular merchandise would remain at the lower price level on the sell list.

There are almost as many ways to boost your cash flow as there are ways to operate a restaurant. For instance, consider the idea contributed by Arnold Ertola of Shenanigans:

CASE IN POINT   Last March our food cost went up to 37%, yet we managed to boost our cash flow considerably during the same period. This came about when we decided that on St. Patrick's Day the first drink of each customer would be on the house. This pre-publicized "gesture"—though not unique or novel—proved to be a profitable marketing idea. It was the best day—liquor-wise—we ever had. We tripled our liquor business that day, and even the following day it was double the usual sales. And we got a lot of steady new customers to boot.

The success of Shenanigan's is all the more remarkable since at the time Mr. Ertola joined Messrs. Robert Sturm and David Owens, the restaurant—under a different name and different orientation—was doing 25% of what it is doing now. The business was on a completely C.O.D. basis. In fact, as Mr. Ertola pointed out, "We came in here completely blind. And for the first four months we treaded water just to get the business above the water line. Because my two partners were involved in the previous ownership, it wasn't a matter of starting out fresh. We had to change the name, the image, and even the interior, and work with the old business' debts. And while we're still a small establishment, our volume of sales and our cash flow are steadily increasing. We have become quite popular with people in this area who are looking for a restaurant with a nice pub atmosphere."

$$$-SAVING IDEA   Still another way to increase your cash flow is to take all the time the law allows you to pay for various merchandise. Take liquor, for example. Purveyors will tell you that you have to pay for the delivered merchandise in 30 days, but in reality you have 42 days. The purveyor has to give you 12 days in addition to the usual 30 days. IT'S THE LAW. But it's also the law that you have to buy liquor from more than one liquor dealer.

In sum—to increase your cash flow it's not enough to know ways to bring up your check average. You also have to save money through careful buying and paying practices. What all this boils down to is this: it is the nickels and dimes you save in the restaurant business that give you a margin of profit, not the dollars.

b. Structuring for Profit

According to Mr. Al Levie of Gulliver's restaurant chain, perhaps the single major reason for the large number of failures in the restaurant business is that most people do not take the trouble—or just don't know how—to structure for profit; to increase their cash flow. Mr. Levie says:

> Here in our Irvine store, everything we do, from the time the guest enters, to the way we receive and greet the guest—including the opening words—to the way we serve the guest, everything is structured. Service, preparation of meals, pouring of drinks, everything is according to written specifications or procedures. There's a French expression, "mise en place," which essentially says that before you start to prepare any item, you have the proper utensils and all the ingredients. Moreover, all the ingredients are measured out so that as you combine them you are not guessing, you are not rushing, you are not doing anything else except follow the procedure in the sequence in which they should occur. And of course, with the exact amount of right ingredients. All this, plus the right staff who really want to please people, gives us a heck of a chance of servicing our guests the way we want to service them, the way they should be served.

CASE IN POINT

> And the proof of the pudding is that this, our first store, though somewhat smaller than the other stores (only 200 seats), does 2.7 million dollars a year. Specifically, we do 1900 lunches a week and 3600 dinners a week, and dinner is ONLY ONE ENTREE. Of course, we do a good job in terms of quality, service, price, and nice environment, not to mention pretty waitresses. But that's the name of the game—putting it altogether by structuring for profit. And it works!

Conversely, Mike Walsh, owner/manager of the well-known and very successful The Holding Company, a businessman's bar and restaurant at Embarcadero Plaza in the heart of San Francisco, has a slightly different approach to effect a profitable restaurant.

> In the restaurant business, the only lasting impression customers will carry with them are the people who wait on them. They don't necessarily remember what they ate or what they drank, or even what they spent, but they will remember how they were treated. So your only tool in the restaurant business is the staff that you have working for you. Accordingly, you have to make sure that they are selling. But to accomplish this you have to teach your employees how to sell; teach them how to serve; teach them how to keep the customers happy. And finally, teach your staff to become aware of the problems or potential problems they may encounter with guests, and teach them how to handle people and incidents that may come up in a restaurant. Don't just throw your employees loose on the floor and hope they survive. That's

CASE IN POINT

no way to run a restaurant. If you want your customers to be satisfied, if you want your customers to come back *and* bring their friends, you provide them service people who know the value of being in rapport with the customers.

The way I structure my restaurant for profit is to ensure that my staff understands that by working for the house, they too are making more money. That is, if they are not pushing cocktails for the house, if they are not trying to satisfy the customers' eating and drinking preferences by selling—not by being pushy but just by making the customers aware of the choices they have in food and liquor, it is they, the employees, who are not making money. Of course, neither is the house.

And the way to insure that the whole place works according to your setup is to "be there." You have to be on the floor. You have to watch your staff work. You have to listen to your customers. You have to watch everything, and listen to everything that goes on in your store.

An additional way of boosting your cash flow is to save dollars and cents by monitoring these on a regular basis, that is, by keeping a scoresheet of financial performance. More, this should be reviewed by management on a regular basis. The two-page financial analysis worksheet shown in Figure 3-1, or a modification of it, can be very useful in keeping score of the major factors that have input on the critical bottom line.

Analyze Your Own Restaurant

A periodic analysis of your restaurant's financial performance may provide some early warning signs of potential problems. Food costs or payroll may be inching up month by month. Some controllable expenses could be increasing while others are decreasing.

Day to day changes in your costs could appear small and possibly go unnoticed. However, examination on a regular basis could uncover undesirable trends, allow you to take corrective action and control situations that could lead to a crisis. Here lies the key to effective management. To help you toward better management, we have included a worksheet on this page, designed to help you analyze how well your restaurant is doing in comparison to the rest of the industry.

Follow these simple instructions for completing the worksheet:

1. Enter your financial data in the first column.

2. Compute the percentages for column 2 dividing the amounts by total sales. (Note — where food and beverage sales are broken down separately compute percentage of food cost by dividing cost of food by food sales and for the beverage cost percentage divide cost of beverage sales by beverage sales.)

3. Calculate the supplementary statistics in accordance with the formulas given.

4. List the appropriate comparative percentages or ratios from this report in column 3.

5. Compute the variances by dividing the difference between the figures in column 2 and column 3 by the figures in column 3. Multiply the result by 100 to express the variance as a percentage.

6. If the variance is greater than plus or minus 10 percent further analysis should be made to determine the reason for that variance.

Worksheet

Complete and Compare Statement of Income and Expenses	Your Figures Dollars	Your Figures (% of Sales)	Restaurant Industry Report	Variance + or −
Sales Food	$	%	%	
Beverages	$	%	%	
Total sales	$	%	%	
Cost of sales Food	$	%	%	
Beverages	$	%	%	
Total cost of sales	$	%	%	
Gross profit	$	%	%	
Other income	$	%	%	
Total income	$	%	%	
Controllable expenses Payroll	$	%	%	
Employee benefits	$	%	%	
Direct operating expenses	$	%	%	
Music and entertainment	$	%	%	
Advertising and promotion	$	%	%	
Repairs and maintenance	$	%	%	
Total controllable expenses	$	%	%	
Income before occupation costs	$	%	%	
Rent, property taxes and insurance	$	%	%	
Income before interest and depreciation	$	%	%	

Supplemental Operating Information	Your Figures	Restaurant Report	Variance + or −
Sales per seat Food	$	$	
Beverage	$	$	
	$	$	
Average receipt per cover (total sales ÷ covers)	$	$	
Daily seat turnover (covers ÷ seats ÷ 365 days)	times	times	
Index of productivity [sales ÷ (payroll + benefits)]	times	times	
Current ratio	times	times	
Accounts receivable ratio to sales	times	times	
Inventory turnover (cost of sales ÷ average inventory) Food	times times	times times	
Beverage	times	times	
Total	times	times	
Return on equity (net profit ÷ net worth)	%	%	

FIGURE 3-1   **Used with permission of Laventhol & Horwath.**

Worksheet

Complete and Compare Statement of Income and Expenses	Your Figures Dollars	Your Figures (% of Sales)	Restaurant Industry Report	Variance + or −
Sales Food	$	%	%	
Beverages	$	%	%	
Total sales	$	%	%	
Cost of sales Food	$	%	%	
Beverages	$	%	%	
Total cost of sales	$	%	%	
Gross profit	$	%	%	
Other income	$	%	%	
Total income	$	%	%	
Controllable expenses Payroll	$	%	%	
Employee benefits	$	%	%	
Direct operating expenses	$	%	%	
Music and entertainment	$	%	%	
Advertising and promotion	$	%	%	
Repairs and maintenance	$	%	%	
Total controllable expenses	$	%	%	
Income before occupation costs	$	%	%	
Rent, property taxes and insurance	$	%	%	
Income before interest and depreciation	$	%	%	

Supplemental Operating Information	Your Figures	Restaurant Report	Variance + or −
Sales per seat Food	$	$	
Beverage	$	$	
	$	$	
Average receipt per cover (total sales ÷ covers)	$	$	
Daily seat turnover (covers ÷ seats ÷ 365 days)	times	times	
Index of productivity [sales ÷ (payroll + benefits)]	times	times	
Current ratio	times	times	
Accounts receivable ratio to sales	times	times	
Inventory turnover (cost of sales ÷ average inventory) Food	times times	times times	
Beverage	times	times	
Total	times	times	
Return on equity (net profit ÷ net worth)	%	%	

FIGURE 3-1   (continued)

4

How to Stay Within Your Restaurant and Food Service Organization's Budget

CHAPTER HIGHLIGHTS

While it's quite important for a corporation to have each one of their restaurants stay within their particular budget, it's a matter of survival for a single store restaurateur—small or medium size—to keep a tight rein on his budget. The way you do it, however, varies with the type, size, and location of your restaurant. The fact is that there are almost as many methods to stay within your budget as there are restaurants. Some single unit operators advocate "bargain hunting"; others state flatly that "small businessmen cannot afford to spend their time on bargain hunting." Again, a number of one-store restaurateurs claim that the only way to stay within the budget is via the "floating food cost" technique, a method of stabilizing the price fluctuation of the products and hence the profit. Still other restaurateurs recommend setting up certain rules—tailor-made for the individual operator—and then making sure to stay within those rules. Thus, the selection of a course of action for holding on to a prescribed budget becomes almost limitless. On a few things, however, most restaurateurs agree. These are:

1. Comprehensive knowledge of food, i.e., meat, groceries, produce (often overlooked yet essential), and liquor is critical.
2. Constant vigil over the fluctuating price structure of all items is essential.
3. Detailed and accurate recordkeeping is a MUST.

Arnold Ertola of Shenanigans has this to say:

> I stay in my budget just by staying within the rules I've set for myself, and the way I do it is by drawing up, that is, forecasting, a six-month budget based on what I know I can afford. The only budgetary items I work differently are liquor and food, simply because that's contingent

CASE IN POINT

upon the volume. But I budget six months ahead on everything else. Thus, furniture, cleaning, janitorial … it's all pre-set. It's all budgeted by my accountant and myself. We decide how much we can spend, and then we spread that amount across the items. We decide what is a reasonable operating capital, and anything else that's left over, we invest elsewhere. We don't put it back into the business.

FLOATING FOOD TECHNIQUE

Now insofar as food is concerned, I use the "floating food cost" technique. That is, I price my menus on a six-month period ahead of time, looking where the costs will be six months from now, and not what they are today. In other words, I forecast my menu prices six months ahead.

$$$-SAVING IDEA

Another way I budget is by buying my menus in large quantity. This is a small restaurant; nevertheless, I buy 5000 menus at one time. I pay a "set-up" charge. That is, I pay for 5000 menus at the time I buy them, and I have them printed whenever I have the need to change prices. It doesn't cost me anything extra, because I've already paid for my printing costs when I bought the menus.

Another way I stay within my food budget is by displaying my "daily specials" without any prices. I price them according to what it costs me that day. Since this is only a lunch-and-bar restaurant, today I may serve Beef Stroganoff, and it will be $3.50. Then tomorrow I may serve Reuben Sandwich, and only charge $2.35. I'm fair with my customers when it comes to prices. I know how much profit I have to get out of the food, and that's all I take from my customers. I value my customers; I want them to come back again and again. I want them to make Shenanigans their steady pub for lunch and drinks. And since we're doing quite well, I guess my policy works.

Jack Rowe, owner/manager of Midway, a small but profitable restaurant in Minneapolis, uses this approach:

ANOTHER CASE IN POINT

The way I stay within my budget is by posting daily my books myself. I have my own sheets on which I break down all my bar and food through the day. I take care of my accounts payable simply by alphabetizing my vendors, and paying the bills myself. The rest of my bookkeeping I leave to my accountant. That's why I'm using an accountant and not a bookkeeper. He's able to set up a system, give me the "big picture" of my business, and do all the detail work. Anyway, every month he gives me a four-page report with all my costs broken down: my month-to-date costs, my year-to-date costs, and a comparison of the actual income and expenses to the forecasted income and expenditure. It's a package. And it's the only way I can stay within my budget. I know what my capabilities and limitations are, and it's worth it for me to pay an accountant to control my books. This way I know that I have accurate records.

Many one-store restaurateurs feel that a judicious inventory control system is an important factor in staying within the budget. This might include a pre-set number of ordering, such as top sirloin, or leg of lamb, which then makes it possible and easy to take visual checks in the kitchen and know how much is there vs. how much is supposed to be there. The other recommendation is to have as few people have access to merchandise as possible. Generally, the restaurateur and the chef/cook are the only persons who have keys to the food store room. Finally, most operators of single restaurants feel that since competition is good in any business, having many purveyors, and being on good terms with salesmen who might give them tips on certain bargain items, are of great help in staying within their budgets.

Mr. Ertola likes to deal with a number of purveyors.

I use quite a few purveyors. Moreover, I make sure that they are aware of this fact. The reason is that if they know that someone else is also serving me, they will give me better service and better prices on certain items. Now on my groceries I can't get a price break. But with my meat and produce purveyors it's different. Their prices change according to whether they want my account, or whether they think they have my account.

Produce and meat purveyors are notorious for giving you low prices coming in, and then sneaking prices up on you. Grocery companies aren't too bad. Nevertheless, I deal with more than one grocery company, so that if I get into a bind, that is, if I'm out of something, the salesman will be more inclined to get it himself if he knows that I have accounts with other purveyors also. But if he knows that he's the only person I called, he might say "I'll be there tomorrow," and I would have to put up with it.

With groceries, it's a matter of service. With meat, produce, or any kind of perishable items, it's a matter of price. Because of this, your best ally is a good salesman who tells you when the prices will go up on certain items BEFORE it happens. For example, I just bought 55 cases of wine, saving $1 on next month's price on each case. Now 55 dollars may not be a lot of money, but when you add up all the 55 dollars I can save, well, that can come to a nice sum.

One of the best ways to stay within your budget was taught to me when I first started out in this business. I worked for a gentleman on the coast who had a small restaurant. It only held 76 customers, but this restaurateur lived on a beautiful 16-acre estate off that little store. And he told me: "Any time you have to call anybody for malfunctioning or broken equipment, watch how they fix it. Don't ever call them again, because every time you call a plumber, an electrician, a carpenter, or whatever, to fix your dishwasher, oven, meat-grinder, and the like, it is the PROFIT dollars you are paying out. And if you can fix it yourself, that's money in *your* pocket and not *theirs*."

I never forgot that lesson. And I guess that's one of the reasons that I can stay within my budget.

An essential but overlooked way of staying within your budget is to have an in-depth knowledge of the produce you buy. Says Mr. Bruno Andrighetto, Vice-President of Lee Ray—Tarantino Co., Inc., South San Francisco (one of the largest produce companies in northern California) and a man with 32 years in the produce business:

The most important things a restaurateur should know about the produce are the area the particular produce comes from, the time of year to use it, and the specific varieties to look for. A restaurateur, for example,

CASE IN POINT

YOUR BEST ALLY: A GOOD SALESMAN

$$$-SAVING IDEA

CASE IN POINT

should know that the southern California oranges are the best oranges available throughout the year. They generally cost a little more, but they are excellent. The Arizona oranges look beautiful, but they have little juice. Florida oranges have lots of juice, but less flavor. On the other hand, the best grapefruits come from Texas and Florida.

WHAT PRODUCE VENDORS ARE; WHAT THEY DO

Before giving a comprehensive rundown on the areas, varieties, and sizes of produce used in restaurants, perhaps a brief account is in order as to what produce vendors are and what they do.

Produce purveyors are service companies. They make selections for their restaurant customers in accordance with the orders, and deliver the produce—at least the larger produce companies, like ours, do—to the customers' doors the same day they order. Most large produce vendors are located at produce terminals. Our facilities are at the Golden Gate Produce Terminal, South San Francisco. Our produce arrives to us all through the night directly from farms. And when we get here early in the morning, it's on our sidewalk. Our salesmen, after making a selection for our regular customers, then sell the rest of the produce right from the sidewalk to the buyers who come to the market. And finally, the two basic items in the produce business are lettuce and tomatoes. These are the items we sell most to restaurants.

Popular Produce List

Oranges

As I said before, the best oranges in the world are the southern California oranges. Sunkist is the first grade; Choice the second grade. There's nothing wrong with Choice oranges, except perhaps a blemish on the skin. That's the only difference. Oranges are packed 40 pounds to a box. Orange sizes are 56, 72, 88, 113, 138, and 163. The larger ones, the 56's, are generally sold to gourmet food stores. The 72's and 88's are used for hotels and restaurants. The 113's and 138's are the juice oranges which the hotels use, while the 163's we ship overseas to other wholesalers. We ship these small oranges to Hong Kong, Japan, and to other parts of the Orient.

Grapefruit

Insofar as grapefruit goes, the best grapefruit comes from Texas and Florida. Grapefruit sizes are 23, 27, 32, 40, 48, and 54. The 23's go to real fine stores and hotels. Hotels prefer 23's and 27's, while the 32's, 40's, and 48's are sold to stores. Grapefruit is packed about 35 pounds to a box.

Apples

The best apples are the Delicious Washington State apples. But the McIntosh, Gravenstein, Pippin, and Jonathan are also very good. Apple sizes are 80, 88, 100, 113, 125, 138, and 163. The 80's usually go to gourmet stores; 88's and 100's to hotels and restaurants; 125's to schools; 138's to airlines; and the 163's we ship overseas to the Orient. Apples are packed about 40 pounds to a box.

Berries

Strawberries are 12 ounces to a basket; blackberries are 8; blueberries are 16; boysenberries are 8; and raspberries are 8 to a basket. Berries are packed 12 baskets to a case.

Cherries

Cherries are sold by weight, so they are packed differently.

Lemons come mostly from Florida and California. There are two varieties: Sunkist and Choice. Lemon sizes are 95, 115, 140, 165, and 200. The 95's and 115's are generally used for skin, because the bigger the lemon, the heavier the skin. Hotels and restaurants use two sizes: the 95's and 115's for the bars, and the 165's or 200's for juice or for kitchen use. Restaurants use the Choice lemon for slices in the kitchen; for bar use, they generally use the real clean lemon, which is Sunkist. Lemons are packed about 38 pounds to a box.

Limes we get mostly from Florida and California. Sometimes, in between season we have to go down to Mexico to get them. But it's just for a short period, maybe two or three weeks. This scarcity can happen anytime during September, October, or November. Limes are generally packed 40 pounds to a box.

Grape varieties are Concord, Lady Finger, Malaga, Muscat, Ribier, Seedless, and Tokay. Ninety percent of the grapes that we sell here come from southern California. Most of the eating grapes come from Fresno down. Grapes are packed 22 pounds to a box.

This delicious fruit comes from Hawaii, and we have it continuously, all year round. Papaya sizes are 8, 10, 12, and 14. There are generally 12 pounds of papaya to a box.

We have *cantaloupes* about nine months out of the year. We start with the Mexican cantaloupe in February, and then we go to southern California and work all the way up to the Fresno area. We have the last California cantaloupes at the end of November. And we don't have any cantaloupes until Mexico starts again in February. Cantaloupes come in sizes 23, 27, 36, 45, and 54. The 23's and 27's are generally for gourmet stores. Most hotels and restaurants use 36's. The 45's and 54's are generally the ones that sell five for a dollar in supermarkets. Melons, i.e., cantaloupes, are packed 80 pounds to a case, and there are 36 cantaloupes. So that means that each one weighs about two and a half pounds.

Other melons are packed differently. The casaba, the crenshaw, the honeydew, and the Persian melon are packed in 30-pound boxes, and generally run in sizes from 4 to 6.

The *honeydew* is a big user. It is very popular, and generally very reasonably priced, so hotels and restaurants get a lot of use out of it; get a lot of yield for the dollar.

Another big user is *watermelon* because it is very reasonable and tasty. Restaurants make watermelon balls to add color and taste to their fruit salads.

Hotels and restaurants use a lot of honeydews, watermelons, cantaloupes, and crenshaws. *Crenshaw* is a big demand item. It is the best eating melon, but generally very expensive.

The two main varieties of pears in use are D'Anjou and Bartlett. But these are not the best eating pears. The best eating pear is the du Comice, a French type of pear. But hotels and restaurants don't use Comice pears; they're too expensive. Besides, Bartlett and D'Anjou are better known.

Lemons

Limes

Grapes

Papayas

Melons

Pears

Peaches

Some ninety-five percent of peaches come from California, while the remaining five percent come from Oregon and the State of Washington. The best peaches come out of the Fresno area. When a restaurateur buys peaches, he should watch that "Fresno" is printed on the box. That is really the best area for peaches.

Avocados

The only real good avocado is the Hass variety. That's the one with the soft dark skin. A dark-skinned avocado that is hard when it's ripe is no good. Avocados come mostly from southern California, specifically Escondido, San Diego, and around there. Many restaurateurs are confused when it comes to buying avocados. Some of them think that when it states "24" on the box, it means a double layer of avocados. That is not the case. The 20's as well as the 24's are a box of single layer avocados. And they generally weigh 14 pounds per box. In other words, whether there are 20 or 24 packed in a box, that's still a single layer. A double layer box contains either 40 or 48 avocados, and generally weighs 28 to 30 pounds.

Tomatoes

We have tomatoes all year round, and we have them from all the areas. There is a price variation of from $3.00 a box to $6.00 a box. The $3.00 ones are local tomatoes, so we sell them cheaper. But as soon as we have a good heavy rain, they are through. Then the $6.00-a-box tomatoes come from San Diego. They are firmer and nicer looking tomatoes, but really not better eating ones. So your best value is your local tomato. But if we're shipping the stuff, we have to go to San Diego, because they are real firm tomatoes, and hold up a lot better. The local tomatoes break down right away.

Tomatoes come in different varieties and sizes: beefsteak, medium, small, cello, and cherry. There are local beefsteak and San Diego beefsteak tomatoes. These are the big, round tomatoes. For stuffed tomato dishes they use a medium size tomato, because the large one would be too much. Then there's the cherry tomato. They are a big item. They have a nice flavor, and go a long way. There are about 40 cherry tomatoes to a basket. So if a person takes two or three cherry tomatoes, he could serve about 15 people per basket.

Lettuce

The biggest lettuce-growing area in the world is the Salinas area in California. Ninety percent of the lettuce comes from there. We get lettuce out of there nine months of the year. Then we go to Arizona and then back to southern California. The weather has a lot to do with the price of lettuce. We just went through the worst drought I have seen in 30 years. The lettuce shot up to $7.00 a carton. The average price for a carton of lettuce is about $5.00 or $5.50.

There are different types of lettuce. Your basic lettuce is the head or iceberg lettuce. Then there is Australian, butter, chicory, escarole, Belgium, red, romaine and limestone lettuce. Some of these are not very well known to the public. Some restaurants use different types of lettuce just to serve something different. Lettuce is packed 24 heads to a carton. If a restaurateur does not want a full case, he can order a dozen heads, that is, a half a carton. Head lettuce is the biggest user, because it gives so much yield for the dollar. And generally people will mix it with either romaine or red lettuce to make the salad more colorful. If you make a Caesar Salad, you've got to use the white heart of the romaine. Some restaurants use chicory, some use escarole, some use red lettuce, and some use butter lettuce in addition to head lettuce as the base. But the gourmet restaurants use mostly butter and limestone lettuce. Limestone lettuce is flown out of Terra Haute, Indiana. They grow it in hot houses all year round.

Zucchini

If you get 100 zucchini, the price is $12.00. But if you get 3000, the price is $3.50. That's how the demand-and-supply impacts the price. Zucchini can be bought locally here in California a few months out of the year. But the rest of the year we have to import it from Mexico. This, of course, makes it much more expensive.

Onions

There are many different varieties of onions: boiling, green, yellow, white, and torpedo. Most of the restaurants use the large yellow onions, except when they need onions for salad. Then they like to have a red onion because it is generally sweeter and softer, and it adds color. The sweetest onion is the early California red onion, called spring onion. It generally gets here about April. They grow it locally. That's really sweet. It's almost like eating candy, and besides, it's very reasonable.

Potatoes

Your best potatoes are the Russet Bakers. They claim that the best ones are out of Idaho, but I would say that Oregon has just as good a potato as Idaho. If I put two baked potatoes in a dish—one from Idaho and one from Oregon—it would be hard to tell them apart. Moreover, the Idaho potatoes are much more expensive. In fact, while we sell a lot of potatoes, we don't sell any Idaho potatoes, because the price is so high. Besides, I can't see any difference in them. Most Idaho potatoes go into the freezer. I guess they are the biggest freezer operation in the world. This is done to keep their price up. And by the time you bring it here, it costs about $3.00 per hundred. That's 3¢ a pound more than the Oregon potatoes. Using 100 sacks a week, as many restaurants do, that's $300 more a week for a restaurateur. And there's nothing wrong with Oregon potatoes. For French fries we use the same potato, the Oregon Baker, but we use the larger ones. They come in 100-pound sacks.

Sweet potatoes

They are rather expensive. Some restaurants serve them during Christmas and Thanksgiving holidays. They generally run 15 to 18¢ a pound. This against the regular potatoes which only run about 5¢ a pound. That's why restaurants generally use sweet potatoes only on holidays or special occasions.

Swiss chard

Swiss chard is Italian spinach. It is a great tasting vegetable that's very nutritious, yet not commonly used, except in Italian restaurants.

Artichokes

Because artichokes are good only when they get frost on them, they should be bought only after the area where they grow has the first freeze. It tenderizes them. Before that time artichokes don't taste good. They are tough, and very expensive. Artichokes should be bought at the end of December or January, as soon as we have our first freeze. When they first come out they are expensive, but good to eat. And by February they are generally quite reasonable. Some gourmet restaurants use fresh artichokes all year round. They just use the bottom—the most tender part—of the artichoke, so it's not too much affected. These high class restaurants use them all year, regardless of the price.

Asparagus

We get asparagus from California and Mexico. Asparagus season really doesn't start until March, when up at the Delta River the farmers begin to send us asparagus. I would say that from March until about September about 90 percent of the asparagus comes from the Delta area. Then we have to go to other places, such as southern California, Imperial Valley, and Mexico to get it, and it gets very expensive. The areas I mentioned are the only three other areas that grow asparagus in this country. Farmers ship tons and tons of asparagus back East every year.

Beans

Beans are a very touchy item. Most people don't know that the best bean in the world is a genuine KY. There are two varieties of beans: genuine KY and improved KY. And the only way you can tell if it is genuine KY is to know what to look for. By feeling a bean you can tell how good it is. *If a bean feels slick; it's tough. If it feels nice and soft like silk; it's tender.* So when you're buying beans, close your eyes and just feel them.

There's also a big difference in price. A genuine KY is generally 5 or 6¢ more than the improved KY, but it's much better.

Some restaurateurs know quality, and demand genuine KY when they're buying this produce. Others don't know, and they'll take the improved KY.

None of these beans come from Kentucky. That's just the "variety" name, that is, Kentucky bean is just a certain kind of bean. It's grown in California, right here, locally.

Cabbage

There's not much you can say about cabbage, except that it's very reasonable.

Carrots

The same thing is true of carrots. There are different varieties, but all carrots taste about the same.

Cauliflour

No problem here either.

Celery

Most restaurants use the outside stocks of celery for their soups, or whatever, and then keep the heart and use it for celery hearts.

Corn

Corn is very seldom used in restaurants. They may use frozen corn, but very little fresh corn.

Leeks

Restaurants use a lot of leeks because they are a good flavor item. Leeks are like shallots—an item that the hospitality industry uses a lot.

Shallots

Shallots look like a piece of garlic, but are not as strong as garlic. They are used for seasoning. Both leeks and shallots are used, especially in sauces, in French cooking.

Brussels sprouts

This is an item that very few people use. Yet they should be using it because it's a very reasonable and good item.

Banana squash

This is another vegetable that is easy to fix and very reasonable to serve. Again, very few restaurants serve it.

To summarize it: the restaurateur should know the different varieties of the produce he buys, the area(s) they come from, and when they are in season, so as to make up his menus accordingly. For example, if Brussels sprouts or banana squash are in season and thus very reasonable, why use expensive zucchini?

One final note I would like to add is that most of the restaurant people have some knowledge about produce. Some know more; some know less. I wish that more people would take the trouble of learning about produce, because the more a restaurateur understands the produce business, the better off we—the produce purveyors—are.

5

Cutting and Controlling
Overhead Cost in Restaurants and
Commercial Food Establishments

CHAPTER HIGHLIGHTS

While some restaurateurs believe that it's not too difficult to police your overhead costs as long as you keep a tight control over your expenses, other restaurateurs hold a diametrically opposite view. They maintain that the only way to assure that your administrative costs are under control is to have an accountant in charge of them. This is how Mike Walsh of The Holding Company feels about it:

CASE IN POINT

Actually, most overhead expenses are fairly easy to police because you know what you need, and you have a tight inventory control. Your telephone is a little more difficult to control—that is, as far as what you allow your employees to do with the phone. You have to set a very tight policy on that. We, for example, put a lock on the telephone, and the only people who have keys to it are the management people. That's the easiest method. There are pay phones that the help can use if they need to make phone calls. They can take incoming calls, but there's no reason for the restaurant to subsidize the employees' phone calls.

Now insofar as printing, stationary, office supplies, kitchen and restaurant supplies are concerned, all you need is an effective inventory control to make sure that everything you're buying is being used for restaurant business only. There are a couple of different inventories that we run. Liquor inventory, for example, we run weekly, and then we run a complete in-house inventory on everything monthly. Everything is accounted for: food, liquor, wine, dry goods, supplies, linen, uniforms, everything that we own.

Your control system can be as tight as you want them to be, but if you don't have any problems with your cost, then there's really no reason to

63

have a daily inventory system. Not if you're running a small place. If you're running a big store, then it's a different matter.

$$$-SAVING IDEAS ON INSURANCE

But even for a one-store owner like me, it's very difficult to save on occupation costs such as rent, property taxes, interest, and insurance. It's extremely difficult, especially with your insurance costs, because the rates are going up for restaurants. Your insurance costs are basically at the mercy of insurance companies at this point. You have to shop around. You go where the prices are the lowest for the same amount of coverage. You have to shop around for brokers on different types of insurance. You can't go to one guy and have him do your whole insurance package. He only handles what he knows, and he doesn't know everything. So the only thing you can do is to shop around.

$$$-SAVING IDEAS ON RENT

Your rent is usually an established figure. You can't do much with that. What you can do with your rent though is to have a good deal when going in. In other words, when you sign your lease, you have to be fully cognizant of what you're committing yourself to. For example, is it a five- or ten-year lease? That's an expense that you're going to be dealing with for five or ten years, every month. So you'd better be careful what you're signing. And are you going to be able to live with that cost? You should consider it not from an optimistic viewpoint. You should weigh it realistically, or even on what you think you'll be doing on a "least" basis rather than on a "hopeful expectation" basis. Many people opening a new restaurant think that they are going to make a lot of money. But that's not the way to look at a new venture. You have to look at your costs based on future *minimum* earnings.

Insofar as labor cost is concerned, your labor percentage is only in relationship to your volume, so it drops proportionately to the height of your volume. For instance, because we've just recently begun doing dinners at night, we have a full staff for dinner but not a booming dinner business as yet. So the labor costs are high, but we do it on an overall basis, and I include the management in that figure. Not myself, but the chef, the chief bartender, the floor managers, and everybody else in the store is included in the labor costs. And that's what I can live with in this operation.

To summarize everything, the only way you can really save money on overhead costs is to review them often. To look at them often. Don't put overhead cost items away in the files and not think about them until the next time the bill comes due. If you review them on a quarterly basis, if you have some system of reviewing so that you can compare the costs on a quarterly basis, you can save some money by tightening at one area or switching to something else at another area. The main thing in the restaurant business is to be on your toes constantly; to be alert. After all, it's the nickels and dimes you SAVE in this type of operation that make you the money, not the dollars.

Other restaurateurs have a completely different viewpoint on the same subject. For instance, here is what F. Edward Fleishell, owner of the chic and successful San Francisco restaurant Le Club, says:

CASE IN POINT

Many restaurateurs consider only the "buy price" of a certain item, instead of the item, plus labor cost, plus overhead cost, when calculating the menu price for that item. Probably that's why you have so many bankruptcies in restaurants. They may be doing great business, and they don't realize that they're losing money until suddenly they have these enormous debts and no money, and they don't understand what went wrong. Often they jump to the wrong conclusion that someone on their staff is stealing, when in fact they may very well have been selling something for $8.00 that cost them $9.00—counting labor and overhead—and they didn't know it. Most successful restaurant owners that I've dealt with over the years rely heavily (and I urge them to rely heavily) upon an accountant. There are accountants who specialize in restaurants. They handle anywhere from ten to twenty restaurants, so they're familiar with the peculiarities of this industry.

The record-keeping function in a restaurant is done principally by an accountant. We have an internal part-time bookkeeper, and a CPA who prepares the monthly statements, so that I know precisely what we're doing. Even though we're a profitable operation, I still want to know whether there's any change in any particular item of expense or profitability, so we know where we're going.

You can get into trouble in a few months and not know that you're in trouble unless you have this kind of control. Some restaurateurs will get only a quarterly statement. Again, it's false economy. They won't know until four months or five months later the errors they have made. This is dumb. Again, though, it goes back to the problem that most people in the restaurant business are not educated in this field and therefore have to rely upon a lawyer for all their licensing problems. And they have to rely upon the accountants for all their bookeeping problems, including not only the sales tax reports, the income tax reports, but all the reports that have to be prepared and sent to the various government agencies. I dare say there's not a restaurant owner I know who prepares these reports himself. They're all done by accountants.   **TROUBLE-SAVING IDEA**

You must realize though that an accountant does nothing more than memorize the errors you've made. He doesn't contribute to the profitability of the restaurant at all. Too often accountants end up being nothing more than bookkeepers. All they do is show what you spent, and what you took in. Well, that's fine, but the real function of accounting is to give you an analysis of where you can improve your business. The average restaurant owner, because of his lack of accounting acumen, hasn't the ability to analyze the financial statements. Many people get financial statements and can't even read them. All they do is look at the last line: net profit $5,000. Great! That's all they look at. The rest, they don't understand. It's up to the accountant to interpret and interpolate what, in fact, the statement is telling them.

In other words, a good accountant should study your balance sheet and tell you, on the basis of his experience, if your cost of liquor is too high; if your cost of food is too high; or if the gas or electricity you're using is too high. He is to point out if something is wrong. Because you shouldn't be using that amount of monthly electricity to turn out the number of meals you're turning out. He is the one to call your attention to the fact if something in your operation is amiss. People may be leaving stoves on overnight, for example, or doing other foolish   **$$$-SAVING ADVICE** and wasteful things. A good accountant, established in the restaurant business, can analyze such things and more, because he has other restaurant accounts. He has experience.

SOUND ADVICE ABOUT
LAWYERS AND
ACCOUNTANTS

If you're going to open a restaurant today, regardless of what your background is you ought to have first of all a lawyer who has handled restaurants, so that he will know about leases; an experienced lawyer who will know about licensing laws; a lawyer who will know about all the federal, state, and city regulations. The lawyer, if he is a good lawyer and specializes in restaurants, normally knows one or two accountants who are experts in the field—accountants who are competent, and know how to set up a set of books, so that they accurately portray the state of your business. That's what all restaurateurs are trying to do, and so many are always behind. For example, at the end of the month you correct your records, and by the 5th or 6th you get them to the accountant, who usually takes two weeks to process them. So the third week of the succeeding month you learn what happened last month. If something is wrong, you are seven weeks behind. At the earliest, you are seven weeks behind. That is, if you watch it and take the steps that the balance sheet directs you to take.

$$$-SAVING IDEA

To put it another way: by looking at your balance sheet you can see where, for example, the labor is too high; where something is wrong. Let's say, for example, that you have increased your gross $2,000, but it cost $3,000 in labor. Of course that is not good business. Therefore, by reducing your staff and selling less, you'd make more money. The problem arises when a restaurateur doesn't know how to read the balance sheet, and unfortunately doesn't get the services of an accountant. In many cases problems are compounded, and the restaurateur often ends up in the bankruptcy courts.

In sum, the accountant is the most valuable person you can have. He can recommend where to buy things, where to get financing, how to fill out financial statements for the bank, how to handle the various credit cards, and the like. Thus, it's very important to have a good accountant, even though he may cost a few pennies more. In the long run, however, he's far cheaper than a young, inexperienced accountant. The latter, in fact, may be training while you are paying him. Moreover, he'll make all the mistakes on *your* time.

You can get by without a lawyer. There are many successful restaurant owners who have only accountants. These accountants look at the lease, go to the landlord and negotiate, and do other vital services—all of which saves you money. Thus, often accountants fulfill the role of semi-lawyers, because they do have a lot of experience, and they have a clear view of the direction in which the business is going. Again, in controlling the overhead cost nothing is more important to a restaurateur than a good accountant. (See the Appendix for a financial overview of the restaurant business. It is presented by one of the best known CPA firms—Laventhol & Horwath—that specialize in restaurants.)

6

Selecting and Dealing Successfully with Restaurant and Food Service Purveyors

CHAPTER HIGHLIGHTS

Contrary to the traditional notion that dealers habitually undercut other purveyors and sell products at the lowest possible prices, today's successful restaurateurs take the opposite stand. Specifically, they go on the assumption that a purveyor is honest until proven otherwise. In line with this thinking, after carefully selecting a purveyor who satisfies their well-defined, stringent criteria, they enter into a "one-stop program" agreement with the dealer. This innovative program, which is profitable to both the restaurateur and the distributor, has proven highly satisfactory for the kitchen manager not only in impressive dollar savings, but also in consistent quality products delivered, consistent good service, and greatly reduced possibility of theft, pilferage, and other losses in the kitchen area.

Criteria for Selecting Purveyors

Going on the assumption that a purveyor is honest until proven differently does not exempt you from doing the thorough groundwork that must be done to ensure that you are selecting the most suitable distributor for your products, meat, and dairy. Here are field-tested ways to best accomplish this task.

1. How to Pick the *Right* Purveyor

First of all, even if you are not directly affiliated, contact one of the large dealer organizations such as NIFDA, CODE, North American, or SYSCO Most of these organizations are co-ops, comprised of dealers who have banded together for purchasing power, exercising quality control, and having the means to enforce definitive standards. Whereas most of the small distributorships could never afford a staff of 10 to 15 people at the head office doing nothing but purchasing, quality control, labeling, and public relations, these large co-ops have their own quality control departments. Their staff go out into the field and deal with the different packers throughout the country. Member distributors of NIFDA, headquartered in Atlanta, North American in Chicago, SYSCO in Houston, and other co-ops, as well as large independent distributors, have well-qualified standards. In most cases these standards are higher than the government standards. For instance, if you said to a purveyor that you wanted U.S. grade choice in a certain product, it wouldn't mean much, because within the grade of choice there may be anywhere from three to five different variations. You can get the top of choice, or the very bottom of choice. So by getting the top line of products of any of these large distributors—most of whom have two or three labels—you are pretty much guaranteed that you are going to get a quality product. Briefly, here are the *preliminary* steps in picking a purveyor who will meet your requirements:

   a. Contact one or several of these large co-ops or independent distributors, and get the names and addresses of their prime dealers in the area.
   b. Set up a personal interview with the recommended purveyors. During your talk with them, explain your program; point out that you are very quality conscious, and listen to their philosophies on business. This last is an often overlooked but important factor. It is essential that you and the purveyor you will deal with have a similar business philosphy.
   c. Inspect the purveyors' facilities.

If you are satisfied on the last two items, get a list of their larger or more prominent customers in the city. Check with the kitchen managers they presently serve, and get these customers' impression of the purveyor service. In other words, go to the listed restaurants, or hotels, or whatever, and make an appointment with the person (the kitchen manager, the director of food purchasing, or the director of food and beverages) in charge of purchasing. Then just sit down—sometimes it takes only ten minutes, sometimes it takes half an hour—and discuss different things about the purveyor's operations such as:

   • Consistency and quality of the products
   • Consistency of pricing
   • Consistency of the delivery service.

Next, while you are evaluating the various purveyors, send each of them—if you have not already left it with them—your product list to be priced. (Figure 6-1 presents sample product list of Victoria Station.) Of course, before you can give your product list to any purveyor, you must compile your entire list of grocery items such as canned vegetables, mustard, catsup, salad bar products, and anything else by brand and pack. In short, you must know your exact needs. When dealers price out this list, you should look for more than just the price. You must check to see how strictly they adhere to your standards.

Scrutinize the list to see if they have substituted products with their own products, though you specified a brand product. This is a very important point in judging the purveyor, since on your initial visit you have made—or should have made—crystal clear how quality conscious you are. You also told them that this is *your* program, your *entire* grocery program, and *not* their program. And if they want to get your account, they have to adhere strictly to your

VICTORIA STATION

GROCERY REQUIREMENTS
(NO SUBSTITUTIONS)
1175

ITEM	SPECIFICATION	PACK	QUOTATION
K-TYPE			
BLUE CHEESE DRESSING	LESLIE/DOXSEE	4 GAL TUB	
FRENCH DRESSING	LESLIE/DOXSEE	4/1 GAL	
ITALIAN DRESSING	LESLIE/DOXSEE	4/1 GAL	
ITALIAN DRESSING	LESLIE/DOXSEE	12/1 QT	
THOUSAND ISLAND DRESSING	LESLIE/DOXSEE	4 GAL TUB	
BEETS	PICKLED KRINKLE CUT (145 CT) NORTHWEST	6 #10's	
BEANS, KIDNEY	CHOICE, DARK RED	6 #10's	
BEANS, GARBANZO		6 #10's	
BEANS, GREEN	NORTHWEST WT #4 SIEVE	6 #10's	
APPLE RINGS	CINNAMON SPICED 75-80 CT	6 #10's	
AU JUS BASE	CUSTOM FOODS, INC.	12/1#	
CHEESE, GRATED	PARMESAN, ROMANO HARD	5 LB	
HORSERADISH	PUREED	12/1 QT	
LEMON JUICE	REALEMON	12/QT OR 4/GAL	
MAYONNAISE	WHOLE EGG	12/QT OR 4/GAL	
OIL, SALAD	COTTONSEED	6/1 GAL	
OLIVES, RIPE	LARGE PITTED, 400 CT	6 #10's	
PEPPERONCINI	140 CT	4/GAL	
PEPPERS, HOT	ORTEGA STRIPS	24/27 OZ	
PEPPERS, RED	DICED	24/2-1/2 CN	
PICKLES, SLICED	LONG SLICED DILLS	6 GAL OR #10's	
PICKLE, SPEARS	KOSHER STYLE	6 #10's	
SAUCE, A-1		24/5 OZ	
SAUCE, BBQ	CATTLEMEN'S SMOKEY	4/GAL	
SAUCE TABASCO		24/2 OZ	
SAUCE TERIYAKI	KIKKOMAN'S	4/GAL	
SAUCE WORCESTERSHIRE	L & P	24/5 OZ	
VERMOUTH, COOKING		QTS	
VINEGAR, RED WINE		4/GAL	
WINE, RED COOKING	BURGUNDY	4/GAL	
WINE, WHITE COOKING	CHABLIS	4/GAL	

FIGURE 6-1   Courtesy of Victoria Station, Inc.

ITEM	SPECIFICATION	PACK	QUOTATION
BACON BITS	GENERAL MILLS/STALEY	20 #	
CATSUP	HEINZ	24/14 OZ	
CHIVES	FREEZE DRIED	6/3 OZ OR 12/1 OZ	
CROUTONS	BROWNBERRY SEASONED	10 LB BOX	
GARLIC POWDER	STANDARD IN BULK	6# TO 30#	
MUSTARD	GREY POUPON	12/8 OZ	
PEPPER	MCCORMICK'S G292 (24-26 MESH) OR LOCAL EQUIVALENT	25 LB OR 6/4 LB	
PEPPERCORN	MCCORMICK'S WHOLE BLACK PEPPER OR LOCAL EQUIVALENT	2/5 LB OR 6/1 LB	
SALT		25 LB OR 50 LB	
SUGAR	DOMINO/AMSTAR-SPECIAL PRINT	2 M	
SUGAR SUBSTITUTE	SWEET & LOW*	3/1 M/CS	
TEA BAG	LIPTON	10/100 BOX	
SANKA		10/100 BOX	
ICED TEA BAG	2 OZ BAG		
CHEESE, SLICED	AMERICAN 24/LB	6/5#	

*NOW BEING DEVELOPED—WEE CAL (DOMINO/AMSTAR) SPECIAL PRINT

Through the courtesy of Victoria Station

FIGURE 6-1   (continued)

VICTORIA STATION

BAR SUPPLIES
0976

ITEM	SPECIFICATION	PACK
OLIVES	STUFFED LARGE QUEENS (300 CT)	4/GAL
ONIONS, COCKTAIL	LARGE, 100 CT	12/QTS
TOMATO JUICE	SACRAMENTO/HEINZ	12/48 OZ
TOMATO JUICE	SACRAMENTO/HEINZ	48/5½ OZ
BEEF BROTH	CAMPBELLS/HEINZ	24/#1
RITZ CRACKERS	#941	12/1 LB
TRISCUITS	#951	12/9.5 OZ
GRAPEFRUIT JUICE	DEL MONTE/ TREESWEET	12/48 OZ
CHEESE	KAUKAUNA, SMOKY CHEDDAR	12/2 LB
CHERRIES	MARASCHINO, LG STEM (200-300)	6½ OR 4/1 GAL
PINEAPPLE JUICE	DEL MONTE/DOLE	12/48 OZ
COCONUT SYRUP	COCO LOPEZ/REESES	12/14½ OZ
BITTERS	ANGOSTURA	12/12 OZ
TOOTHPICKS	ROUND, LG CARTON	12 BOXES (800-1000)
STRAWS	5¼" RED	CARTON (1000)
SPECIAL STRAWS	10" RED OR GREEN	CARTON (1000)
GRENADINE	MR. & MRS. T'S/ROSES/ ANGOSTURA	12/25 OZ
LIME JUICE	ROSES	12/25 OZ
SWEET & SOUR	TRUE(VS)/QUICKWAY/ FLORIDAN	CASE OF 12
NUTMEG	SCHILLING OR EQUIVALENT	CASE OF 12/1-3/8 OZ
ORGEAT SYRUP	GARNIER HOLLAND HOUSE	12/25 OZ
ORANGE FLOWER WATER	FUNEL	24/4 OZ
FROZEN ORANGE JUICE	NATIONAL BRAND/ PRIVATE LABEL	12/32 OZ
SIMPLE SYRUP	ANGOSTURA OR EQUIVALENT	12/25 OZ

Through the courtesy of Victoria Station

FIGURE 6-1   (continued)

VICTORIA STATION

CLEANING SUPPLIES
0875

ITEM	SPECIFICATION	PACK	QUOTATION
BLEACH		6/1 GAL	
CLEANSER			
GARBAGE CAN LINER	40 GAL POLY		
GARBAGE CAN LINER	4 GAL POLY		
ALUMINUM FOIL	18 IN x 2,000 IN	ROLL	
TOILET TISSUE	CROWN POM 199	96/CS	
PAPER TOWEL	CROWN MARATHON JR #069 (9½ x 9½)		
SEAT COVERS			
EASY OFF		12/16 OZ	
SARAN TYPE FILM	18 IN	ROLL	
HAND SOAP	PINK LANOL	6/1 GAL	
KLEENEX TISSUE		36/125's	

Through the courtesy of Victoria Station

FIGURE 6-1 (continued)

program. It is very important to know at the beginning of a possible business relationship if purveyors are likely to think that they have a better program than you have and substitute a product. If they are substituting products the very first time on their price list, they are going to substitute products all down the line.

To sum up, the *next* barometrical indicators that you can use in selecting purveyors are:

a. The quickness with which they reply in pricing out your product list. This will show the degree of their interest in getting your account.
b. The strictness with which they adhere to your product list.
c. The prices quoted on the product list.

The "price," however, indicates much more than just dollars and cents. Specifically, on the basis of the quoted price on any given item on your list you should be able to tell, in most cases, whether or not the purveyor substituted a product. Thus, if you have done your homework, as all successful restaurateurs do, you know approximately what the product cost the dealer. The difference must be only the freight charge. If the product is quoted a dollar or two dollars higher or lower, chances are the purveryor has substituted a different product. For example, if you know that a case of some grocery product cost $7.00 or $8.00, and it is quoted $2.00 higher, that's a 25% variance in price. Now, if a product varies 20¢, that may be freight, or it may be the purveyor's buying power. If it's higher, it also might be that on your initial visit you gave the purveyor the impression that you're willing to pay for what you want, even if it has to be imported. And that brings up another factor to be considered: some canned vegetables are better from certain parts of the country. For instance, beets are best from the Northwest, i.e., Oregon; Midwest is second, and the New York area is third. Most quality restaurants will not accept beets from Texas or the South. The quality and color are somewhat different.

CASE IN POINT

A well-known restaurateur in Austin, Texas commented: "If every one in Texas is buying Texas beets, and we buy Northwest beets—even if it means paying a higher price—I think our salad bar will show the difference."

On the other hand, with certain products such as catsup, the home location is immaterial. For example, Heinz catsup is the same high quality whether it is produced at their plant in Pittsburgh, Pennsylvania, Muscatine, Iowa, Fremont, Ohio, or Tracy, California. It is when you are buying beets and other grown canned products that you're getting into a difference. Your distributor might think that he's doing you a service if he is buying a cheaper product and charging you accordingly less. Then it is *your* job to tell him: "Thank you for getting us an inexpensive product, but though we're cost conscious, we don't want it. We're willing to pay more for a better product."

Again, if you don't like the quality of a certain canned product, it may not be the region of the country that is the problem. It may be the time of the year. Restaurants have to live with the problem of the seasons, and there's nothing anybody can do about it. When it is the end of the year and, for example, Northwest beets are out of season, or if it is the tail end of the season and not much is being picked, the only thing to do is to go to a different product.

One point cannot be overemphasized: Do your homework and know the exact cost from the manufacturer for the key items on your product list. Knowing the amount, all you have to do is figure in an approximate freight charge, and you can know within a dime what the purveyor paid for the product. Next, you tack on your agreed-upon percentage mark-up, and that's what you should be paying for the product.

The percentage mark-up must be figured out so that both you and the purveyor can profit, yet be fair to each other. That is the whole game: he's got to make money, and you've got to make money. If at a later time you are not charged the proper amount, you should call the distributor and ask for the reason. Again, you should go under the assumption that if it is the wrong amount, it was a mistake. Of course, if such a thing occurs too often with this particular purveyor, it becomes more than a mistake. It becomes a problem, necessitating a careful reappraisal of the vendor.

2. The One-Stop Program

A good rule of the thumb before going into an agreement with a purveyor is to shop around. Check out three or four different vendors before committing yourself to a one-stop program with one of the purveyors. And that is exactly what a one-stop program means: dealing with only one distributor for your groceries—one purveyor for your meat, one purveyor for your dairy items, and one purveyor for your liquor. The principles, with some variations, within the one-stop program are:

a. Your Guarantee

Guarantee the purveyor 100% of your grocery (or meat, or dairy, or liquor) purchases.

b. Prompt Payment

Pay your bills on time, i.e., pay the bills within 30 days.

c. Fair Play

Never leave the purveyor "hanging" with a product. In other words, if he's buying a product specifically for you, and you decide to change the product on your menu, you do not act upon your decision until he has delivered and you have used up all of that particular product that he has in store for you.

d. No Salesman

Leave no doubt in the purveyor's mind that you don't want any salesman; that you want to be a *house account*. The reason for this is simple: sales commission raises the price on every product at least 3%, sometimes more. However, in order to ensure that your account is not taken for granted after a while, insist that the purveyor assign a house-account representative, or that he or his delegate check weekly or biweekly to see if the products and deliveries are satisfactory at your store.

e. One Delivery Per Week

Take one delivery per week. Tell him that the order will always be phoned in either Monday or Tuesday, and you want delivery next day, in the morning.

Justification for the last two principles: first of all, with no salesman involved, and being a house account, you have knocked the price down by at least 3%. Second, by having one delivery per week, the purveyor's profits increase, and you gain by it also.

In the past, every one of the 90 restaurants in the highly successful nation-wide Victoria Station chain had at least three or four deliveries a week from different grocery products distributors. That meant that out of this company's total product purchasing for a restaurant—which was anywhere from $5,000 to $7,000 per month, depending on the size of the restaurant—they have had as many as ten to 12 deliveries per week. Dividing say $7,000 at ten deliveries, that's $700.

Then Victoria Station, after much research and analysis, made the decision to go on the one-stop program. This meant that now each restaurant has only one delivery per week, or four deliveries per month of grocery products. Dividing the same $7,000, one purveyor thus comes out with a much nicer total dollar delivery. The individual Victoria Station restaurants also gained, because the kitchen manager has only one truck of grocery products per week backing up to the door. The time saved for him is tremendous, plus the fact that there are fewer people walking in and out of the back door. This practice also cuts down the possibility of theft, pilferage, and other losses.

"This method is working extremely well in all our units," said George McCullagh, Director of Support Services, Victoria Station, Inc. It was Mr. McCullagh and Mr. James Mitchell, Vice President-Operations, of the same corporation, who modified and implemented this program for Victoria Station.

f. Price List

Ask the purveyor for a price list which, by mutual consent, may vary in period covered from one month to three months. If it's a one-month price list, it is to be sent to you at the beginning of each month, and it is to be valid until the end of the month.

This serves two purposes: (1) The kitchen manager no longer has to call and ask about price when ordering for the restaurant. He can simply take his Food Order Form (see sample form in Figure 2-2), take a quick inventory of his products, figure out his needs in writing, and place the order on the telephone. This saves many hours for the kitchen manager, and ergo it means many dollars saved. (2) Because you guaranteed to the purveyor that you're going to buy from him everything you need during the period, he doesn't have to worry that you will buy from some other dealer who is trying to undercut him by a dime on a certain product. Undercutting means loss to the purveyor not only because his product then sits in his warehouse, but also because he has to carry that money tied up in inventory.

A successful North Carolina corporation used to have a purchasing agent in each of their ten restaurants in various states. Then they switched to the one-stop program, and now they have the ordering as only a small function of the kitchen manager's job. In other words, whereas the manager in charge of ordering for his restaurant used to spend the entire

CASE IN POINT

BENEFITS OF THE ONE-STOP PROGRAM

CASE IN POINT

Monday morning bargaining with various purveyors, and deciding from whom he was going to buy, now, with the new purchasing policy, the head office has taken over this responsibility. The result is that the kitchen manager spends only about 20 minutes every Monday morning ordering products for the entire week for his unit.

g. Personality Conflicts

The purveyor doesn't have to worry about personality conflicts. Because the deal is between the purveyor and the director or manager of purchasing at the head office, if there is a change in kitchen managers or general managers the distributor need not worry that he might lose the account. He knows that the new kitchen manager will be told by the head office about the one-stop program and the purveyor who supplies the product list.

h. Handling of Problems

In case any problems arise, the kitchen manager has to try to work it out with the purveyor. If this doesn't help, the kitchen manager has to call the purveyor's director of sales, or the president, or whoever the one-stop program agreement was made with, and inform him of the problem(s). If the kitchen manager cannot work it out locally, he or the unit manager should phone the director of purchasing at the head office. This verbal description of the problem should be backed with mailed detailed documentation. Thus, the director of purchasing can ascertain whether the complaint(s) is justified, and act accordingly.

AN ESSENTIAL INGREDIENT OF THE ONE-STOP PROGRAM

But to go back one step: when setting up a one-stop program, a meeting with everyone involved is a MUST. Moreover, this should be a high level meeting. The president, or the director of sales from the distributor, the director of purchasing, and the unit or general manager and the kitchen manager of the particular restaurant have to be the attendees. If this seems to imply that the one-stop program works only when the restaurant manager personally knows the purveyor's policy makers, it is because that is exactly the case. With this setup, however, when there is a problem, the kitchen manager can directly communicate with the distributor's top people, and thus have a good chance of solving the problem.

To put it another way, the kitchen manager should not accost the driver with a problem. He should talk to the president, or the director of sales of the purveyor.

A PROBLEM-SOLVING TECHNIQUE

Now if it is a one-time problem—i.e., the truck broke down, and there wasn't delivery till noon, right in the middle of lunch—well, that can happen every now and then. However, if it is a continual problem—i.e., the distributor is continually out of some product—then it is the director of purchasing who should contact the top man at the purveyor's office, and make him fully aware of the situation. The best way of exposing everybody to the problem is to hold a meeting which includes all the people who were at the initial meeting, and at which the problem(s) should be discussed. In this way, neither side can say that they were not made cognizant of the problem(s). Moreover, this discussion should be documented, the purveyor given a certain amount of time to correct the problem, and a waiting period established. If the vendor fails to resolve the problem, then you should look for another distributor.

Such meetings are an important element in the one-stop program, which is based on fair play by both parties. The fact is that it is not always the distributor's fault when a problem arises. It could very well be that the kitchen manager is not ordering properly. To avoid this:

- Each kitchen manager must have an operations manual
- Each kitchen manager must have a copy of the purveyor's 30-day price list, which must reach him on the first of the month
- Each kitchen manager must have an entire product list for his restaurant.

With these tools the kitchen manager can order off his product list whatever he needs. Then, when he receives the products, he must check that the prices on the invoice are the same as on the list he has received on the first of the month from the purveyor. Finally, the prices are monitored on a spread sheet every month by the aforementioned purveyor's price list.

In sum, the advantages for choosing the one-stop program are:

- To relieve the kitchen manager of the time-consuming task of shopping the market on a weekly or more frequent basis, and then to check and sign for the many different deliveries from many different distributors.
- To receive products with consistent quality and continual availability.
- To receive the specified items on the product list at a continuously fair price.

To ensure that the one-stop program works, you must tell the selected purveyor that:

- You want top quality product, but at the same time he should be aware that you *are* cost conscious.
- You want quality product on a consistent basis.
- You don't want to be overcharged on any product.
- You want continual availability of the product.
- You are willing to pay for any specially requested product.
- You want good service, which means that if they receive your order on Monday, they must deliver that order—complete—on Tuesday.
- You will be fair to him, and he has to be fair to you. This means that you will live up to your one-stop program agreement as long as he does.
- You are cognizant of the fact that he's got to make money, and he has to be cognizant of the fact that you've got to make money.

CAUTIONS

Before entering into a one-stop program with a purveyor, shop around, and check references. Make sure that the business philosophy of the purveyor you chose is similar to yours.

After checking the reliaiblity and availability of the purveyor, go on the assumption that he is honest until proven otherwise. Nothing terminates a business relationship faster than the expectation by one party that it will be cheated. Such an attitude is self-defeating.

3. Local Distributors vs. Commissaries

If you are in charge of purchasing for a restaurant chain, it is of utmost importance to decide which is more beneficial to your company: pricing or control.

If your priority is pricing, then you can be more competitive by choosing to go through local distributors at unit level. If yours is a small product list, and if you have the capabilities for monitoring the policies of local distributors, you should be able to control your units by purchasing locally. This will make you very competitive.

If your priority is control, then you should set up a commissary, i.e., your own distribution point, and bring everything into that distribution center. For example, if you use 500 cases of Heinz catsup a month, then you would have to bring 500 cases of catsup into your commissary, and then redistribute it to your restaurants. The sole purpose for setting up commissaries is control, not pricing. The fact is that at times commissaries are above competitive pricing at the local level, but the company is in full control of all purchases.

7

Maximizing Customer Satisfaction in Restaurants and Institutionalized Food Operations

CHAPTER HIGHLIGHTS

One of the most effective ways of pleasing the customer and increasing your sales with no increase in personnel is to ensure that your staff's objective is to satisfy the customer and not themselves. This can be accomplished if you hire people with the right attitude and personality. When your employees have the point of view and goal that run parallel with your marketing objectives, you won't have, for example, a lot of "sandbagging," i.e., waste of food, time, and effort in your restaurant, which in turn tends to reduce customer satisfaction and hence your profit margin. In other words, you can maximize your customers' satisfaction by having competent, responsive, and sincere personnel not only in the dining area and the kitchen area, but in the bar as well. Since in restaurant business the name of the game is making money, this makes sense. In fact, such approach pays off in dollars and cents, because in the final analysis the service you provide is what sets your restaurant apart from other restaurants of comparable quality, price, and locale.

According to Mike Walsh of The Holding Company:

> What you are selling in the restaurant business is SERVICE. Customers can buy drinks. They can buy food. They can buy whatever you're selling right down the street. The only thing that sets you apart is what you do with your staff. It is your employees that people are going to remember when they leave your restaurant. And that's why your personnel *have* to be people-oriented. For example, you can have—skill-wise—the best bartender in the world, but he can't talk, he's not a bartender. At least, he is not an asset to you. Similarly, if the waitress can't keep one or several people at the table happy, she's really a detriment to you. The "personal touch" is important in any service business, but in the restaurant business it's absolutely essential.

CASE IN POINT

THE ESSENTIAL "PERSONAL TOUCH"

79

People go to a restaurant to get away from the many problems in the outside world. They don't want any hassle. They want to relax and enjoy themselves. They want somebody to take care of them. And that's what you—the restaurateur—must provide if you want your customers to be pleased; if you want those customers to come back again and again to your restaurant.

And that is the reason I hire people strictly on a personality basis. If I like them, I assume that everybody will like them, because I'm looking at them just as a customer would. They don't necessarily have to have prior experience, because previous experience sometimes can be negative. Somebody else taught them a certain job, and I have my own specific way I want them to do that same job. That's why I prefer inexperienced applicants. I can teach them a lot easier than experienced people, whom I have to re-train. Nevertheless, I have hired some good people *with* experience. But only because I really liked them and their personality.

Even in the kitchen I hire completely off personality. The reason for this is that the chef has to deal with my waitresses, the dishwasher, and everybody else. And he's got to be able to get along with them. If you have a bunch of happy employees and a grumpy chef, nobody is happy. So you have to make the whole place—the dining area, the bar, and the kitchen—work in harmony to ensure as high a customer satisfaction as possible.

Mr. A. Levie of Gulliver's goes one step further.

SECOND CASE IN POINT

We are a highly structured company. We believe that by structuring our staff, i.e., teaching our staff the proper servicing and communicating techniques, we are also insuring customer satisfaction. Of course, we realize that unless an employee has basically the proper attitude, we can't teach that person to respond properly to the customer. That's why the right attitude is all-important to us; that's why when selecting personnel, we are very careful that they measure up to our criteria. We insist on having a staff who have a "service" attitude; who really want to please the customers. For example, if a chef or a cook does what we call "sandbagging," which can mean anything from frying or broiling a steak or a hamburger patty for a non-existent customer to overcooking meat or vegetables, and anything in between, that person will not last long with us. Pleasing the customer is paramount to us.

Mr. Arnold Ertola of Shenanigans says:

THIRD CASE IN POINT

Because we are a small restaurant, our greatest asset is the friendly atmosphere, the personal touch we can give our customers. People like to go to a restaurant where the owner, the bartender, the waitresses or waiters know their names, and recognize them when they walk in. My waitresses are very good at remembering customers' names, and knowing their preferences. For instance, we have a very nice salad bar where customers serve themselves. But there are some customers who prefer not to get their own salads. For those customers, my waitresses bring the salads to their table without their asking for this extra service. I believe in this very strongly, and consequently, I insist that my staff provide the customers that "personal touch." We built our reputation on being a quality and friendly place. And my staff and I *are* our customers' friends.

Mr. Jack Lee, marketing director of the exclusive l'Epicure restaurant chain, well known for their French cuisine as well as their traditional southern hospitality, has still a different approach.

> To maximize customer satisfaction, we have, unlike many other restaurant chains, a chef in addition to several cooks in each of our three restaurants. We prepare everything from stock. We cook all our own soups; all our sauces. We cut our own meat in each restaurant. When in quality magazine ads we tell our guests that at l'Epicure they get fresh, top quality meat, that is exactly what we serve them.
>
> Because we want to keep our guests satisfied, and because we only have three restaurants, we can monitor them well. If, for example, the food cost in one of our restaurants becomes too high, the chef may be wasting food. If it gets too low, the chef may have become a little too conscious of his food cost and may be cutting his meat a little thinner to bring his cost down. But since our whole orientation is to keep our guests pleased, we stop such practices immediately. In other words, we monitor our restaurants on a regular basis to ensure our guests' satisfaction.
>
> We apply the same method to the liquor costs. We watch it very closely. If it starts to get too good, we suspect that possibly the bartender is trying to impress the management by short-pouring the guests. Or, if the liquor cost rises, there is the possibility that the bartender is becoming careless. Such cases are immediately investigated, and proper action taken. Since we, in marketing, pride ourselves on being the focal point of communicating with the customers, insofar as the kind of service they want and the prices they are willing to pay, we act as sort of watchdogs for the customers of our restaurants.

FOURTH CASE IN POINT

MONITOR RESTAURANT
FOR QUALITY CONTROL

Bartenders

Considering that it's a well-known fact that a bartender can make or break a restaurant, especially the businessman's bar-and-restaurant and the pub-type of restaurant, it is not surprising that restaurateurs regard a good bartender as one of their chief assets. Nevertheless, there is a wide difference of opinion of what constitutes a "really good" bartender. According to Mike Walsh of The Holding Company:

> As far as I'm concerned a top-notch bartender is one who can have one stranger converse very soon with another stranger. To my mind the bartender—because he has a reason to talk to everybody at the bar, and everybody has a reason to talk to him—is a bridge, or, if you will, a communicator between two strangers sitting at the bar. And once the two people are talking to each other, the bartender isn't tied down to these two customers anymore. He can go down the bar and talk to somebody else. He's got those two guys happy as clams. He doesn't have to do

CASE IN POINT

anything more with them, except to keep supplying them with drinks. They're having a fine time enjoying the bar and each other's company.

In other words, I believe that the bartender's chief responsibility, besides serving drinks, is to start a conversation between two complete strangers. After all, people come to a bar for two reasons: for the drinks, and to meet people.

BARTENDER'S CHIEF RESPONSIBILITY

When you are a bartender in a busy place like ours, you meet some 500 people a day. You can't possibly talk to all of them; you can't keep them all entertained. And if you try to make everybody happy, you're going to end up making nobody happy. So the way to solve the problem is to get everybody talking to each other. And a good bartender accomplishes this by finding out, almost as soon as the person sits down and orders a drink, what the customer's likes and dislikes are. What does he or she want to talk about? What is he interested in? What does he do for living? What is his hobby? Then, if the person occupying the next bar stool has anything in common with the first customer, the bartender involves both persons in a mutually interesting topic, and stays around only until the conversation between these two gets rolling.

Subjects? There is always sports; frustration in the office; "good old alma mater"; and, of course, the weather. Sure, it's all lightweight talk, but that's what bar customers are there for. They want to discuss something with somebody, but nothing serious. They have enough serious matters in their place of work, or at home, or both places.

A good bartender is valued so high because for most people it's quite difficult to walk up to a complete stranger and start a conversation. On the other hand, it's very easy to walk up to a bartender and say "Hello," because the bartender is supposed to talk to you. That's why a really good bartender will have, within a short time, everybody talking to everybody else. And when these customers leave, they will think that the bartender is the greatest guy in the world. And that's how it should be, because it takes a special talent to do what he does.

Mr. Levie of Gulliver's has a different idea of what constitutes a good bartender.

CASE IN POINT

When we select a bartender, we have a certain criteria relative to the type of person we want. One thing we try to avoid; this is what we call the hard-core bartender.

I look upon a bartender as a doctor of mixology. That's his forte. That means that basically he is a combination of psychologist, friend, sports analyst, and also somebody to lean on as far as the guests are concerned. Consequently, we look for people with a certain personality and ability who can handle all types of guests in all types of situations, PLUS possess mechanical skills.

RIGHT PERSONALITY, RIGHT ATTITUDE

We give our bartenders good equipment, and all the tools they need, including a detailed bartender's training manual. But unless they have the right personality, the right attitude toward our guests, toward our operation, they won't do for us. I'll even go further. I prefer a college graduate, and I don't care what his degree is in. But that tells me something about his personality. It tells me that he wants to amount to something. That's important to me, because every college graduate I hire—man or woman—is a potential manager for me.

Obviously I cannot advance everybody, but I want to consider every qualified applicant that way. I want to foster my managers from within, so I do look for a college degree. I also take into account their physical appearance. Then I check their experience. This is important in terms of whom they worked for, how frequently they changed jobs, why they left their last employer, and other good questions like these. I consider their skills, and try to determine whether they are the right kinds. I also try to find out the way they are thinking; the goals they have. And primarily, I want to find out what their attitude is. In other words, I want to know if they have a negative attitude, or if they are eager to join our team.

We spend a great deal of time—at least two or three interviews—trying to ascertain whether the people who apply can become part of our team. But we think it's worth it.

How to Deal with a Problem Customer

An important aspect of maximizing customer satisfaction is how a problem person is handled in the restaurant, i.e., in the dining area or in the bar. To cite Mike Walsh of The Holding Company:

Anytime you're dealing with a problem person, you must remember that each person is an individual with an individual problem; you must remember that you want to solve a specific problem.

CASE IN POINT

When you talk to a person who is determined to cause trouble, keep in mind that you want to have that person leave your premises, quiet down, or just stop the disturbance. It's very important that you remember that *this is all* you want to accomplish. In other words, you can never let your ego get into it. *You've got to keep your ego out of the situation.*

PROBLEM-SOLVING IDEAS

It doesn't matter what that person is saying. What you want to do is to solve the problem. But that is when many people make a mistake. They get involved in it; their feelings get involved in it. They get angry.

You cannot *afford* to get angry. You are there to solve a problem in your bar or dining area. And you solve it by asserting some authority over the person you're dealing with. Whether it's a man or woman, whether they're drunk or sober, you have to exert your authority. *But you never want to force them into a corner. You always want to provide them a graceful way of getting out of the situation.*

They know that you're going to win; they know that you have everything on your side, your whole staff and the police department. Moreover, you have lawyers and insurance. So all you want to do is to get them out. If you're dealing with an ugly drunk, for example, you just want him out of your place.

He can call you anything he wants to call you. If he leaves, that's what you want. If you get involved with him, you've made the biggest mistake you can make, because that's what—in general—the troublemaker wants.

All in all, there are three things that you have to do:

1. Remember that each case, each person is unique.
2. Remember WHY you're negotiating with the person, so NEVER get emotionally involved in the situation.
3. Keep constantly in mind WHAT you're doing: you want the problem person to leave your premises, so you give the person "a way out," and *never* back the person into a corner.

8

Restaurant and Food Service Sanitation Codes

CHAPTER HIGHLIGHTS

Contrary to popular impression, the federal government has established and published food service sanitation code guidelines which must be adhered to by the states. Consequently, each state has published brochures on its own sanitation code guidelines for the food service industry. However, these brochures are not sent automatically to every restaurateur; you have to write for them. (A sampling of the contents of California, Illinois, and New York states' sanitation code guidelines, as well as a directory of the Health Departments of the 50 states, are at the end of this chapter.) The states' sanitation codes vary quite a lot. Some states barely meet the federal government's requirements, while others go beyond the federal guidelines, and require much stricter rules than does the federal government. California, for example, is very lenient, while Illinois is very stringent. Moreover, Illinois and some other states are going to require *within the next few years* that one of the management—the owner or manager in a restaurant—be certified in the sanitation codes by the particular state. This is a recent development. And while not all the states are in this initial move, in a growing number of them the trend seems to be toward sanitation codes certification.

Doug Scott, Director of Food Purchasing of the successful multi-state and Canada restaurant chain, Victoria Station, Inc., has this to say:

> I think a lot of confusion comes from the fact that you've got federal guidelines and state guidelines. And the states vary tremendously from the federal guidelines. To the single unit operator who has only one restaurant in one state, all he or she would have to do is become familiar with that state. But for us, as a chain, we have to conform in each area to what that state wants. I think the biggest problem though with the sanitation codes is just lack of education. I think very few restaurateurs are really knowledgeable on what sanitation is insofar as a restaurant is concerned.

CASE IN POINT

That's why verbal communications between restaurant operators and health inspectors are not enough, especially since there's a high rate of turnover of both restaurant staff and health inspectors. If you want to play it safe, there are several avenues in which you can get information on your particular state's sanitation codes. You can always contact either the national or the local Restaurant Association, the state Department of Health, or the Food and Drug Administration (FDA). They all have to make this information public. All you have to do is to request it.

I don't know about other people, but I've found in almost all states that the Health Department is more than happy to supply us with information, because the more we do, the easier their job. Similarly, whether you have or haven't the written sanitation codes, if you are honest and open with the health inspectors, and if you set your standards higher than those of the Health Department, you'll never have any problems. In fact, whatever the standards are for the Health Department, ignore them. Just go for the highest possible standards in all cases. Then how can you have problems? On the other hand, if you're lax in this very important area, you're asking for trouble."

Michael Walsh of the Holding Company says:

SECOND CASE IN POINT

In addition to the written guidelines that we get from the State of California, Department of Health, the inspectors give us a written notice, stating everything they want done, and a time period, something like three weeks or a month. Then they come back and re-inspect at that time. If it's not done, I think they give you another period of time to do it in. They're very lenient. If you don't do it then, I think they fine you.

As far as I'm concerned, the major problem here in California is that we've gone a year and a half between inspections. There's no schedule for the health inspectors. They just drop in, which is fine. But if you're clean, they'll write you up as a clean restaurant, and probably won't be back for quite awhile. Which is all right. But if they were here more often, they'd keep you on your toes. Of course, I realize that it's a problem of logistics. It's probably an almost impossible job to inspect a particular restaurant more often. After all, there are 2400 liquor licenses just in the city of San Francisco, which means that there are probably 5000 eating establishments in the city.

Oh, I'm sure that everybody gets inspected periodically. But if you inspected a restaurant a month, or five restaurants a day, and had 5000 to do, by the time you got back to the ones with problems, and you wrote up all your forms, well, you can see that it's almost an impossible job.

Another problem is that a lot of one-unit restaurateurs don't read the local state sanitation codes. The fact is that most people don't know what the codes are, but they keep their restaurant clean. You can't have a successful restaurant without keeping it clean. That's the only way. You set up your own level of sanitation criteria—which is usually better than the state's—and if you keep it at that high level by constant inspection, you won't have to worry about inspectors or the sanitation codes. But you or your managerial staff has to get down on hands and knees and look under the stove and other places, or the man that does the kitchen or does the floor at night won't be down on his hands and knees cleaning it.

J. Edward Fleishell, owner/operator of Le Club, says:

THIRD CASE IN POINT

First of all, sanitation codes prescribe minimal standards of cleanliness. If you're running a restaurant any way near correctly, you're far above the sanitation code problem. We've never had a problem like that. When we took over the restaurant it was appallingly filthy. The flues were greasy; the potato baskets were re-used; the air conditioning was incredibly dirty. We took probably a pound of grease out of the air conditioning. We spent thousands of dollars putting the place in shape, so that the kitchen is as clean as the dining room. Every year we have a crew of painters that come in and completely paint the kitchen. We have a service on the flues and vents. We have a service on air conditioning, so that everything is immaculate. I'd rather see a dirty dining room than a dirty kitchen— because the kitchen is where it's all at. This is far above the municipal laws on cleanliness.

We very seldom see a health inspector because the standard is so far lower than what we maintain just on the average. It's sort of like the Department of Alcoholic Beverage Control. The average good restaurant never sees a liquor investigator because it doesn't even come near having a problem with the law. The average good restaurant won't even think of serving minors, watering drinks, or changing brands and serving an inexpensive brand for an expensive brand. In sum, if you run a clean restaurant, you won't have any problems with sanitation codes or health inspectors.

REPRESENTATIVE EXCERPTS FROM SEVERAL STATES' DEPARTMENTS OF HEALTH AND SANITATION REGULATIONS

• State of Illinois Food Preparation and Employee Health Requirements

• California Restuaurant Act Sanitation Requirements and Health Requisites for Restaurants

• Table of Contents of New York State Sanitary Code for Food Service Establishments

• Directory of Departments of Health State Officials for All Fifty States

These selections are intended as representative. The reader may obtain health and sanitation regulations in full by writing to the state Departments of State.

ILLINOIS*

ARTICLE II

FOOD PREPARATION

Rule 2.07—*General.* Food shall be prepared with the least possible manual contact, with suitable utensils and on surfaces that prior to use have been cleaned and sanitized.

Rule 2.08—*Raw Fruits and Raw Vegetables.* Raw fruits and raw vegetables shall be washed thoroughly before being cooked or served. Fruits and vegetables to be served raw shall be washed in sanitized utensils.

Rule 2.09—*Cooking Potentially Hazardous Foods.* Potentially hazardous foods requiring cooking shall be rapidly cooked to heat all parts of the food to a temperature of at least 140 degrees F., except that:

   (a) Poultry, poultry stuffings and stuffed meats shall be cooked to heat all parts of the food to at least 165 degrees F. with no interruption of the cooking process.

   (b) Pork and pork products shall be cooked to heat all parts of the food to at least 150 degrees F.

   (c) Rare roast beef shall be cooked to an internal temperature of at least 130 degrees F., and rare beef steaks shall be cooked to a temperature of 130 degrees F. unless otherwise ordered by the immediate consumer.

Rule 2.10—*Dry Milk and Milk Products.* If reconstituted, dry milk and dry milk products may be used in instant desserts and whipped products, or for cooking and baking purposes.

Rule 2.11—*Liquid, Frozen, Dry Eggs and Egg Products.* Liquid, frozen, and dry eggs and egg products shall be used only for cooking and baking purposes.

Rule 2.12—*Reheating.* Potentially hazardous foods that were cooked and then refrigerated shall be heated rapidly to 165 degrees F. or higher throughout before being placed in a hot food storage facility. Steam tables, bainmaries, warmers, and other hot food holding facilities are prohibited for the rapid heating of potentially hazardous foods.

Rule 2.13—*Reconstitution.* Nondairy creaming agents shall not be reconstituted for consumption on the premises in quantities exceeding one gallon.

Rule 2.14—*Product Thermometers.* Metal stem-type numerically scaled indicating thermometers accurate to ± 3 degrees F. shall be provided and used to assure attainment of proper internal cooking temperatures of all potentially hazardous foods.

*Courtesy of Roy W. Upham, D.V.M., Chief of Division of Food and Drugs.

Rule 2.15—*Thawing Potentially Hazardous Foods.* Potentially hazardous foods shall be thawed:

(a) In refrigerated units in a way that the temperature of the food does not exceed 45 degrees F.; or

(b) Under potable running water at a temperature of 70 degrees F. or below, not to exceed two hours with sufficient water velocity to agitate and float off loose food particles into the overflow; or

(c) In a microwave oven only when the food will be immediately transferred to conventional cooking facilities as part of a continuous cooking process or when the entire, uninterrupted cooking process takes place in the microwave oven; or

(d) As part of the conventional cooking process.

ARTICLE III—PERSONNEL

EMPLOYEE HEALTH

Rule 3.01—*General.*

(a) No person while affected with a disease in a communicable form or while a carrier of such disease, or while afflicted with boils, infected wounds, or acute respiratory infection, shall work in a food service establishment in an area and capacity in which there is likelihood of transmission of disease to patrons or to fellow employees, either through direct contact or through the contamination of food or food contact surfaces with pathogenic organisms. No such person shall be employed in such an area and capacity in a food service establishment.

(b) When suspicion arises as to the possibility of transmission of a disease from any person through an item of food, the regulatory authority or its representative is authorized to require any or all of the following measures:

(1) The immediate exclusion of that person from any food-handling activities;

(2) The immediate exclusion of the food in question from distribution and use; and

(3) The adequate medical and bacteriological examination of the person, of his associates, and his and their body discharges.

PERSONAL CLEANLINESS

Rule 3.02—*General.* Employees shall thoroughly wash their hands and the exposed portions of their arms with soap and warm water before starting work, during work as often as is necessary to keep them clean, and after smoking, eating, drinking, or using the toilet. Employees shall keep their fingernails clean and trimmed.

CLOTHING

Rule 3.03—*General.*

(a) The outer garments of all persons, including dishwashers, engaged in handling of food or food contact services shall be reasonably clean.

(b) All clothing shall be cleanable unless it is discarded after a single use.

(c) Employees, while in preparation, handling or service of food, shall wear hairnets, headbands, or other effective hair restraints to prevent the contamination of food or food contact surfaces.

CALIFORNIA RESTAURANT ACT*

Article 2. Sanitation Requirements for Restaurants
(Article 2 repealed and added by Stats. 1961, Ch. 633)

28540. The floor surfaces in all rooms in which food or beverage is stored or prepared, utensils are washed, or refuse or garbage is stored, and the floor surfaces of toilet, dressing, or locker rooms and of walk-in refrigerators, shall be of such construction and material as to be easily cleaned. They shall be smooth, in good repair, and kept clean.

The floors of rooms in which food or beverage is served shall be clean and kept in good repair. The use of sawdust on floors of food preparation rooms is prohibited.

(Added by Stats. 1961, Ch. 633.)

28541. The walls and ceilings of all kitchens shall be of light-colored, smooth, washable material and kept clean and in good repair. The walls and ceilings of food storage rooms and toilet rooms shall be of such construction as to be easily cleaned and shall be kept clean and in good repair.

This section shall not be applicable to storage rooms where foods or beverages in unopened bottles, cans, cartons, sacks, or other original shipping containers, are stored, but such storage rooms shall be kept free from vermin and in a sanitary condition.

(Added by Stats. 1961, Ch. 633.)

28542. Walls and ceilings of all rooms shall be cleaned as often as is necessary to maintain them in a clean condition. In rooms or areas where food is prepared, or where utensils are washed, acoustical tile may be used, if it is not installed less than six feet above the floor and where used it complies with all applicable requirements of this section and Section 28541.

(Added by Stats. 1961, Ch. 633.)

28543. All restaurants shall be so equipped, maintained, and operated as to control the entrance, harborage and breeding of vermin, including flies. When flies or other vermin are present, effective control measures shall be instituted for their control or elimination.

(Added by Stats. 1961, Ch. 633.)

28544. Light shall be provided in all areas and rooms of a restaurant. The working surfaces in rooms or areas in which food or beverages, other than alcoholic beverages, are prepared or in which utensils are washed shall be provided with at least 10 foot-candles of light. Food and utensil storage rooms, and toilet and dressing rooms shall be provided with at least four foot-candles of light, as measured 30 inches above the floor.

*Courtesy of Director of Department of Health.

During general cleanup activities, adequate light for efficient conduct of such activities shall be provided in the area being cleaned.
(Added by Stats. 1961, Ch.633.)

28545. Ventilation shall be provided for dissipation of disagreeable odors and condensation in all rooms of a restaurant where food or beverages are prepared, stored, or served, where utensils are washed, in garbage storage rooms, and in all toilet rooms and dressing rooms.

At or above all cooking equipment, such as ranges, griddles, ovens, deep-fat fryers, barbecues, and rotisseries, there shall be provided mechanical exhaust ventilation equipment, as required to effectively remove cooking odors, smoke, steam, grease, and vapors.

All food preparation and dishwashing areas shall have sufficient ventilation to provide a reasonable condition of comfort for the employees working there, consistent with the job performed by the employee.
(Added by Stats. 1961, Ch. 633.)

28546. Hot and cold running water under pressure shall be provided in all areas in which food is prepared or utensils are washed. The water supply shall be of a safe, sanitary quality.
(Added by Stats. 1961, Ch. 633.)

28547. Toilet facilities shall be provided convenient to the employees on the premises. Where there are five or more employees of different sex, separate toilets shall be provided for each sex. Toilet rooms shall be separated from other portions of the restaurant by tight-fitting, self-closing doors.
(Added by Stats. 1961, Ch. 633.)

28548. Handwashing facilities, in good repair, shall be provided for employees within or adjacent to toilet rooms and shall be equipped with hot and cold running water. Handwashing detergent or soap and sanitary towels or hot-air blowers shall be provided at handwashing facilities in permanently installed dispensing devices.

No person shall begin or resume work in a restaurant after visiting the toilet without first wasing his hands. Legible signs shall be posted in each toilet room directing attention to this requirement.
(Amended by Stats. 1963, Ch. 544.)

28549. A room or enclosure, separated from toilets or any food storage or food preparation area, shall be provided where employees may change and store their outer garments. No employee shall dress or undress or store his clothing in any other area on the premises.
(Added by Stats. 1961, Ch. 633.)

28550. All toilets, lavatory facilities, and change rooms shall be maintained in a clean and sanitary condition.
(Added by Stats. 1961, Ch. 633.)

28551. Toilet paper, handwashing detergent or soap, and sanitary towels or hot-air blowers shall be provided at all times when the restaurant is in operation.
(Amended by Stats. 1963, Ch. 544.)

28552. All plumbing shall be installed and maintained so as to prevent contamination of the water supply and minimize the possibility of con-

tamination of foods and specialized equipment used in the washing of utensils.
(Added by Stats. 1961, Ch. 633.)

28553. All multiuse utensils and all show and display cases or windows, counters, shelves, tables, refrigeration equipment, sinks, dishwashing machines and other equipment or utensils used in connection with the preparation, service, and display of food, in the operation of a restaurant, shall be made of nontoxic materials and so constructed, installed, and maintained as to be readily cleaned, and shall be kept clean and in good repair.
(Added by Stats. 1961, Ch. 633.)

Article 6. Health Requisites for Restaurants, Itinerant Restaurants, Vehicles, and Vending Machines
(Article 6 added by Stats. 1961, Ch. 633)

28686. All employees preparing, serving, or handling food shall wear clean, washable outer garments or other clean uniforms and shall keep their hands clean at all times while engaged in handling food, beverage, or utensils. All such employees shall wash their hands and arms with soap or detergent and warm water before commencing work after using toilet facilities, and before returning to work, and at such other times as are necessary to prevent contamination of food.

All such employees shall wear hairnets, caps, headbands, or other suitable coverings to confine their hair when reasonably required to prevent the contamination of foods, beverages, or utensils. Wherever practical, employees serving food shall use tongs or other implements rather than their hands. The use of tobacco in any form by any employee while handling or serving food, beverage, or utensils is prohibited. No employee or other person shall use tobacco in any form in any room or space used primarily for the preparation of food, and the employer shall post and maintain "No Smoking" signs in such room or places.
(Amended by Stats. 1972, Ch. 254.)

28687. No person shall be employed in a restaurant, itinerant restaurant, vehicle, or in connection with a vending machine, who, in the opinion of the local health officer, is affected with, or a carrier of, any disease in a stage which is likely to be communicable to persons exposed as a result of the affected employee's normal duties as a food handler.
(Added by Stats. 1961, Ch. 633.)

28688. When information as to the possibility of disease transmission is presented to the local health officer, he shall investigate conditions and take appropriate action. The health officer may, after investigation and for reasonable cause, require any or all of the following measures:

(a) The immediate exclusion of such employee or owner from the restaurant, itinerant restaurant, vehicle, or affected vending machine operation, by the health officer.

(b) The immediate closing of the restaurant, itinerant restaurant, vehicle, or affected vending machine operation, until no further danger of disease outbreak exists in the opinion of the health officer.

(c) Adequate medical examination of the owner, employee, and his coemployees, with such laboratory examination as may be indicated; or should such examination or examinations be refused, then the immediate exclusion of the refusing owner, employee, or coemployee from that or any other restaurant, itinerant restaurant, vehicle, or affected vending machine operation, until an adequate medical or laboratory examination shows that he is not affected with or a carrier of any disease in a communicable form.

(Added by Stats. 1961, Ch. 633.)

28689. The state department shall adopt and approve first aid instructions designed and intended for use in removing food which may become stuck in a person's throat. Such instructions shall be limited to first aid techniques not involving the use of any physical instrument or device inserted into the victim's mouth or throat.

The state department shall supply to the proprietor of every restaurant in this state such adopted and approved instructions. The proprietor of every restaurant shall post the instructions in a conspicuous place or places, which may include an employee notice board, in order that the proprietor and employees may become familiar with them, and in order that the instructions may be consulted by anyone attempting to provide relief to a victim in a choking emergency.

In the absence of other evidence of noncompliance with this section, the fact that the instructions were not posted as required by this section at the time of a choking emergency shall not in and of itself subject such proprietor or his employees or independent contractors to liability in any civil action for damages for peesonal injuries or wrongful death arising from such choking emergency.

Nothing in this section shall impose any obligation on any person to remove, assist in removing, or attempt to remove food which has become stuck in another person's throat. In any action for damages for personal injuries or wrongful death neither the proprietor nor any person who nonnegligently under the circumstances removes, assists in removing, or attempts to remove such food in accordance with instructions adopted by the state department, in an emergency in a restaurant, shall be liable for any civil damages as a result of any acts or omissions by such person in rendering such emergency assistance.

(Added by Stats. 1975, Ch. 1142.)

NEW YORK*

CHAPTER I—STATE SANITARY CODE

PART 14

SERVICE FOOD ESTABLISHMENTS
(Statutory Authority: Public Health Law, §225)

*Courtesy of Albert T. Squire, Director of Burea of Food and Sanitation.

DIRECTORY OF STATE OFFICIALS*

ALABAMA

STATE DEPARTMENT OF PUBLIC HEALTH
State Office Building, Montgomery 36104

Ira L. Myers, M.D.   (205) 832-3121
State Health Officer

   Bureau of Environmental Health
   William T. Willis, Director   (205) 832-3176

      Division of Inspection
      Director   (205) 832-3175 FOOD SERVICE

ALASKA

STATE DEPARTMENT OF HEALTH AND SOCIAL SERVICES
Pouch H-01, Juneau 99811

   Section of Environmental Health
   Pouch H-06F, Juneau 99811   FOOD SERVICE

   Sidney D. Heidersdorf, Chief   (907) 465-3120

ARIZONA

STATE DEPARTMENT OF HEALTH SERVICES
1740 West Adams Street, Phoenix 85007

   Bureau of Sanitation
   411 24th Street, Phoenix 85008   FOOD SERVICE

   John H. Beck, M.P.H.   (602) 255-1160
   Chief

      General Sanitation Section
      A.J. Battistone, Manager   (602) 271-3151

      Food Protection Section
      Mason A. Lang, B.S.   (602) 271-3151
      Manager

ARKANSAS

STATE DEPARTMENT OF HEALTH
State Health Building, 4815 W. Markham
Little Rock 72201

Rex C. Ramsay, Jr., M.D.   (501) 661-2111
State Health Officer

   Division of Sanitarian Services   (501) 661-2171
   James M. Wallace, Director

   Jack Lusby, Assistant Director   (501) 661-2171

      Food Services Section
      William Teer, Supervisor   (501) 661-2171

*Through the courtesy of Department of Health, Education, and Welfare, Public Health
Service, Food and Drug Administration, Rockville, MD 20857.

CALIFORNIA

STATE DEPARTMENT OF HEALTH
714 "P" Street, Office Bldg. #8
Sacramento 95814

Jerome A. Lackner, M.D.   (916) 445-1248
Director

  Food and Drug Section
  Chambers F. Bryson, Chief   (916) 445-2263 FOOD SERVICE

COLORADO

STATE DEPARTMENT OF PUBLIC HEALTH
4210 East 11th Avenue
Denver 80220

Anthony Robbins, M.D.   (303) 388-6111 FOOD SERVICE
Executive Director

  Office of Health Protection
  Dr. Thomas Vernon, Director   (303) 388-6111

CONNECTICUT

STATE DEPARTMENT OF HEALTH
State Office Building, 79 Elm Street
Hartford 06115

Douglas S. Lloyd, M.D.   (203) 566-2279
Commissioner

Dennis Kerrigan, Acting Deputy   (203) 566-2197 FOOD SERVICE
Commissioner

  Food Service Section
  Paul M. Schur, Chief

DELAWARE

STATE DEPARTMENT OF HEALTH & SOCIAL SERVICES
Administration Building, Delaware State Hospital
New Castle 19720

Patricia C. Schramm, Ph.D.   (302) 421-6705

  Bureau of Environmental Health
  Donald K. Harmeson, Chief   (302) 678-4731

    Office of Food Control   FOOD SERVICE
    Frederic Stiegler
    Program Director

DISTRICT OF COLUMBIA

DEPARTMENT OF ENVIRONMENTAL SERVICES
Presidential Building, 415-12th Street, NW.
Room 307, Washington 20004

Herbert Tucker, Director   (202) 629-3415 FOOD SERVICE

  Food Protection Division
  Foster Robertson, Chief   (202) 629-5965

John W. Grigsby   (202) 629-5965
Shellfish Sanitarian

FLORIDA

STATE DEPARTMENT OF BUSINESS REGULATION
725 S. Bronough
Tallahassee 32304

Jackson J. Walter, Executive Director   (904) 488-7114

Division of Hotels and Restaurants   FOOD SERVICE
Anthony Ninos, Director

GEORGIA

STATE DEPARTMENT OF AGRICULTURE
19 Martin Luther King Drive
Capitol Square, Atlanta 30334

Thomas T. Irvin, Commissioner   (404) 656-3600

General Sanitation Unit   (404) 656-4871 FOOD SERVICE
Lovett Fletcher, Acting Director

HAWAII

STATE DEPARTMENT OF HEALTH
Kinau Hale Building, 1250 Punchbowl Street
P.O. Box 3378, Honolulu 96801

George A. L. Yuen, Director   (808) 548-6506

Vern C. Waite, M.D.   (808) 548-6506
Deputy Director

James S. Kumagai, Ph.D., Deputy Director of (808) 548-4139
Environmental Health

Sanitation Branch   (808) 548-3225
Peter Goo, Chief

Harold Matsura, Chief Sanitarian, Island of (808) 961-7371
Hawaii, Hilo, Hawai

David Nakagawa, Chief Sanitarian, Island of (808) 244-4228
Maui, Wailuku, Maui

Theodore Inouye, Chief Sanitarian, Island of (808) 245-4323
Kauai, Lihue, Kauai

IDAHO

STATE DEPARTMENT OF HEALTH AND WELFARE
State House, 700 West State Street
Boise 83720

Milton Klein, Director   (208) 384-2336

Milk & Food Quality Control Section   FOOD SERVICE
Carroll E. Despain   (208) 384-2437
Supervisor

ILLINOIS

STATE DEPARTMENT OF PUBLIC HEALTH
535 West Jefferson
Springfield 62706

Paul Q. Peterson, M.D.   (217) 782-4977
Director

Office of Environmental Health   (217) 782-6550
Leroy E. Stratton, Associate Director

Division of Food and Drugs   (217) 782-2015
Roy W. Upham, D.V.M., M.S. Chief

INDIANA

STATE BOARD OF HEALTH
1330 West Michigan Street
Indianapolis 46206

William T. Paynter, M.D.   (317) 633-8400 FOOD SERVICE
Secretary and State Health Commissioner

Retail Food Section
Robert L. Jump, Chief   (317) 633-0369

IOWA

STATE DEPARTMENT OF HEALTH
Lucas State Office Building
Des Moines 50319

Norman L. Pawlewski   (515) 281-5605
Commissioner of Public Health

Ronald D. Eckoff, M.D.   (515) 281-4910
Director, Community Health

Consumer Protection Division
   Food Products Control   FOOD SERVICE
   Earl M. Revell, Chief   (515) 281-8602

KANSAS

STATE BOARD OF AGRICULTURE
503 Kansas Avenue
Topeka 66603

William W. Duitsman, Secretary   (913) 296-3556

Donald L. Jacka, Jr., Assistant Secretary

Bureau of Food and Drugs
Building 321

James Pyle, Acting Director   (913) 862-9360
                             ext. 541

MARYLAND

STATE DEPARTMENT OF HEALTH & MENTAL HYGIENE
201 W. Preston Street
Baltimore 21201

Neil Solomon, M.D., Ph.D.   (301) 383-2600
Secretary

Environmental Health Administration
Donald H. Noren, Director   (301) 383-2740

MASSACHUSETTS

STATE DEPARTMENT OF PUBLIC HEALTH
600 Washington Street, Boston 0211

Jonathan Fielding, M.D.   (617) 727-2700
Commissioner

  Division of Food and Drugs
  George A. Michael, D.Sc.   (617) 727-2670
  Directory

MICHIGAN

STATE DEPARTMENT OF PUBLIC HEALTH
350 North Loga Street
P.O. Box 30035
Lansing 48909

Maurice S. Reizen, M.D.   (517) 373-1320
State Health Officer

  Division of Food Service Sanitation   FOOD SERVICE
  David Hodgson, Chief   (517) 373-2936

KENTUCKY

STATE DEPARTMENT FOR HUMAN RESOURCES
Capitol Annex
Frankfort 40601

Peter D. Conn, Secretary   (502) 564-7130

  Division for Consumer Health Protection
  Irving Bell, Director   (502) 564-3722

  Dudley J. Conner   (502) 564-3722
  Assistant Director

    Food Control Branch
    John Draper, Manager   (502) 564-3127

LOUISIANA

STATE DEPARTMENT OF HEALTH AND HUMAN RESOURCES
P.O. Box 3376
Baton Rouge 70821

William O. Cherry, M.D.   (504) 389-5796
Secretary of State Health Officer

  Sanitarian Services   FOOD SERVICE
  J. C. Watson, Acting Chief   (504) 568-5181

MAINE

STATE DEPARTMENT OF HUMAN SERVICES
221 State Street
Augusta 04330

David E. Smith, Commissioner   (207) 289-2376

Bureau of Health
George E. Sullivan, M.D.
Director

Division of Health Engineering
Donald Hoxie, Director   (207) 289-3826

MINNESOTA

STATE HEALTH DEPARTMENT
State Department of Health Building
717 Delaware Street, SE., Minneapolis 55440

Warren Lawson, M.D.   (612) 296-5460
Commissioner

Section of Environmental Field Services   FOOD SERVICE
Charles B. Schneider, Chief   (612) 296-5335 (INSPECTIONAL)

MISSISSIPPI

STATE BOARD OF HEALTH
P.O. Box 1700, 2423 North State Street
Jackson 39205

Alton B. Cobb, M.D.   (601) 354-6646 FOOD SERVICE
Executive Officer

Division of Food & General Sanitation   (601) 354-6616
Paul M. Rankin, Director

MISSOURI

STATE DEPARTMENT OF SOCIAL SERVICES
DIVISION OF HEALTH
Broadway State Office Building
High & Broadway, P.O. Box 570
Jefferson City 65101

Herbert R. Domke, M.D.   (314) 751-4330
Director

Joseph B. Reichert   FOOD SERVICE
Deputy

Food Service & Lodging Sanitation
Conn B. Roden, Chief   (314) 751-4679

MONTANA

STATE DEPARTMENT OF HEALTH & ENVIRONMENTAL SCIENCES
W. F. Cogswell Building
Helena 59601

Arthur C. Knight, M.D.   (406) 449-2544
Director

Food & Consumer Safety Bureau   FOOD SERVICE
Vernon E. Sioulin, Chief   (406) 449-2408

NEBRASKA

STATE DEPARTMENT OF HEALTH
301 Centennial Mall South
Third Floor, Lincoln 68509

Henry D. Smith, M.D.   (402) 471-2133
Director

Division of Housing & Environmental   FOOD SERVICE
Health   (INSTITUTIONS)
Fred Jolly, Director   (402) 471-2541

NEVADA

STATE DEPARTMENT OF HUMAN RESOURCES
505 East King Street, Room 600
Carson City 89710

Bureau of Consumer Health Protection   FOOD SERVICE
Al Edmundson, Chief   (702) 885-4750

NEW HAMPSHIRE

STATE DEPARTMENT OF HEALTH AND WELFARE
8 Loudon Road
Concord 03301

Robert E. Whalen, Commissioner   (603) 271-3331

Division of Public Health
61. S. Spring Street
Concord 03301

Maynard H. Mires, M.D.   (603) 271-2526
Director

William T. Wallace, M.D.   (603) 271-2526
Deputy Director

Bureau of Consumer Protection
Public Health
State Laboratory Building
Hazen Drive
Concord 03301

Gilman K. Crowell, Chief   (603) 271-2747

William F. Oakman, Chief
Inspector

NEW JERSEY

STATE DEPARTMENT OF HEALTH
Health-Agriculture Building
John Fitch Plaza—S. Warren Street
P.O. Box 1540
Trenton 08625

Joanne E. Finley, M.D., M.P.H.   (609) 292-7837
Commissioner

Food and Milk Program   (609) 292-1180   FOOD SERVICE
Joseph W. Prince, Chief   (INSPECTION &
                                                                CERTIFICATION)

NEW MEXICO

STATE DEPARTMENT OF HEALTH AND ENVIRONMENT
P.O. Box 968
Santa Fe 87503

George Goldstein, Ph.D., Secretary   (609) 392-1180

Food Protection Unit   FOOD SERVICE
Gus Werner, Manager   (505) 827-5271

NEW YORK

STATE DEPARTMENT OF HEALTH
Tower Building, Empire State Plaza
Albany 12237

Robert P. Whalen, M.D.   (518) 474-2011
Commissioner

Bureau of Food & Institution Sanitation   FOOD SERVICE
Albert T. Squire, Director   (518) 474-3291

NEW YORK CITY DEPARTMENT OF HEALTH
125 Worth Street
New York, 10013

Pascal J. Imperato, M.D.   (212) 566-7150
Commissioner

Shirley A. Mayer, M.D.   (212) 566-7154
First Deputy Health Commissioner

Jean B. Cropper, M.P.H.   (212) 566-8023
Deputy Commissioner for Environmental
Health Services

Bureau for General Operations   FOOD SERVICE
Zigmund (Irving) Feldman   (212) 566-8210
Director

NORTH CAROLINA

STATE DEPARTMENT OF HUMAN RESOURCES
325 North Salisbury Street
Raleigh 27611

Dr. Sarah T. Marrow, Secretary   (919) 733-4534

Division of Health Services
225 No. McDowell Street
Raleigh 27602

Jacob Koomen, Jr., M.D., M.P.H.   (919) 733-3446
Director

Food, Lodging & Environmental   FOOD SERVICE
Sanitation Program   (919) 733-2261
Stacy Covil, Program
Supervisor

NORTH DAKOTA

STATE DEPARTMENT OF HEALTH
State Capitol
Bismarck 58501

Jonathan B. Weisbuck, M.D.   (701) 224-2372   FOOD SERVICE
State Health Officer

OHIO

STATE DEPARTMENT OF HEALTH
450 E. Town Street, P.O. Box 118
Columbus 43216

John H. Ackerman, M.D.   (614) 466-2253
Director

  Bureau of Environmental Health   FOOD SERVICE
  Ray B. Watts, Chief   (614) 466-5190

OKLAHOMA

STATE DEPARTMENT OF HEALTH
Northeast 10th & Stonewall
P.O. Box 53551
Oklahoma City 73105

Joan K. Leavitt, M.D.   (405) 271-4200
Commissioner

  Consumer Protection Service   (405) 271-5455   FOOD SERVICE
  Lloyd Parham, Chief

OREGON

STATE DEPARTMENT OF HUMAN RESOURCES
318 Public Service Building
Salem 97310

Richard Davis, Secretary   (503) 378-3034

  Health Division
  1400 S. W. Fifth Avenue
  P.O. Box 231
  Portland 97201

  Kristine Gebbie, Administrator   (503) 229-5032

  Edward Press, M.D., Deputy Administrator   (503) 229-5806
  & State Health Officer

    Office of Protective Health Services   FOOD SERVICE
    Douglas Pike, Chief   (503) 229-5861

PENNSYLVANIA

STATE DEPARTMENT OF HEALTH
Health & Welfare Building
7th & Forster Sts., P.O. Box 90
Harrisburg 17120

Leonard M. Machman, M.D.   (717) 787-6436
Secretary

Division of Food Control   FOOD SERVICE
Leroy C. Corgin, Jr. Chief   (717) 787-4315

PUERTO RICO

DEPARTMENT OF HEALTH
Bldg. A, Psychiatric Hospital Grounds
Rio Piedras, Box 9342
San Juan 00908

Jaime Rivera Dueno, M.D.   (809) 951-8259

Environmental Health Services and   FOOD SERVICE
Consumer Protection
P.O. Box 10427
Caparra Heights Station
Caparra Heights 00922

Jorge Chiriboga, M.D.   (809) 767-9264
Assistant Secretary for Environmental Health

RHODE ISLAND

STATE DEPARTMENT OF HEALTH
75 Davis Street, Providence 02908

Joseph E. Cannon, M.D.   (401) 277-2231
Director

Division of Food Protection & Sanitation   FOOD SERVICE
Frederick A. Siino, Chief   (401) 277-2833

Manuel T. Canario, Jr.
Deputy Chief

SOUTH CAROLINA

STATE DEPARTMENT OF HEALTH AND ENVIRONMENTAL CONTROL
J. Marion Sims Building, 2600 Bull Street
Columbia 29201

Albert G. Randall, M.D., M.P.H.   (803) 758-5445
Commissioner

Bureau of Environmental Sanitation   FOOD SERVICE
E. Carl Fox, Chief   (803) 758-5684

Richard K. Rowe, Assistant Chief

Division of Food Protection
Williard Horton, Director   (803) 758-5476

SOUTH DAKOTA

STATE HEALTH DEPARTMENT
State Office Building #2
Pierre 75701

Edward DeAntoni, Ph.D., Acting State Health   (605) 224-3361
Officer & Secretary

Division of Sanitation & Safety   FOOD SERVICE
Gerald M. Nelson, Director   (605) 224-3141

Melvin O. Nelson, Radiation Specialist

TENNESSEE

STATE DEPARTMENT OF PUBLIC HEALTH
Cordell Hull Building, Nashville 37219

Eugene W. Fowinkle, M.D.   (615) 741-3111
Commissioner

Division of Hotel and Restaurant   FOOD SERVICE
Inspection
Ed Puckett, Director   (615) 741-2511

TEXAS

STATE DEPARTMENT OF HEALTH
1100 W. 49th, Austin 78756

Fratis L. Duff, M.D.
Commissioner

Division of Food and Drugs   FOOD SERVICE
Robert L. Henna, Director   (512) 458-7248

UTAH

STATE DEPARTMENT OF SOCIAL SERVICES
150 West North Temple
Salt Lake City 84103

Dr. Anthony W. Mitchell   (801) 533-5331
Executive Director

Food Service Section   FOOD SERVICE
Richard A. Sweet, Supervisor   (801) 533-6163

VERMONT

STATE DEPARTMENT OF HEALTH
60 Main Street
Burlington 05401

A. Marshall McBean, M.D.   (802) 862-5701
Commissioner   ext. 251

Environmental Health Division   FOOD SERVICE
Ms. Joan Bouffard, Chief of Food/Lodging   (802) 862-5701
   ext. 234

VIRGIN ISLANDS

DEPARTMENT OF HEALTH
Knud-Hansen Memorial Hospital
P.O. Box 7309, St. Thomas 00801

Roy L. Schneider, M.D.   (809) 774-0117
Commissioner

John S. Moorehead, M.D.   (809) 774-0117
Deputy Commissioner for Health Services

Division of Environmental Health   FOOD SERVICE
Richard J. Maloney, M.P.H.   (809) 774-6880

VIRGINIA

STATE DEPARTMENT OF HEALTH
James Madison Building
109 Governor Street
Richmond 23219

James B. Kenley, M.D.   (804) 786-3561
Commissioner

Bureau of Tourist Establishment Sanitation   FOOD SERVICE
Joseph W. Moschler, Director

WASHINGTON

STATE DEPARTMENT OF SOCIAL AND HEALTH SERVICES
M/S OB-44, Office Building #2
Olympia 98504

Harlan P. McNutt, M.D.   (206) 753-3395

Occupational Health Section (M/S LD-11)

Terrance Strong, Head   (206) 753-3468

Charles Bartleson, Food Coordinator   (206) 753-2555 FOOD SERVICE

WEST VIRGINIA

STATE HEALTH DEPARTMENT
State Office Building
1800 East Washington Street
Charleston 25305

George Pickett, M.D., Director and State   (304) 348-2971
Epidemiologist

Environmental Health Services   FOOD SERVICE
Robert McCall, Director   (304) 348-2981

WISCONSIN

STATE DEPARTMENT OF AGRICULTURE, TRADE & CONSUMER
PROTECTION
801 West Badger Road, Madison 53713

Gary E. Rohde, Secretary   (608) 266-7100

Arthur R. Kurtz, Deputy Secretary   (608) 266-7102

Section of Hotels & Restaurants   FOOD SERVICE
Roy K. Clary, Chief   (608) 266-8336

<u>WYOMING</u>

STATE DEPARTMENT OF HEALTH AND SOCIAL SERVICES
State Office Building
Cheyenne 82991

W. Don Nelson, Director   (307) 777-7657

Environmental Surveillance and Control   FOOD SERVICE
Service
Robert L. Coffman, M.P.H.   (307) 777-7951

9

OSHA and What It Means
to Restaurant and Food Service Managers

CHAPTER HIGHLIGHTS

There is more misconception in the restaurant industry about the government Occupational Safety and Health Act (OSHA) of 1970 than about any other government (federal, state, or city) regulations. Most restaurateurs, for example, don't know that if they have ten or fewer employees during any calendar year, the "small employer exemption" applies to them, and they don't need to keep OSHA records. (See page 20, "SMALL EMPLOYERS," in the enclosed latest brochure from the U.S. Department of Labor, Bureau of Labor Statistics, Report 412-3.)

However, if there is "an accident which results in the death of one or more employees, or the hospitalization of five or more employees, it must be reported by telephone or telegraph within 48 hours to the nearest Area Director of the Occupational Safety and Health Administration." (See Appendix A of the OSHA brochure for addresses of area offices.) Similarly, workers' compensation insurance has nothing whatsoever to do with OSHA. Specifically, "There is no direct connection between workers' compensation laws and recordkeeping requirements under the Occupational Safety and Health Act." (See page 22 of the 1978 OSHA brochure.)

To comply with OSHA's regulations, all you have to do (if you employ no more than ten persons) is to report any occupational injury or accident that requires medical care. If it's only a first aid case, the injury or accident does not have to be reported. (See page 11, "FIRST AID.") You also have to post "in a conspicuous place the Summary (OSHA No. 200 form) by February 1 of each year, and leave it there until March 1." Samples of the needed OSHA forms (Nos. 101 and 200) are also enclosed. A clear diagram showing when to report and when *not* to report an accident is shown in Figure 9-1. This diagram is from the OSHA brochure, but since it illustrates an important point, it is also included here.

Guide to Recordability of Cases Under the Occupational Safety and Health Act

**(In addition, any accident which results in a death or hospitalization of
5 or more employees must be reported by telephone or telegraph within 48
hours to the Area Director of the Occupational Safety and Health Administration.)**

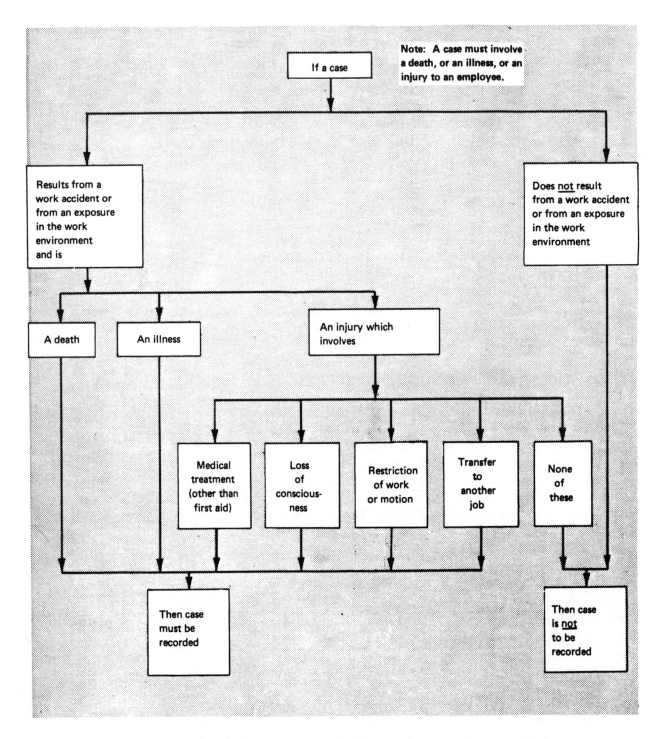

FIGURE 9-1   From Report 412-2 U.S. Department of Labor, Bureau of Labor
                Statistics, 1975.

NOTE: Because certain OSHA regulations are somewhat dynamic, i.e., in a state of flux, for the latest ordinances check with OSHA, U.S. Department of Labor, Bureau of Labor Statistics, Washington, D.C., 20212.

To quote Mike Walsh of The Holding Company:

> My interpretation of OSHA is that it is a protective agency to watch over employees' health and welfare. They want to make sure that your employees are not climbing shaky ladders, using bad electric plugs, walking down rickety stairs, and that sort of thing. They're a very tough agency. You do everything by OSHA rules, or you don't do it. There are very strict standards that they set up when you're in the construction business, for example. Your Building Inspectors that come around are all governed by OSHA. OSHA is a monumental agency. You have to have certain types of plugs and cables and other things—all OSHA approved. They're very tight. They make sure that everything works well. They're a very conservative group, because—in my estimation at least—they're over-protective. I don't know whether that's good or bad. If they save a couple of people's fingers and arms, I guess it's worth it.
>
> But let's say you open a restaurant that had been completely approved by the Building Department, the Fire Department, and everybody else. Both the Building Inspector and the Fire Department still come by periodically to check things out. Especially in a metropolitan area like the one I'm in, the Fire Department is a very strict agency, because they're very touchy about high rise fires. So they're very strict about what you can and cannot do. They work along with the Building Department and the Health Department, which are all state agencies. But I would imagine that OSHA is heavily involved in all three as advisors or regulatory agencies.
>
> To make sure that you don't get into any trouble with any of the agencies, including OSHA, you have to check all of your appliances, equipment, and electrical and gas outlets. You have to go from wall to wall, from top to bottom periodically, or you have your manager(s) do that. You delegate the responsibility of checking the linen closet to make sure it's kept clean, and that you don't have mice or dust or rags piling up. You have to periodically inspect every square foot of your restaurant and your equipment. We have somebody going through this restaurant— every nook and cranny—at least once a week. I'm a cleaning and safety freak. I like to see everything neat and put away. Somebody checks every part of the restaurant about every two weeks to make sure that someone else has really checked it every week. In other words, it's check and double check. I check my managers; the managers check the help; and the help check each other—which doesn't necessarily mean it gets done. But at least we try. This place runs like a clock. It stays fairly close to what I expect it should be. And at the same time there is less possibility of violating OSHA or any other state or federal law.

CASE IN POINT

According to J. Edward Fleishell of Le Club:

> Most restaurants rely almost totally on their accountant to set up recordkeeping systems such as OSHA. The federal government gives you posters such as OSHA's Job Safety and Health Protection. These

ANOTHER CASE IN POINT

have to be posted. But so far as reports are concerned, most restaurant operators—because the average restauranteur more often than not is not a college graduate but a fellow who worked himself up from bartender, waiter, or busboy—rely on their accountant. That's why the whole concept of recordkeeping is probably the weakest link in most restaurants.

A Midwest restaurateur sums up the feeling of most operators, both one-unit and restaurant chains:

STILL ANOTHER CASE IN POINT

> OSHA can get real touchy. If you don't do it right, you can be in a lot of trouble. You need the exact facts; you need an expert on OSHA. I'd get it from the horse's mouth—from OSHA. And more specifically, from the nearest OSHA regional office.

(See Appendix B of the brochure for the addresses and telephone numbers of all OSHA regional offices.)

To provide accurate, up-to-date information on OSHA and OSHA-related recordkeeping and reporting requirements, the brochure "What Every Employer Needs to Know About OSHA Recordkeeping" follows. In addition, there are sample OSHA forms for every possible occasion.

10

Targeting and Getting the Most Out of Restaurant and Commercial Food Marketing/Advertising Dollars

CHAPTER HIGHLIGHTS

Marketing is not just promotion through advertising. Marketing involves study, analysis, definition of the "product (restaurant) personality," development of specific strategy, and implementation/follow-through of that strategy. To develop a successful marketing strategy, you have to define your marketing objectives based upon the type, class, and personality of your restaurant and your target customers, and compare the total picture to the competition in the marketplace. Once you have come up with a definition or "positioning statement," you have to follow through. And you accomplish the latter by having everything—from the items on the menu to the attitude of your staff, to the type and level of advertising in various media—present the same image statement about your restaurant. Thus, if your restaurant is a steak house, or a seafood restaurant, or an ethnic restaurant, or a white tablecloth dinner house, every item, every word, every action, and primarily the total feeling in your restaurant and in your advertising should reinforce that image. And because advertising (communicating to the potential audience that your product is available) is only one of the many elements that constitute marketing strategy, you should never advertise just for the sake of advertising. In other words, to get the most for your money, make sure that you have a valid objective based on a carefully developed marketing strategy *before* you advertise.

Basic Building Blocks of Marketing

Two essential phases have to be performed before an effective marketing strategy can be developed:

1. Study Analysis
2. Defining/Positioning

1. Study and Analysis

To begin with, you have to determine what, in fact, your restaurant is. Are you a steak house? Are you a gourmet house? Are you a family restaurant? How important is price value to you? Who is your competition? On a scale that runs from a very inexpensive type of restaurant chain like the Sizzler, to the more expensive, finer European style restaurant like Bourgogne or Ondine's (in San Francisco), or Antoine's (in New Orleans), or Seth Jones (in Raleigh), or the Palace (in New York), where do *YOU* fit? Where in that continuum do you *WANT* to fit? And where in that continuum is there a potential for growth? To arrive at a definition of what your restaurant is or should be, make a thorough study of all areas of the restaurant, including food, service, atmosphere, and price structure. Then, based on an analysis of these variables, make a decision as to the type of food you should serve, the price/value relationship, the atmosphere you want to create, and the type and extent of care and service you want to give your customers. (Actually, you define yourself in line with what you perceive your audience's demands are.) This might mean a complete revision in the make-up of your restaurant; it might mean a shift in the emphasis of the restaurant; or it might mean no change at all.

Says Jon Larrick, Vice President of Marketing of Saga Enterprises' highly successful Velvet Turtle restaurant chain:

CASE IN POINT

> When I joined the company a few years ago, my posture was that we needed to define what we were. We couldn't tell people what we were if we couldn't define ourselves. And until we could articulate it, it would be very difficult to advertise to people why they should come to one of our 18 Velvet Turtle restaurants.
>
> Management agreed with me, and so we conducted a thorough study. We talked to the founders, to management, to employees, and to many, many customers, and we came up with what we called a "positioning statement"—a definition of what The Velvet Turtle is. Basically, we defined ourselves as a casually elegant, white tablecloth dinner house, contemporary California style, serving a variety of uniquely prepared specialty dishes, as well as steaks, prime rib, and lobster, cooked and served by people *who care*. Next, we communicated to all levels of the organization not only our positioning statement, but also the quality we wanted to offer in the restaurant. We did this so that everybody in the company would have a clear picture of the image we wished to project, of what, in fact, we as a company wanted to be. As a direct result of our defining ourselves and our goal, we made a very important shift in the emphasis of the restaurant. We moved from a heavy emphasis on prime rib, steak, and lobster, to serving a wider variety of uniquely prepared specialty dishes. In our attempt to upgrade the type of food we serve, we now are selling more specialties like Pacific Cold-Water Abalone, Roast Duckling l'Orange, Rack of Lamb—for which we've become very well known, Beef Wellington—which we've recently added to the menu, and Fresh Fish in Season.

"POSITIONING STATEMENT" OF A RESTAURANT

Other equally successful restaurateurs who run steak houses or other limited-menu types of dinner houses may disagree with The Velvet Turtle's management insofar as one type of restaurant having more potential for long term growth than another. Nevertheless, according to the latest trade reports, many limited-menu houses that want to stay competitive are adding more items to the menu. Actually, different restaurateurs interpret differently the study done for the National Restaurant Association which states that in any two-week period about 50 million American families dine out...and that these customers spend $44 billion or more at some 375,000 eating establishments...and that the day is not far off when fifty percent of the consumers' food dollars will be spent away from home in outside dining places.

2. Defining/Positioning

Defining Your "Product Personality"

The product personality of a restaurant is not one simple thing that you can put on a plate and present, saying, "Here it is." It is the waitress or waiter; it is the uniform; it is the pictures on the walls or the flower on the table. It is the manager greeting the guest at the door; it is the well-designed menu; it is the clean washroom. In other words, it is the totality of a restaurant that comprises its product personality. And it all must satisfy your customers' needs.

To go one step further, restaurant operation perhaps can be best explained by making an analogy to a manufacturing company. The latter has a plant, a production facility: that's your kitchen. The kitchen is used to prepare the food element of your product. The chef is the production manager. He's making food instead of watches, plastic toys, integrated circuits, or whatever. The manufacturing company maintains a sales organization and a distributing center. Your sales organization includes your waiters/waitresses, and bartenders. And they are your distributors as well. They do a combination of selling and distributing the product from the kitchen (the plant) to the customer. Thus, when the production manager, i.e., the chef, prepares an item, he has to think in terms of that item satisfying a particular customer's demands. And when the waitress serves a guest, she has to think in terms of what that particular customer wants; what she can sell that person. Consequently, when you walk into a restaurant and the waitress comes over and opens the menu and says with a smile, "Today we've got a special on this," or "This is particularly good today," or "May I suggest this?", she sells more and adds more to the customer's satisfaction than the waitress who, it seems, couldn't care less if the customer is pleased or not.

By comparing the restaurant field to any other field, the concept of marketing, which is in fact satisfying the target customer, falls into place. And by using marketing methodology, it is easier to determine if your product personality responds to the customers' needs and preferences, whether you operate a single store or a restaurant chaim.

Defining Your Target Customers

To respond positively to your customers' requirements, you have to define the people you are trying to reach in terms of standard demographics: income, age, and geography. But you also have to look at life style. Life styles are changing. Age is no longer a major factor. Income is a factor, but income alone

WHAT CONSTITUTES A RESTAURANT'S PERSONALITY

no longer divides people. Many blue-collar workers have yearly incomes equal to or exceeding those in the professional and technical fields. Consequently, the standard blue-collar and white-collar division no longer breaks down according to income. People in any category, with any life style, can eat anywhere they want, and it is up to the particular restaurant to make people of certain life styles comfortable. Simply put: people will go where they feel comfortable; where they feel wanted.

For example, if you defined yourself as a dinner house and your target customers are people looking for a pleasant, relaxing dinner experience, you should emphasize the dining aspect, i.e., the food instead of the bar business. This does not mean elimination of the bar. There could very well be a cocktail lounge, but it should be associated with the restaurant. It should be for guests who might want a cocktail before dinner, or a drink after dinner. The point is that if you define your customers as people who are looking for a quiet dinner experience, your emphasis should be on the dining area. On the other hand, if your target audience is the young, swinging single set, then the emphasis should be on the bar and cocktail lounge, and possibly a rock band to make the young people feel more comfortable and thus boost your liquor sale.

DIFFERENT CUSTOMERS HAVE DIFFERENT NEEDS, DIFFERENT WANTS

In sum, different audiences have different needs, different wants. They want to spend their money different ways, and you have to define who *YOUR* target audience is in order to make sure that you give them what they are looking for, what they want. If you give the right product to the wrong people, it's just as abortive as if you give the wrong product to the right people. You are bound to lose either way. That is why it's so very important that you define your restaurant in line with what you perceive your audience's needs are. That is why the definitions of your product personality and your target customers have to be compatible, if you want your restaurant to be successful.

Importance of Location

Location is a very important factor in the restaurant field. Specifically, on what street the restaurant is located; whether it has easy access and sufficient parking area; whether it is in a safe neighborhood, and if possible, whether the people who live within its trading area are your target customers.

If you want to appeal to people in the $25,000 or more income bracket, you wouldn't put your restaurant in the area of low-income houses. It would be illogical, as well as highly unprofitable. On the other hand, if your customers are in the $10,000 income bracket, locating your restaurant in a wealthy suburb wouldn't be appropriate either.

COMPETITION CAN HELP YOU OR HURT YOU

In addition to being in the right area, and on an accessible street with sufficient parking place, you also have to check whether you are near your competition. Competition can help you or hurt you. If you are on a street that becomes a "restaurant row," that is advantageous for business. Conversely, if it's an inconvenient location, and you are the only restaurant in the area, it may be very difficult to get customers. However, if there are eight restaurants in the area, even if it is five miles from town, it becomes the "place to go." Consequently, the pie gets bigger, and everybody gets a larger share of it.

Price Value Relationship

When you make a pricing decision, you have to consider several factors. Obviously, you have to look at the cost of the item, since each item has to have a minimum profit margin or contribution to stay on the menu.

If the retail price of abalone, for example, went up from $7.50 to $15.00 a pound, you could double the price on your menu. Of course, the probabilities are that people would stop buying abalone, so it would have to come off the menu. The fact is that no restaurateur who wants to stay in business can afford to leave items on the menu that do not contribute to the profitability of the store. So you do have to consider the cost of items, but you also should look at your total menu.

The cost of a dinner in a restaurant is not just $8.50 for a steak. It's made up of a cocktail, maybe two, maybe a carafe of wine, possibly an appetizer, and maybe some dessert in addition to the entree. So it's not $8.50 for the steak that counts; it's $22.00 for the check, or $26.00, or $35.00. That's what people notice. You can raise the price of an entree a quarter or fifty cents and get no complaints, as long as other items on the menu are reasonable. Customers will remember the size of the check they pay when they leave the restaurant, and not the price of an entree.

WHAT CUSTOMERS
REMEMBER

You should weigh price in terms of value to the customer, not as price alone. And if you have done your basic work in defining your product personality, you will find that determination of price value will be an integral part of your definition. Moreover, if you don't price your items properly, your customers will let you know. Consumers today know food costs, and consequently are willing to pay certain amounts for certain kinds of food. You change prices on the menu, and you, no doubt, will notice a shift in the items that customers buy. For example, if the retail price of fish goes up, the customers are aware of that fact. And if you don't raise the price of fish on your menu, people will recognize fish as being a bargain, and will order that entree over some other item. Thus, when you consider pricing, you have to look at your target audience. What kind of people are coming to your restaurant, what do they expect to find in your restaurant, and what do they expect to pay for that kind of service? In the final analysis, it is the customer who establishes the price. If you overprice an item, your sales will drop off on that item, and so you really gain nothing by it.

Theme vs. No-Theme Restaurant

If you are a theme restaurant, then everything you do should carry out that theme. A good example of this is the very successful Victoria Station restaurant chain. Their theme is railroad, and they stress this theme through their logo (see illustration) as well as by both the outside and the inside of their restaurants which are refurbished boxcars and cabooses placed around a central waiting room filled with British Railways artifacts. By contrast, there are other, equally successful restaurants that do not have a theme; one of them is The Velvet Turtle, whose management says:

CASE IN POINT

> We're not a theme restaurant. We don't have a theme to hang our hat on. We're not a "nostalgic" early 1920s restaurant; we're not a funky restaurant. We are a very basic dinner house, almost traditional, but not

The Old Logo

The New Logo
Courtesy of Velvet Turtle

stuffy, and our new logo reflects this philosophy (see illustrations). We don't use the turtle as a theme. We don't have our staff running around looking like turtles, nor do we have turtle-shape menus or serve turtle soup.

Because we believe that people coming to The Velvet Turtle are looking for a fine dining experience, good quality food at a good price value, it's even more important for us to maintain our image and ensure that everything we do makes the same statement. We have to be very careful to maintain that fine line between being too elegant and perhaps intimidating people; or being too casual and not living up the reputation of quality that we want.

We are not in the business of selling steaks; we're not in the business of selling prime ribs; we're not in the business of selling martinis. We are providing pleasant dining experiences. And that's why people come back to The Velvet Turtle; they like the total experience in our restaurants.

Planning the Advertising Strategy

Creative Strategy

To develop an effective strategy, whether you are an individual operator, or the marketing director of a restaurant chain, you must go back to the definition of the restaurant and ascertain point by point not only what your restaurant is and what you are trying to sell, but also who is your target audience. There is no best advertising media for a restaurant per se. It depends on a lot of things. It depends on your target audience; it depends on how much you can spend; it depends on what sort of creative direction you want.

Mr. Larrick of The Velvet Turtle says:

CASE IN POINT

After we defined our restaurant, we had to develop a creative strategy. Having defined ourselves as a "white tablecloth dinner house, offering a variety of uniquely prepared specialty dishes, served by people who care, and at an appealing price value," we asked ourselves, how are we going to get this message across to the public? We can't write a two-paragraph definition about what The Velvet Turtle is and put it in the newspapers. That's not going to motivate people. In fact, people won't read it, because nobody, except us, cares what our definition is. So, together with our advertising agency, Honig, Cooper, and Harrington in Los Angeles, we developed a creative strategy based on our positioning statement.

What we've done in our advertising is to emphasize the variety of fine foods we serve; the people who care; and the price value. Basically, we are telling people what we are and what we're trying to sell.

The nice thing about our advertising is that we are not gimmicky; we are not themey. We are as straightforward as we can be about what the customer can expect when he or she walks into one of our restaurants.

CAUTION: When you advertise and set up an expectation, make sure that you fulfill it. Because if you build up an expectation, and a guest walks into your restaurant and does not get what you have promised, you will do more harm than if you have not advertised at all.

The Media Question

Once you have developed a creative direction and know whom you want to reach, generally that dictates the type and level of media. According to Mr. Larrick:

CASE IN POINT

We derive two benefits from our advertising. We have a general image campaign in quality magazines that displays in beautiful four colors our uniquely prepared food. Then we have more specific retail advertising that we use during promotion periods, such as Mother's Day, St. Patrick's Day, Secretaries Week, in local newspapers as well as radio. We may say, "Come into The Velvet Turtle this Mother's Day." That's very specific retail selling. It is meant to convince people to visit us today. The other is directed to the future, trying to build our long-term image for the restaurant; trying to reinforce our positioning in the marketplace, and strengthen our image with people who have visited our restaurants. Of course, we're also reaching out to make new friends, and invite them to come in and try us out.

The media we use is dictated, to some degree, by our creative strategy. Since we have 16 restaurants in California, plus one in Seattle and one in Houston, we use as many regional magazines as we can. We are also in local newspapers—usually in the restaurant sections. In addition, we're on news and easy listening radio stations. We don't go on rock stations because that's not our audience. We also use outdoor billboards, and occasionally we use direct mail to zero in on a very tight geographic area.

CAUTION: In using the media you have to be very careful that the people you reach are your target audience. For example, if your target customers are fairly well educated, up-scale higher income individuals, you would have to go into the media such as quality magazines and metropolitan newspapers that they are likely to read. Similarly, if your target customers are the less educated individuals, earning lower income, you would advertise in sports magazines and local newspapers they are likely to read.

The Most Profitable Media for Restaurant Advertising

The fact is that there is no way of ascertaining which media works better, which is more effective for advertising a restaurant. It's very difficult to measure the effectiveness of advertising. There are many things that can affect an individual in choosing a particular restaurant. These factors can range from the product personality and the location, to word of mouth. If you could run an ad in the newspaper and give a separate phone number, or run a coupon, then perhaps you could track how many people respond to your ad. But in the long run, it's very difficult to say that one media works better than another one.

Different media can do different things for you.

WHAT VARIOUS MEDIA
CAN DO FOR YOU

Radio, for example, is thought of more as a retail vehicle. Marketing professionals believe that people respond most quickly to radio and newspaper. If people open a newspaper and look in the restaurant section, they are looking for a restaurant. It's just like the yellow pages of the telephone book. If a person looks in the yellow pages for a restaurant, that person is ready to go for dinner. If that same person sees an outdoor board or reads a magazine ad for a restaurant, it may sink into his mind. Magazine advertising—especially four-color display—attempts to create an image in the reader's mind about a particular restaurant. It is not saying, "Put the magazine down. Get in your car, and come here right now." The objective of magazine ads is to plant an image in the people's mind. Most marketing professionals are of the opinion that the various media works together, each reinforcing the other. For example, people driving down the street see an outdoor board. Then they hear about a particular restaurant on the radio and see it advertised in the newspapers. Finally, the wife might say to the husband, "Why don't we try that place? I've heard a lot about it." Then perhaps the husband says, "If it's the same place the Roberts went to, okay. Jim told me the food was great, and the prices reasonable."

In sum, it takes a lot to convince people. You have to continually talk to the public. You have to talk to people because there are other restaurateurs talking to them, trying to get them away from you. You have to constantly remind them of *what you are*; of *what you are serving*; of *your price value*. And the total impact of it is that people will visit your restaurant and fulfill their expectations, and subsequently become steady guests.

CAUTION: Don't deal with anybody who says he will do a great ad for you and build up your business until you have first come up with your positioning statement. In other words, before signing up with an advertising agency to produce an ad for you, you should determine what your product personality is; what your objectives are; what response you want of the person who sees the advertising; what it is you want the potential customer to feel about you. In sum, you should not advertise just for the sake of advertising. You should have a purpose behind it. You should say, "I'll spend this amount of money for advertising, but then I'm going to watch my customer count to make sure it works."

Advertising can go wrong for a number of reasons.

It can go wrong because you are saying the wrong things to the right people. It can go wrong because what you are saying to the people isn't true. For example, if you say in your ad that you have the best price value in town, and the customers walk in and they pay twice as much in your restaurant as they do anywhere else, without getting any more for it, they are not going to come back. And you are just wasting your money advertising.

Advertising can go wrong because you are using the wrong media, the wrong time slot, or the wrong newspaper. You may be saying the right things, but you may not be reaching your target audience. For example, if you want to reach adult businessmen via radio, it would be a mistake to go on rock stations. Similarly, if you are advertising on TV and you want to reach housewives, you should go on in the daytime because that's when they watch TV. If you want to reach school children, you should go on Saturday morning when they're home. And if you want to reach businessmen, you should go on in the evening, during the evening news, or put your ad in the *Wall Street Journal,* or the sports or the financial page of the daily newspaper.

WHEN ADVERTISING FAILS

In all of your advertising, however, there are certain things that must be observed if you are to get the most for your marketing/advertising dollars. These are:

- The message has to be right!
- The message has to be honest!
- It has to say what you are!
- It has to be direct!
- It has to be noticed!

Implementation/Follow-Through

The main thing in controlling the implementation or follow-through of your positioning statement is to ensure that everything, both in your operation and in your advertising, makes the same statement, conveys the same feeling about the restaurant. Under this quality control umbrella you include the kind of people you hire; the kind of service you give; the kind of food you serve; the plates you put it on; the prices you charge; and the drinks you pour. Similarly, your ads in magazines and newspapers have to communicate the same statement as your radio and TV commercials.

Often people develop an idea, but they execute their idea in 22 different ways. They will have a fine tablecloth dinner house, and they will hire a lot of youngsters who don't have the training or knowledge to serve a fine dinner. Or they will have a funky-fun contemporary place and have a lot of stuffed shirt waiters who intimidate the customers. Both of these are likely to result in the failure of the restaurant.

On the other hand, if you define yourself properly, i.e., in terms of what your customers' demands are today, and you offer your product at a proper price value, and then follow through by delivering the product you advertise, you should be well on your way to having a successful, profitable restaurant.

PART TWO
Kitchen Staff Management

11

Key Ingredients to Successful Kitchen Staff Management

CHAPTER HIGHLIGHTS

According to successful restaurateurs the key ingredients to successful kitchen staff management are: (a) total involvement of employees, (b) pride of staff in place of employment, (c) pride of staff in their own job, (d) effective supervisor/manager, (e) open communications line between manager and staff, (f) opportunity for employees to be creative, (g) unstructured environment, (h) structured environment, (1) higher-than-average wages, (j) average union wages, (k) selection of applicants who will be in rapport with the customers, with the particular environment, and most importantly with the other employees, and (l) effective training. While some restaurateurs place high wages on top of the list for successful kitchen staff management, others claim that money alone cannot effect employee involvement. Still others say that employee pride in the restaurant cannot be developed unless the owner/operator is respected, and the restaurateur can gain such respect by an in-depth knowledge about food and/or kitchen operations, and knowledge about managing people. Specifically, he or she must know the art of management via delegation, responsibility, incentive for creativeness, and praise. In short, the restaurateur should emphasize the human factor that plays such an important part within the management-employee relations.

Restaurant owners have interesting ideas on just what constitutes successful kitchen staff management. Arnold Artola of Shenanigans says:

> Kitchen staff management, as in my case, which is a small restaurant, is making the employees feel that they have the freedom of a certain amount of creativity as well as responsibility in their work. My cook, for example, is given a certain amount of freedom by allowing him to add a little bit to the recipe—my recipe. However, I also expect him—because we're a small establishment—to accept perhaps more responsibility than if he worked in a large restaurant. I find that giving such privileges keeps

CASE IN POINT

the staff in line with less effort because they respond to responsibility and the chance to be somewhat creative. In a restaurant of this size, the kitchen consists of one cook, an assistant, and a dishwasher. By giving the cook a little extra responsibility that he might not get in a larger establishment, we make him feel more pride in his job, and it takes a little bit less management to watch him.

Specifically, at Shenanigans the cook does all the primary ordering on a day-to-day basis. I set the standards for ordering, but the cook takes care of the ordering. He's also responsible for all sanitation in the kitchen. Of course, all cooks are responsible for sanitation in the kitchen, but my cook is made to *feel* that he's responsible for it. Simply put, it's not that he *has* so much more responsibility; it's that he is *made to feel* that he has more responsibility.

You can accomplish this fine but very important difference by *asking* your staff to do things, instead of *telling* them to do things. All you have to do is be a little more friendly and suggest that this be taken care of, or that be performed. Then, if it's not done, you become a little more aggressive. But give people a choice where they feel they're getting a choice, and you're going to get much more out of them. Never put people in a position where they feel they're being ordered around. I have to be put in a corner to give somebody a direct order. I like giving people a choice, making them feel it's their choice.

SECRET OF SUCCESSFULLY MANAGING KITCHEN STAFF

The same principle applies to all of your kitchen staff. *You make them feel* that they're part of the restaurant by making them part of the decision-making policies. That is, policy decisions not concering the way you run your business, but those that concern the customer. For example, if I'm going to make any changes in menu or other things, I usually ask my help what they think of it. And I go by the consensus. You'll find that your employees are fairly responsible, even when it comes to something like whether a waiter or waitress should or shouldn't be allowed to smoke on the floor. You'll find that people given a certain amount of choice will make the same decisions you would, because a responsible individual will react in a certain way to certain situations. I try to make all such decisions a group effort. Once again, however, we're talking about a small business. On a corporate level these things won't work. Here we act not quite as a family, but in such a way as to make everybody feel that he or she has a part of the business. It gets back to responsibility. If you give people a little bit more responsibility, they'll respond better to you, and you'll get more work out of them.

STAFF SELECTS NEW HIRE

By the same token, it is my staff that select the kind of responsible and responsive people that we need in our place. It's rather interesting. I do very little job interviewing. My idea of a job interview is that if somebody comes in and I feel he or she has the job qualifications—the initial qualifications to work—and I need somebody, I'll hire him or her. But this is with the stipulation that at the end of two weeks we're going to sit down and talk about it. We then discuss what kind of job these new people have done, or thought they have done, and other things. If they don't fit into our mold, then at the end of the two weeks they're terminated. It's sort of a trial period during which the rest of the staff weed out people not suitable for our place. They'll force them out if they don't fit in.

People in a job interview are always going to tell you what you want them to say. They're going to answer your questions the way they feel you want them to answer. So It's silly to ask questions. What you do is to put them in a work situation, with the stipulation that at the end of a certain period their progress is going to be reviewed, and they'll either fit in or not fit in. I've had people that did not fit in on three previous jobs in a row, yet they fit in fine with me. Conversely, there are people that fit in fine here, and do not work well in some other restaurant. I just had a waitress switch from days to nights. She had a day lunch job somewhere, and worked nights here. She worked one day in that other restaurant, and then called me and asked if she could go back on days here because the environment in the other place was totally different.

Here at Shenanigans we are informal to the degree that we have to be informal to make money, because we have to get right down on the level with the customer. We can't put the customer higher than we are, and we can't get below him. We have to be at the same level. That's why the staff in the public area have to know what they're doing; have to fit into our mold. And when it comes to people who are not up front and don't deal with the public, I simply judge them by the fact of whether they want to work or not. It's very simple. You are either going to work and get along with everybody, or you're not. It's not that complicated. People either work hard or they don't. The people who work the best are the people who are motivated by money.

ONE WAY OF DEALING WITH CUSTOMERS

In other words, the person who works the hardest for you, the best for you, is the one who wants his or her paycheck. These people have a certain pride, and their motivation is taking care of themselves. Such applicants are going to be your best employees because they're motivated to do their job, and ergo, they're going to fit into that particular mold. I've had waitresses that didn't fit in because they were too busy socializing at the bar with the customers. The other waitresses forced them out, because they themselves were working too hard; because they were doing their work, while the socializing ones were not. The same thing applies in the kitchen. If a person is working, he or she doesn't have time to not fit into the mold. I'm not creating a mold of what I think a perfect employee should be. It's a work mold.

WORK MOLD

But because of our particular work mold, I pay above union scale; I have to. Because to operate a restaurant like this, you have to manage with fewer people, which in turn is more work load for each person. For example, you get a man who tends bar for you. Well, it's common in small restaurants for the bartender to be the cashier as well. My bartender handles, say, $1,500 a day. He takes in all the money for the food checks and liquor. In other words, there's no cashier. He's bartender-cashier. The waitresses pay him for the food and drinks. In my opinion a person should be paid for the responsibility of taking care of that money. I only have three waitresses. I could have four waitresses and pay them less. I have three good waitresses. It's cheaper for me to pay them a little bit

PAYING STAFF ACCORDING TO RESPONSIBILITY

more and have less help. Still, it's not only money that counts. It's also pressure. There's no pressure here, unless the person brings it on himself. I'm not talking about work pressure such as lunch or cocktail time; I'm talking about pressure from management. Here, nobody's standing behind the staff screaming at them. If there's a problem, it's taken care of later. Nothing is ever done in front of the customer or during work time. I'd be cutting off my nose to spite my face by getting somebody upset while in the middle of working.

WHY A SMALL
ESTABLISHMENT PAYS
HIGHER WAGES

Here's a good example of why a small establishment pays more. It's better for me to pay a cook above average wages and get a good cook, than to pay a mediocre cook average wages. It's the same thing with your help. If you pay them a little more, you get better help. In other words, you get what you pay for. You can go to an establishment like Gulliver's where they pay a set wage because they have a set job to do. It's all done by the manual. They always have ten people who want jobs there. For a small establishment like this, my whole crew doesn't add up to as many waitresses as one Gulliver's restaurant has. I've got to have reliable, competent people, so I have to pay more. I pay more than places like Gulliver's or Charley Brown's, all corporate restaurants. I pay well above what a person would get in a large restaurant. The only people who are paid higher wages are in your privately owned bars and restaurants. But they have to pay more to get good people away from large restaurants, because it's a little easier to work for a corporation than for a one-unit owner. The work isn't easier at restaurant chains, but you don't have to think. The thinking is all done for you. The waiters or waitresses don't have to worry about what to say to the customer; they tell them what to say to the customer. It's all pre-set. In an establishment like this, it's not. In a small restaurant there's more opportunity for creativeness or individualism, but at the same time, it makes the job a little harder. There's a bit more pressure on the person to be an individual to the customer. Your individuality is lost in a corporation, while in a smaller place there's no uniform, no written procedures for serving, talking, or anything like that.

CRITERIA FOR HIRING
STAFF FOR A SMALL
RESTAURANT

That's why I think if you're a small restaurant owner, you have to be honest about what you expect from an applicant. When I hire people I expect them to fit in. I expect them to get along. If they don't get along, it's one of the main reasons I get rid of them. The only other thing I'd say is that in a place like this, you have to be a little more pliable. If a customer wants something that maybe isn't on the menu or is a little bit of trouble for the employee, that employee has to understand that in a small restaurant, he or she has to make an effort to please the customer. In other words, I have to make sure that my employees understand that they have to be pliable, flexible, and courteous. They have to have the right attitude. I don't want them saying, "Well, it's too much trouble," or "The cook is too busy." Probably the best way to put it is that I don't like negativeness.

If you have a person who gets along famously with the customers, but has trouble with the rest of your staff, you should get rid of him or her. It's not worth it to try to keep such employees. They can't affect as many customers as they can employees. If they're getting along with five customers but have three waitresses upset, they're not getting along with 15 customers. It is a negative situation. And with all the other problems that a small restaurant owner has, you don't need any negative situations.

Insofar as basic incentive or motivation is concerned, whether the people work in a large or small restaurant, the only real incentive or motivation has to be dollars earned in a day. That has to be the initial motivation because a person has to survive. But we, being a small restaurant, can give two additional advantages. First, if I have fairly good days, I have a tendency to go in the cash register and spread it around a little bit. Maybe five, maybe ten dollars. Or if the waitresses are putting in an extra hard day, I'll add five dollars to each of their tip jars. And of course, at Christmas I give the staff bonuses. I can't give my business away. I'm still a small, growing business, but I do what I can. I believe that the best way to give incentive is by giving out bonuses. These things make the staff feel that you're dividing the profits, which then makes them feel as if they are part of the business.

MOTIVATION: MONEY, PLUS

Secondly, I can give my employees a fairly pressure-free environment as far as dealing with me. I don't believe in pressure techniques. Besides, it won't do you any good whatsoever to pressure your employees. Screaming and yelling at your staff will only make things worse. I'm not easy to work for in a lot of ways, but I don't believe in shouting or reprimanding an employee in front of customers. Another thing I won't do is correct anybody if I'm in here as a customer. If I'm in here at night as a customer, and I see something wrong, I won't say anything until the next day—because, say I'm a customer and I've had three drinks, I don't feel that I'm in a proper frame of mind to be saying anything to anybody until later.

J. Edward Fleishell of LeClub proposes a different approach to successful kitchen staff management.

Before you can maximize the contribution of your employees, it's very important that the staff respect you, the owner. This becomes even more important when the owner, like myself, owns a restaurant as a secondary occupation. Employees may view it as a sort of hobby or game for you, and consequently you have to earn their respect by proving to them that you know what is quality food and wine.

CASE IN POINT

One way of gaining this respect is being recognized by other people as a food or wine connoisseur. In my case, whenever there was an article that I wrote, or one that was written about me, it helped to reinforce our employees' conclusion that when it comes to food, I know what I'm talking about. In other words, because I have earned the respect of our staff, I'm at a point where they don't debate with me the propriety of a specific thing. They, in fact, ask for my opinion. When my manager buys wine, for example, he comes to me and asks me to try the particular wine and see if I agree that it is a good wine. It took some time to achieve this milestone though. When I bought the place, rumor had it that it was an ego trip by a lawyer; that it was a tax write-off for a lawyer. Well, I called all the staff together, and said that I wanted to explain why I have gone into the restaurant business. I told them I'd always wanted to own one;

HOW TO GET RESPECT FROM EMPLOYEES

NEW WAY OF JUDGING
KITCHEN OPERATIONS

that I knew absolutely nothing about managing a restaurant but quite a lot about eating in a restaurant. So I intended to judge everything from the standpoint of the customer. And I, the customer, would know whether they were doing it correctly or not. After all, when I go to the ballet, though I can't dance the ballet, I sure as hell can tell you if I'm seeing a good ballet. So I informed the staff that we'll apply the same rules here at Le Club. In general, this arrangement worked out well, and became difficult only in some circumstances. But, of course, I dealt with them on a professional level.

RESTAURANT STAFF ARE
PROFESSIONALS

The fact is that if you are a restaurant owner you must bear in mind that you're dealing with professionals, people whose life is the restaurant business. Whether it's the chef, the cook, the manager, the bartender, the waiters or the waitresses, they are all professionals. So when you see something that is not done right, or a product that is not made correctly, you have to handle it very carefully because you don't want to offend people who take pride in their work; people whom you truly like and respect. Conversely, since nobody is infallible, they too can be wrong, and it is your responsibility to tell them. But *how* you tell them is as important as *what* you tell them.

PROBLEM-SOLVING IDEA:
HOW TO TELL THE CHEF
HE IS WRONG

Let me be specific. We were making crepe suzettes that were not up to the quality I'd expect in our restaurant. They were as good as the ones served at other restaurants, but maybe other restaurants don't know how to make them either. Anyway, this brought up a problem of how do you tell someone that he's making them incorrectly? How do you change a 15-year habit pattern? Luckily, Jack Shelton, the nationally known gourmet and food columnist, wrote about our restaurant. He critized our crepe suzettes. Knowing that the staff read the article, the very next day I went to the restaurant and ordered crepe suzettes. When I was served, I asked the chef if he would spend $5.00 of his money on those crepe suzettes. He answered, "No. Not really." I said, "Well, let me show you the way I was taught to make them. See if it'll make any difference." So then a friend and I showed the chef the correct way to make crepe suzettes, which is to carmelize the sugar first. The chef wasn't offended. He took my suggestion in the way it was given: constructively. And I was happy that from then on our customers were getting top quality crepe suzettes.

A RESTAURANT IS
EITHER SHOW BUSINESS
OR GOOD CUISINE

It's a curious fact that most restaurants serve crepe suzettes by pouring some liquor from a bottle, putting a match to the liquor, and bursting flames all over your plate. This is absurd! You should burn out the alcohol before you serve crepe suzettes. But again, it's either show business or cuisine. You usually can't have both. If you have good cuisine, going through these gyrations doesn't improve your reputation. More often than not, such things will hurt it. Flaming your crepe suzettes in front of you is all right, provided they let the flame burn out. More often than not, they buy this cheap flaming brandy that could light lamps. So you end up literally eating liquor—with some crepe suzettes. This is not the correct way to do things. Similarly, you'll find when waiters bring you a bottle of wine that they go through the litany of what they saw in a movie. They'll present the wine label to you just as they think it's done in

LITANY OF SERVING
WINE

Europe. This is utter hogwash! It's not done that way in Europe at all. And the only people who are not aware of this are the people who don't visit Europe. In most French restaurants—except the top starred restaurants where Michelin is prominent and the place is filled with American, German and Japanese, but no French diners—they pull the cork from the bottle, and put the bottle on the table. When you want to drink wine, you pour it yourself. But here in America, we have this tradition of the waiter or waitress filling the glass with wine—all the way up to within a quarter of an inch from the top. Someone has to teach them. All you have to do is show them how to do it. It's like opening champagne. Apparently, in many of these so-called show business restaurants the louder the pop of the cork, the happier the captain. This is completely erroneous. This is not the way to open champagne. If you're doing it correctly, champagne should make no pop when you open it. Although there are times you can't help it. Sometimes the cork just comes rolling out, and you do get a pop. But essentially, you should just ease it out, so that it just fizzes a little, and then you lift the cork out. That's the correct way—not the big pop of the cork. I drink only wine and champagne, and I drink it all the time. It's not a ceremonial occasion for me. For example, when I cook, I always drink champagne. It serves as an inspiration for me.

CORRECT WAY TO OPEN CHAMPAGNE

But to come back to how to maximize employees' contributions. I think another way you can do it is through motivation. You cannot motivate through money though, because employees never earn enough money. So it cannot be money. I think you can motivate through pride. And pride is having a business card that says you are the manager of a particular restaurant. Our staff gets reinforced in their pride every time our restaurant gets a favorable write-up, or award. Yet we don't even post our awards out in the restaurant. We put them in the office. We don't seek awards, even though whenever the people who give out awards come to town, they eat in our restaurant. Here's an example. A certain airline called me and asked to come down and be a guest at a restaurant awards affair. I said, "You're not giving us an award, are you?" He responded with, "Do you want one?" I said, "No. Definitely not." Because we just don't care about things like that. It's pleasant, but not necessary. We have recognition where it counts, which is from the clientele, from the critical food writers, and others.

MOTIVATE YOUR STAFF THROUGH PRIDE

Another ingredient of successful kitchen management is observing strictly the chain of command. To me, the biggest mistake a restaurant owner can make is to undercut middle management. That almost guarantees failure of kitchen management. In our particular situation—that of a small restaurant—the manager has complete authority. Long ago I had a bad situation where some employees called me privately to complain about something. In order to ensure that the manager was not undercut, I had to impress upon the callers that they must bring the problem to the manager. I told them, "Don't call me. I own the restaurant, but the manager is your supervisor. You work for him; you talk to him. I want you to bring your problem to him. If it's not resolved, then I'm going to resolve it. But not until he's had a chance to do

PROBLEM-SOLVING IDEA

OBSERVE CHAIN OF COMMAND

something about the problem." Convinced, they talked to him, and the situation cleared up very nicely.

ESTABLISH TOP AUTHORITY;ESTABLISH STANDARDS

You can't circumvent a manager. You have to follow some chain of authority, or else you have chaos. Every place must have standards. Many restaurants—husband/wife restaurants—run into that exact problem. Husband wants things done one way, wife, another; and the manager doesn't know whom to listen to. And the result is that nothing happens consistently. When a restaurant is run like that, there's no consistency in doing things; there's no consistency in dealing with the staff. The trick in the restaurant business is to be consistent. This is the secret of MacDonald's and the other fast-food places. They do one thing in a consistent way. The same principle applies to a restaurant. You don't want to go into a restaurant one day and have a great sauce,and then next day get a lousy sauce. It's better to have a lousy sauce all the time than to have the quality of a sauce or anything else on a roller-coaster. People get used to a certain quality, whether it's good or bad. So if they come to a restaurant, at least they know what they are going to get.

ENFORCE QUALITY CONTROL

To put it another way, you have to have quality control in the restaurant business, just as you have it in any other business. And one of the responsibilities of the manager is to enforce quality control, both in product and service. That is, if top management is smart enough not to undercut or interfere, and thus sabotage the manager's authority.

12

Setting the Right Climate to Boost Your Kitchen Productivity

CHAPTER HIGHLIGHTS

Successful restaurateurs agree that their dedicated kitchen personnel is one of the key elements in their profitable business operation. Now, committed staff don't just "happen." These established restaurant operators are able to keep productive, enthusiastic employees because of carefully planned, affirmative personnel practices.

To motivate your employees positively so that their productivity and your sales increase, you have to set the right climate in your operation. This you can do by establishing a sound personnel policy which includes a clear definition of each employee's areas of responsibility, fair wages and benefits, raise and promotion based on merit, open communication lines, appropriate education/ training, and participation-type of recreational activities. Such practices are good business tactics because they foster a dedicated kitchen staff who take pride in their job and place of work.

Utilizing Human Resources

Once you determine that your existing and added-on personnel tally up to your written job description, you should start motivating every one of your staff to utilize the available human resources. Note how the following restaurant operators credit their employees as being the essential components in their "success formula."

"The most important factor in our success and growth," says the management of Victoria Station, a company that operates a chain of phenomenally successful restaurants throughout the country, as well as in Hawaii and Canada, "remains the enthusiasm and dedication of our people."

Then, "Our key personnel contribute considerably to 'Perry's' success," says Perry Butler, co-owner of the well-known San Francisco store that grosses well over a million dollars per year.

Obviously, these and other restaurateurs who gross in the millions are successful in motivating their employees. You too can positively motivate your staff by setting the right climate. And you can provide proper job environment through sound personnel policies.

CASE IN POINT   Because too much time and productivity were wasted by the waiters in bickering as to who should have what station in the dining area every day, Joe Barlotta, a Chicago restaurateur specializing in fine Italian cuisine, decided to do something about the potentially explosive situation.

After much thought, he drew a Work Distribution Chart (Figure 12-1) and assigned his five waiters to a different station each day, i.e., he rotated the staff, so that every one of the waiters was given a chance to wait on the "good" stations.

WORK DISTRIBUTION CHART					
Lunch	Station A	Station B	Station C	Station D	Station E
TUESDAY	Waiter #4	Waiter #2	Waiter #1	Waiter #5	Waiter #3
WEDNESDAY	#5	#3	#2	#4	#1
THURSDAY	#1	#5	#4	#3	#2
FRIDAY	#2	#4	#3	#1	#5
SATURDAY	#3	#1	#5	#2	#4
Dinner					
TUESDAY	#3	#1	#2	#5	#4
WEDNESDAY	#1	#5	#4	#2	#3
THURSDAY	#5	#3	#1	#4	#2
FRIDAY	#4	#2	#3	#1	#5
SATURDAY	#2	#4	#5	#3	#1

FIGURE 12-1

Barlotta then went one step further in ensuring that every one of his staff knew his or her responsibilities. He wrote up a detailed Job Profile (Figure 12-2), i.e., job description for every job category in his restaurant. The time and effort spent on this project proved well worth it. The bickering stopped; the staff's productivity and sales increased; the store was doing much better than before.

The Ten-Point Kitchen Productivity Booster Checklist

Here are ten proven ways of increasing productivity and sales of your kitchen staff:

JOB PROFILE—HEAD WAITER OR HOSTESS

Responsibilities

Your primary responsibility is to provide quality service for the patrons. This includes greeting the guests in a pleasant manner, escorting them to a table, pulling out their chairs, and after they are seated, giving each person a menu. You also must see to it that within a short time a glass of ice water is placed before each patron, that presently the waiter/waitress assigned to that station takes the guests' orders, and that the time between courses is not unduly long.

If there is a delay in service, check the reason. If there is congestion in the kitchen, or an understaffed steam table, or an inadequate supply of clean dishes or silverware, talk to the manager *after* the peak time. If there is a delay in service because the waiter is reluctant to make the trip to the kitchen unless he has several orders, or because he is too busy talking to another employee, remind him in a low but firm voice that the patrons are waiting for the next course, and *after* the peak time have a talk with him.

You are also responsible for the appearance and atmosphere of the dining room. This includes attractively set tables in a clean, well-ventilated and lighted room, as well as the appearance of the help.

Each day, before meal time, you must check with the head chef about the entrees and desserts, and the items that should be "pushed."

Finally, do not forget to say "thank you" or something similar to each departing guest or group. The last impression the patrons take with them is as important as the first greeting.

Type and Level of Skill

This job requires not only that you supervise the waiters/waitresses, cashier, and the bus boys or girls, but also that you are able to handle all types of people, both patrons and kitchen staff. Moreover, you have to be alert for any signs of waste or inefficiency, and attend to any potential problem immediately, and with the utmost tact and diplomacy.

Specialized Knowledge

You must know how to manage people, i.e., how to supervise people, and how to organize efficiently the services, so as to please the patrons and at the same time eliminate waste both in human resources and in merchandise.

Personal Attributes

Since you are the first impression the guests receive of the restaurant, you must be affable, courteous, alert, and intelligent, in addition to being neat in your appearance, smooth in your movements, and gracious in your manner.

FIGURE 12-2

1. Identify and define in *writing* the responsibilities of each job. Via the Job Profile (a definitive description of each job within your kitchen operation), make it crystal clear as to the type, level of skill, knowledge, and personal attributes required to successfully perform each task or function. Thus the employee will know just exactly what is required of him or her.

2. Estimate and state to the employee the expected workload to be performed at an acceptable level and quality and timeliness. Also, make it clear to him or her that any exception in quality or timeliness will have to be explained to the employee's supervisor IMMEDIATELY.

3. Assure each employee by words *and* action that superior performance will be recognized and rewarded in a fair and equitable manner. Rewards for good performance can take many forms: salary increase, profit sharing, bonus, stock-buying option (where the company has stock), promotion, additional education, or training. The main thing in any incentive program is that the rewarding of increased productivity of an employee be based strictly on merit.

4. Make sure that the lines of communication are open. Free-flowing dialog between management and staff aborts rumors before they can do any harm to the morale, and makes for a dynamic relationship. Besides, nothing creates frustration faster than when an employee tries to talk to his/her supervisor about an internal or external problem, and he/she is brushed off with a "Don't bother me. I'm too busy" remark. When frustration level increases, employee's performance declines.

5. Create an open, friendly atmosphere in your kitchen operation. You may have beautiful style and decor, and the right lighting in your restaurant, but if hostility and pettiness rule your kitchen area, the "bad vibes" become visible in sullen faces and pervade your public space. As a result, the customers feel uncomfortable, and your sales fall off.

6. Make affability, courteousness, and intelligence the criteria for any employee of yours, such as bartender, head waiter or hostess, waiter or waitress, whose function is to constantly interface with the customers. Quality food and drinks can be had in many stores, but the restaurant with superlative help is the one that will be really profitable.

CASE IN POINT

When Lou Vincent took over a medium-size New York East Side restaurant, the cash flow hardly met the expenses. Vincent did three things to improve business and boost income: first, he changed the name of the restaurant to "Vincent's Tavern"; second, he changed the interior, giving the restaurant an old-fashioned tavern look; and third, he hired a head bartender whom he had met some time before in a Cincinnati bar, and who had impressed him very much.

Vincent called the young man and offered him higher wages and moving expenses to New York. The young man accepted the offer.

Within six months, business—almost equally divided between bar and food—doubled. The restaurant, now in its third year, grosses over a million dollars.

Vincent credits the geniality and intelligence of his head bartender with a large part of his thriving restaurant's success. "Not only does he know how to give out good vibes to the customers," said Vincent, "but he motivates all the restaurant help, so that they are really productive."

7. Show the kitchen staff that you care about them, and they will care about your business. More, they will take pride in their work, and increase their productivity, thus increasing your sales.

8. If your corporation has a management training program, make sure that all of your staff knows about it. Advertise all the men and women who graduate from this training program. Most successful restaurant chain operations have their own intensive management training programs.

Victoria Station has a management training program which is in three phases: (a) two weeks of daily classes at corporate headquarters for familiarization with all aspects of this company-owned chain restaurant food preparation, service, accounting and other procedures; (b) ten weeks of on-the-job training in the restaurant in cooking, bussing, waiting, bartending, administration, and floor management; (c) one-week seminar back at the headquarters. (More than half of the trainees come from employee ranks, a fact that speaks well of the management of Victoria Station.)

9. Provide recreational activities for your employees. These can range from ping-pong or pool (if there's an extra room or some space on the premise), to horseshoes (in the back of the restaurant), or financing a bowling league, or putting up the money for the winning bowling team's first prize. None of these activities cost much money, yet you'd be surprised how much it does to the morale of the kitchen staff to be able to relax and have fun in simple recreational activities between peak times (such as breakfast and lunch, or lunch and dinner). On shift basis, of course.

10. Conduct periodic evaluation (Kitchen Staff Audit) of every one of your personnel. This means from the bus boy/girl through the line manager, and all the way up to the manager. Moreover, make sure that all your employees know just *exactly* when these periodic evaluations are performed by his or her supervisor. And finally, establish the policy that the employee reads his or her evaluation report. (A sample kitchen audit form, "Periodic Restaurant Evaluation Report," for line managers is shown in Figure 12-3.)

The management of a well-known national and international restaurant chain agrees with single store operators that periodic review (evaluation) of each employee makes for better management-worker relationship, *and* keeps the employee on his toes, so to speak.

By observing the above, you can effect productive and loyal staff who will care whether your business prospers. They will want your sales to increase, because they will have a share in it.

PERIODIC RESTAURANT EVALUATION REPORT

VICTORIA STATION
PURVEYOR OF PRIME RIB & POTABLE SPIRITS ®

UNIT_____

DATE_____ TO _____

UNIT MANAGER_____

COMPLETED BY_____

TOTAL POINTS THIS SECTION_____A

TOTAL WEIGHTING SECTION 4 _80_ B

SAMPLE	
WEIGHTING	6
SCORE	2
WEIGHTING X SCORE	12

FINAL SCORE	A ÷ B

SECTION FOUR
KITCHEN OPERATIONS

FOOD PREPARATION	YES	NO*
4.1 — ITEMS PREPARED PROPERLY		
4.2 — ITEMS COOKED PROPERLY		
4.3 — SPECIFICATIONS ADHERED TO		
4.4 — PLATES POSITIONED PROPERLY AT PASS-THRU		
4.5 — QUANTITY OF ITEMS PREPARED AS PER DAILY FORECASTING		
4.6 — FORECASTING DONE PROPERLY BY KS & MOD		
4.7 — KS HANDLES ALL MEAT HIMSELF AS IS POSSIBLE		
4.8 — MUSHROOMS WASHED, COOKED & PORTIONED PROPERLY		
4.9 — SHRIMP CUT, WASHED & STORED PROPERLY		
4.10 — ALL OTHER ITEMS PREPARED AND HANDLED ACCORDING TO SPEC		
4.11 — MINIMUM REHEATS REMAINING		
4.12 — EMPLOYEE MEALS WHOLESOME, HOT, PORTIONED AND ON TIME		
4.13 — SETUPS & GARNISH OKAY		
4.14 — PORTION OKAY (SCALES USED)		
4.15 — PLATES CLEAN (NEAT APPEARANCE)		
4.16 — HOT FOOD, HOT PLATES		
4.17 — POTATOES OPENED PROPERLY		
4.18 — ENTREE POSITIONED PROPERLY		
4.19 — SOFT COPIES HANDLED PROPERLY		
4.20 — FOOD HANDLED PROPERLY		
4.21 — MEAT ITEMS CARVED PROPERLY AND OF NEAT APPEARANCE		
4.22 — STEAKS ARE GOOD LOOKING & PROPER WEIGHT		

FIGURE 12-3 Courtesy of Victoria Station, Inc.

<u>PERIODIC RESTAURANT EVALUATION REPORT</u>
SECTION FOUR

<u>FOOD PREPARATION (CONT'D)</u>   <u>YES</u>   <u>NO*</u>

4.23 — CARVING & WORK AREA NEATLY
      MAINTAINED AT ALL TIMES (DURING
      SHIFT)   _____   _____

      *EXPLAIN_____

      _____

      _____

      _____

      _____

      _____

      _____

      _____

      _____

      _____

      _____

      _____

      _____

W	15
S	
W x S	

      _____

      _____

      _____

      _____

                                                    <u>YES</u>   <u>NO*</u>

<u>SALAD BAR CORRECT & FILLED</u>

4.24 — SETUP PROPERLY COMPLETED (ICE
      LEVEL & CROCKS)   _____   _____

4.25 — DRESSING RECIPES POSTED & MADE
      PROPERLY   _____   _____

4.26 — BEANS, BEETS DRAINED PROPERLY   _____   _____

4.27 — LETTUCE FRESH & PROPER MIXTURE   _____   _____

4.28 — SPECIFIED ALTERNATES USED   _____   _____

4.29 — PLATES CHILLED DURING SHIFT (NOT
      FROZEN)   _____   _____

FIGURE 12-3 (continued)

Through the courtesy of Victoria Station

PERIODIC RESTAURANT EVALUATION REPORT
SECTION FOUR

SALAD BAR (CONT'D)	YES	NO*
4.30 — PLATE CHILLERS FILLED AFTER SHIFT	_____	_____
4.31 — BACKUP PREPARED DURING & AFTER SHIFT	_____	_____
4.32 — ALL CROCKS ROTATED & CLEANED AT THE END OF DINNER SHIFT	_____	_____
4.33 — UTILIZING PROPER ONE GALLON PLASTIC CONTAINER FOR RESUPPLYING SALAD BAR (NO ALUMINUM)	_____	_____
4.34 — ALL ITEMS CLEANED, COVERED & STORED PROPERLY AFTER LUNCH & DINNER	_____	_____
4.35 — ALL SALAD BAR ITEMS PREPARED ACCORDING TO FORECAST	_____	_____

_____

_____

_____

_____

_____

_____

_____

_____

_____

_____

```
W                    5

S

W x S
                   [____]
```

FOOD COST CONTROL	YES	NO*
4.36 — IS FOOD COST CONSISTENTLY WITHIN 1% OF POTENTIAL	_____	_____
4.37 — IS FOOD HANDLED IN SUCH A WAY AS TO AVOID WASTE	_____	_____
4.38 — GOOD CONSISTENT PR CUTTING PERCENTAGES	_____	_____
4.39 — DOES THE KS UNDERSTAND AND USE THE P & L & OTHER SUPPORT DOCUMENTS TO HELP CONTROL FOOD COST	_____	_____
4.40 — DOES THE BEST CARVER WORK 5 BUSIEST SHIFTS?	_____	_____
4.41 — DOES HE KNOW & UNDERSTAND THE IMPORTANCE OF UTILIZATION OF PRIME RIB	_____	_____
4.42 — ARE THE CUTS EVENLY CUT & NEAT IN APPEARANCE	_____	_____

PERIODIC RESTAURANT EVALUATION REPORT
SECTION FOUR

FOOD COST CONTROL (CONT'D)   YES   NO*

4.43 — ARE RIBS PROPERLY COOKED

4.44 — ARE RIBS AND BUTTS PROPERLY
        TRIMMED

4.45 — ARE THE KNIVES IN GOOD CONDITION
        AND SHARPENED

4.46 — P.R. NOT HANDLED WITH HANDS

4.47 — DOES THE KITCHEN SUPERVISOR
        HANDLE ALL THE MEAT HIMSELF
        WHERE PRACTICAL

4.48 — IS FORECASTING DONE PROPERLY TO
        KEEP PR REHEATS TO A MINIMUM

4.49 — ARE PRIME RIB YIELD PERCENTAGES
        CONSISTENT AND WITHIN SET
        PARAMETERS

4.50 — ARE PRIME RIB PERCENTAGES
        REVIEWED DAILY WITH THE CUTTERS

4.51 — ARE TOP SIRLOIN STEAKS NEAT IN
        APPEARANCE, PROPER THICKNESS,
        TRIMMED TO ¼ INCH FAT THICKNESS
        AND STORED NEATLY ACCORDING TO
        DEGREE OF DONENESS

4.52 — HAS BUDGETED COST BEEN ACHIEVED

4.53 — IS THE STEAK BAG CHECKED DAILY AND
        CORRECTLY COMPLETED DAILY

4.54 — ARE REEFERS, WALK-IN AND STORAGE
        AREAS KEPT SECURE AT ALL TIMES

4.55 — DOES THE UNIT DO INTERNAL COSTING
        OR WAIT FOR MONTHLY RESULTS

4.56 — DOES HE INSIST ON ADHERING TO
        SPECIFICATION AT ALL TIMES

4.57 — BASIC COST CONTROLS IMPLEMENTED

4.58 — YIELD TESTS COMPLETED REGULARLY

4.59 — TOP AND RIB CUTTING SUMMARIES
        REVIEWED DAILY

*EXPLAIN_____

FIGURE 12-3 (continued)   Through the courtesy of Victoria Station

PERIODIC RESTAURANT EVALUATION REPORT
SECTION FOUR

FOOD COST CONTROL (CONT'D)

_____

_____

_____

_____

_____

_____

_____

_____

_____

_____

_____

_____

_____

_____

_____

_____

_____

W		15
S		
W x S		

	YES	NO*

PURCHASING
4.60 — ORDERING TIMELY & IN PROPER
      AMOUNTS
4.61 — MERCHANDISE RECEIVED ON
      SCHEDULE BY MANAGEMENT
      PERSONNEL ONLY
4.62 — WEIGHTS, QUALITY, TYPE & PRICES
      CHECKED AND VERIFIED
4.63 — MERCHANDISE STORED IN REEFERS
      AND STOREROOMS IMMEDIATELY
      UPON RECEIVING
4.64 — PLATFORM SCALE CLEAN, OPERABLE,
      USED

Through the courtesy of Victoria Station　　　　　　　**FIGURE 12-3 (continued)**

PERIODIC RESTAURANT EVALUATION REPORT
SECTION FOUR

PURCHASING (CONT'D)	YES	NO*
4.65 — UTILIZING PRICE COMPARISON & GETTING BEST POSSIBLE PRICES	____	____
4.66 — MAINTAINS GOOD RELATIONS WITH PURVEYORS	____	____
4.67 — ARE CREDIT REQUESTS PROPERLY USED	____	____

*EXPLAIN_____

_____

_____

_____

_____

_____

_____

_____

_____

_____

W		5
S		
W x S		

MAINTENANCE	YES	NO*

EQUIPMENT

	YES	NO*
4.68 — ARE DISHWASHER WASH & RINSE TEMPERATURES AT PROPER LEVELS	____	____
4.69 — IS EQUIPMENT IN GOOD REPAIR AND WORKING PROPERLY (OVENS CALIBRATED)	____	____
4.70 — ARE KNIVES PROPERLY SHARPENED & MAINTAINED	____	____
4.71 — DOES THE UNIT PRACTICE PREVENTIVE MAINTENANCE (I.E., SCREWS TIGHTENED, HINGES OILED, ETC.)	____	____
4.72 — THERMOMETERS IN ALL REFRIGERATORS	____	____
4.73 — SHARPENING STONES MAINTAINED & CLEANED	____	____
4.74 — GREASE TRAP MAINTAINED	____	____

*EXPLAIN_____

_____

_____

_____

FIGURE 12-3 (continued)   Through the courtesy of Victoria Station

PERIODIC RESTAURANT EVALUATION REPORT
SECTION FOUR

EQUIPMENT (CONT'D)

_____
_____
_____
_____
_____

W	4
S	
W x S	

	YES	NO*

KITCHEN
4.75 — WALLS, CEILING AND HOOD
4.76 — FLOOR AND DUCKBOARDS, DRAINS AND
            UNDER EQUIPMENT
4.77 — PREP AREA (INCLUDING SINKS)
4.78 — OVENS CLEAN (CALIBRATED)
4.79 — GRILL & RANGE (NO ALUMINUM FOIL)
4.80 — REEFERS (INCLUDING UNDER COUNTER)
4.81 — WALK-IN (ORGANIZED: SALADS, FOOD,
            BAR, FLOOR CLEAN)
4.82 — PASS-THROUGH & LANTERNS
4.83 — FOOD STORAGE (SHELVES ORGANIZED)
4.84 — FOOD CONTAINERS ON FLOOR
4.85 — KNIFE DRAWERS (ORGANIZED, CLEAN)
4.86 — CLEANING SUPPLIES IN KITCHEN
4.87 — STEAM TABLE (NO LINEN UNDER HOTEL
            PANS)
4.88 — ALL WOOD CUTTING COUNTERS,
            BOARDS, CLEAN & SANITARY
4.89 — ALL EQUIPMENT KEPT CLEAN ON DAILY
            BASIS (OVENS, RANGE, HOOD,
            BROILER, CAN OPENER)

*EXPLAIN_____

_____
_____
_____
_____
_____
_____
_____
_____

W	4
S	—
W x S	

PERIODIC RESTAURANT EVALUATION REPORT
                    SECTION FOUR

DISHWASHING AREA	YES	NO*
4.90 — STAINLESS STEEL, MARLITE, CLEANED & POLISHED	_____	_____
4.91 — COFFEE CUPS (NO STAINS)	_____	_____
4.92 — SHELVES & BREAKDOWN AREA ORGANIZED	_____	_____
4.93 — DISHWASHING MACHINE (IN, OUT, UNDER)	_____	_____
4.94 — SERVICEWARE, CHINA & SKILLETS NOT CHIPPED, SILVER NOT BENT	_____	_____
4.95 — PRE-SOAK FLATWARE AND WASH TWICE	_____	
4.96 — CLEANING SUPPLIES ABOVE CLEAN SERVICEWARE	_____	_____
4.97 — ALL STORAGE RACKS	_____	_____
4.98 — ARE POTS, PANS, MUSHROOM SKILLETS AND OTHER IMPLEMENTS BEING CLEANED PROPERLY	_____	_____

*EXPLAIN_____

_____

_____

_____

_____

_____

_____

_____

_____

W	4
S	—
W x S	

SANITATION	YES	NO*
4.99 — ARE GOOD PERSONAL HYGIENE STANDARDS MAINTAINED BY THE KITCHEN SUPERVISOR AND HIS STAFF	_____	_____
4.100— IS FOOD ALWAYS HANDLED IN A SANITARY FASHION	_____	_____
4.101 — ARE FOODS PROPERLY REFRIGERATED	_____	_____
4.102— DO ALL REFRIGERATORS HAVE WORKING THERMOMETERS	_____	_____
4.103— ARE HEALTH DEPARTMENT REPORTS SATISFACTORY AND/OR ARE VIOLATIONS TAKEN CARE OF IMMEDIATELY	_____	_____
4.104— ARE FOODS PROPERLY COVERED DURING STORAGE	_____	_____
4.105— ARE POISONOUS AND TOXIC MATERIALS PROPERLY STORED, IDENTIFIED	_____	_____
4.106— IS KITCHEN KEPT IN SANITARY CONDITION WITH MINIMUM PRESENCE OF VERMIN, FLIES, ETC.	_____	_____

FIGURE 12-3 (continued)   Through the courtesy of Victoria Station

PERIODIC RESTAURANT EVALUATION REPORT
SECTION FOUR

SANITATION (CONT'D)	YES	NO*
4.107— IS A COMPREHENSIVE CLEANING SCHEDULE IN USE AND SUPERVISED	_____	_____

*EXPLAIN_____

_____

_____

_____

_____

_____

_____

_____

_____

_____

_____

W	8
S	—
W x S	

ORGANIZATION	YES	NO*

STOREROOM & KS ROUTINE

	YES	NO*
4.108— STOREROOM & REEFERS ARRANGED ACCORDING TO A SPECIFIED LAYOUT & HEALTH DEPT. REQUIREMENTS	_____	_____
4.109— WALK-IN BEING UTILIZED FOR FULL CASE STORAGE & WORKING REEFER BEING USED FOR LEFTOVER & OPENED CONTAINERS	_____	_____
4.110 — THERMOMETERS MAINTAINED IN REEFERS	_____	_____
4.111 — GOOD UTILIZATION OF SPACE IN ALL STORAGE AREAS	_____	_____
4.112 — ARE ALL FOOD ITEMS ISSUED ACCORDING TO DAILY NEEDS	_____	_____
4.113 — DOES THE KS FOLLOW A DAILY ROUTINE	_____	_____
4.114 — DOES HE HAVE & FOLLOW AN ORDER-DELIVERY SCHEDULE	_____	_____
4.115 — DOES HE HAVE A COMPLETE & ORGANIZED FILING SYSTEM	_____	_____

*EXPLAIN_____

_____

_____

_____

_____

FIGURE 12-3 (continued)

PERIODIC RESTAURANT EVALUATION REPORT
SECTION FOUR

STOREROOM & KS ROUTINE (CONT'D)

_____	
_____	W ___8
_____	S ___
_____	W x S
_____	

	YES	NO*
STEAK BAG SHEETS		
4.116 — FILLED IN PROPERLY	_____	_____
4.117 — PERCENTAGE COMPUTED DAILY	_____	_____
4.118 — BEEF INVENTORY INITIALLED BY MOD	_____	_____
4.119 — YIELD TESTS COMPLETED & SENT TO 150	_____	_____
4.120 — ARE CUTTING SUMMARIES KEPT CURRENT DAILY	_____	_____
4.121 — IS THE FORECASTING SHEET COMPLETELY FILLED OUT DAILY WITH THE MOD? IS IT FOLLOWED	_____	_____

*EXPLAIN_____

_____	
_____	W ___2
_____	S ___
_____	W x S
_____	

MISCELLANEOUS

	YES	NO*
KITCHEN PERSONNEL		
4.122 — DOES KS HIRE GOOD PEOPLE? ARE THEY ON TIME AND CONSCIENTIOUS	_____	_____
4.123 — ARE THEY NEAT IN APPEARANCE & CLEAN (UNIFORM)	_____	_____
4.124 — ARE THEY SCHEDULED FOR THE JOB FOR WHICH THEY ARE BEST SUITED	_____	_____
4.125 — ARE THE BEST PEOPLE WORKING THE BUSIEST SHIFTS	_____	_____
4.126 — DOES THE KITCHEN & DISHWASHER AREA HAVE THE PROPER SALES PER MAN HOUR RATIO	_____	_____

FIGURE 12-3 (continued)   Through the courtesy of Victoria Station

PERIODIC RESTAURANT EVALUATION REPORT
SECTION FOUR

MISCELLANEOUS (CONT'D)   YES   NO*

4.127— DOES THE KS SPEND AN ADEQUATE
        TIME IN THE KITCHEN AND OTHER
        WORK AREAS TRAINING &
        SUPERVISING PERSONNEL   _____   _____
4.128— IS PERSONNEL DIRECTED &
        SUPERVISED BY THE KS, NOT LEFT
        ON THEIR OWN   _____   _____

        *EXPLAIN_____

        _____

        _____

        _____

        _____

        _____ | W   10 |

        _____ | S   _ |

        _____ | W x S |

        _____

13

How to Resolve
Everyday Kitchen Crises

CHAPTER HIGHLIGHTS

According to the majority of restaurateurs, the most critical kitchen crisis is having to fire the chef or the cook right before lunch or dinner. The breakdown of cooking equipment at equally crucial time rates as the second worse kitchen crisis. As far as the first item is concerned, some restaurateurs recommend ''staying close to potential problems'' as a way of solving such kitchen crises, while others advise planning ahead as a way to avoid crises brought on by temperamental kitchen staff. Still other restaurateurs claim that by having extensively trained back-up staff, nobody is indispensable, and thus no chef or cook can create a kitchen crisis. In regard to the breakdown of cooking equipment, if it is only the ice machine, the slicing machine, or a similar machine that fails, it's relatively easy to resolve such problems. You can buy ice, or you can do the slicing by hand. If you lose your grill or oven, however, you do have a big problem. And the way to resolve it is by improvising, by changing the menu to something you can cook. The most important thing is to keep your menu and yourself in a position where there is always a back-up plan that can be used whenever problems like that occur. In other words, by being prepared for any foreseeable types of problems that can arise with equipment, you are able to resolve them much more easily. Of course, a problem can surface that defies any back-up plan, and one that cannot be improvised around.

Mike Walsh of The Holding Company puts it this way:

> If you have a small menu like ours, and lose the ability to cook *CASE IN POINT* hamburgers, you're in trouble. But you can improvise around it. We had a kitchen fire a year and a half ago, and we didn't have a grill for almost a month. We improvised by serving corned beef and cabbage, which we cooked on a temporarily installed gas burner. We served hot sandwiches. We did anything and everything we could think of. And most important,

149

we were honest with our customers. I told my waitresses to explain to the customers what had happened, and they were very understanding. Actually, it proved to be sort of fun for us and a guessing game for our customers to see what we were going to serve each day. We winged that period quite well.

Doug Scott of Victoria Station has a different view.

CASE IN POINT

I think the main crisis would be finding yourself in a crisis. The whole idea of having a crisis would tend to indicate that you have problems elsewhere. I think the name of the game is to avoid crises by planning ahead; by having foresight. If you have equipment problem, that's normally people related, because if you take care of the equipment, maintain it, clean it, provide regular service, you very rarely have equipment trouble. The same thing is true with groceries or produce. If you establish a close working relationship with your purveyors, I don't think you're going to have product problems either. Good purveyors will always come through for you, again depending on what type of relationship you have with them. As far as I'm concerned, whether it's equipment or product crisis, it's somehow people related.

Most restaurateurs concur that while major kitchen appliances can create problems, it can never be as big a problem as dealing with kitchen staff personalities. States Mike Walsh:

CASE IN POINT

I don't think you can deal effectively with kitchen prima donnas. You survive them. I think that's about all you can do. They're always the same. Every time you have a kitchen, i.e., a restaurant, you have a problem. Everybody back in the kitchen is affected. It's the heat. It's the type of job. It is, in fact, the very nature of the job. Let's be honest: working in the kitchen is a very tough job. It's a high pressure, very coordinated, high speed activity in most places. Or a very artistic creation in other places. It takes a lot of talent to do that. Or, if not talent, a lot of endurance. It's a job that not many people are suited for. Matter of fact, it's a job that most people don't want, or wouldn't take. Consequently, you have to take these factors into consideration, and work with all of your kitchen staff—including the prima donnas—as well as you can. And the way you do it is by staying close to the problem. You eliminate as

MEDIATE LITTLE PERSONAL GRIEVANCES QUICKLY; DON'T LET THEM GROW INTO BIG PROBLEMS

many problems as you can by being around all the time; by checking to make sure that all the little personal grievances that people build up between each other do not grow into great big problems. I try to mediate them quickly, and get them out of the way. In other words, I keep the rapport among my staff, so that the group in the kitchen is an entity, working for the same end, so that all my staff are part of the team.

If anybody has a problem with anybody else, we work it out that day. It doesn't go on until the next day. We resolve any potential trouble immediately. We deal with a problem directly, or directly after. I mean, if it happens during lunch, we deal with it directly after lunch. We don't do it in the middle of the lunch or dinner crunch. Generally, you can't do that. But if you have people with personalities that are very difficult to deal with, sometimes you have to bend. If they are good enough to keep, you bend around them, and you guide the other people to bend around them. However, if they get to be a real problem, you have to eliminate them, and get somebody that you and your staff can work with. There are a lot of people with talent out there. And talent isn't the only thing you're looking for in the kitchen. They have to deal with management; they have to deal with the help; they have to deal with the waitresses; they have to get along with the rest of the team. They don't have the latitude—at least in my place they don't have the latitude to go into a giant ego trip. Especially in the restaurant business there has to be teamwork, if the place is to succeed.

RESTAURANT BUSINESS IS TEAMWORK

When it comes to having an employee with a drinking problem, you can do two things. If you have an employee who is coming in to work under the influence of alcohol, or drugs, or anything that affects his working ability, it's basic that you cannot have him on the premises. It's dangerous for the customers; it's dangerous for the other employees, and for the employee himself. In such cases you cannot make an exception, no matter who he is.

HOW TO DEAL WITH AN EMPLOYEE'S DRINKING PROBLEM

If it happens only once, you send him home with a warning. You explain the problems that his "condition" creates for you, and most people have good enough sense to realize what they're doing, and avoid a repetition. Now if they're good enough to keep, you keep them, if it happens only once. More specifically, you keep them on a one-time basis. The second time, however, it's the one, two, three, and you're out kind of story, as far as I'm concerned. In my restaurant everybody gets two shots. The third shot is goodby. And I don't care if you're dead, if your whole family was in a train wreck. It's still "Good-by!"

Insofar as closet cases go, I have worked with them in different restaurants. These are the people who aren't outwardly drunk, but somehow you can sense that they are "on" something. With people like that, I don't do anything. I mean, if I can't actually ascertain their "condition," but just assume it, and they're not stumbling or falling down, and they are performing well, I don't think their problem is any of my business. Their personal life is their business. And if they have to have whatever they're taking to keep them going, that's fine—as long as they're doing what I require them to do in my restaurant. However, if they do things that are detrimental to themselves or to other employees, or to the business, then obviously it becomes my problem. If they were doing a good job for me and they had a drinking problem, I'd do what I could for them. I'd counsel them, and advise them perhaps as to where they could get professional help. I think as an employer, I should help them—up to a certain point.

DEALING WITH CLOSET CASES

If he were a friend of mine, I'd have to treat him differently. Actually, I think I'd be harder on a friend working for me than I would be on any other employee. But again, if it doesn't get into my realm, I don't feel it's any of my business.

And this brings up a very important point in the restaurant business: the employer-employee relationship. Without doubt, it's tremendously easier if you keep such relationships on an employer-employee basis. You can do that in a very friendly way, yet keep it business-like. If you

THE EMPLOYER - EMPLOYEE RELATIONSHIP

treat your employees like family, and give them all the slack, you're really putting them in a difficult position. They don't own the restaurant; they can't understand the problems that go hand-in-hand with restaurant; they don't understand the costs. You are the only one who understands all the problems you have. Yet you're giving them the availability of having a tremendous advantage. That is, they can use the restaurant, or abuse the restaurant at will. It takes years of hard work to develop a place, and keep it going. You don't pass that information on to an employee. That's why you establish a set of rules, and you don't break them. Whatever rules work well for your restaurant, you must enforce. If you're going to allow your employees to drink on the premises, if you're going to allow them to sit down and eat after hours, or come in and use the place on their days off, it's up to you. Or, if you don't allow any of it, that's up to you, too. The important thing to remember is whatever set of rules you decide to use in your restaurant, enforce them, keep them enforced.

ENFORCE YOUR SET OF RULES

Don't bend them because you have become friendly with some of the help. That's inviting trouble. In other words, when you hire an employee, you give him or her all the rules that you require for the job. If he or she breaks them, you have a warning system. I don't think employees should be fired summarily just because they break a rule once. But you warn them. You give them a chance to reinstate themselves as good employees. If they continue to break it, then you fire them.

Doug Scott of Victoria Station, Inc., looks at these problems somewhat differently.

CASE IN POINT

I think that most people in the food industry, particularly people who are working with the preparation of food, tend to be temperamental. That is probably a pretty widespread trait of chefs, cooks, and other kitchen personnel. At Victoria Station we have a term for situations that are caused by unexpected or irrational actions or reactions of various personnel. We call it "crisis management." This term covers situations where you have to consider all possible ways just "to get the door open." Let's say, for example, that a key employee quits or doesn't show up for work, and you can't replace him in time for lunch or dinner. In other words, all of a sudden you're in a position where you have to pull other employees from their regular stations to try to fill the gap. Generally, in cases like that there will be a breakdown in one area or another, and you are in the middle of crises management, unless you have planned ahead.

CRISIS MANAGEMENT

To put it another way, most restaurants go through a turnover in August or early September because the young people—the summer help—are going back to school. At Victoria Station restaurants we have a younger employee group than many other restaurants. Some of our key positions, in fact, are filled with young people.

YOU HAVE TO PLAN AHEAD

Actually, when you think about it, everybody is a key employee. If you don't have a dishwasher, that'll tie you up just as badly as not having a cook. Because many of our employees are students, we tend to go through a turnover every year in August or September. Consequently, you have to plan ahead for such possibilities. Restaurant employees, in general, are somewhat transient, anyway. And it isn't only the dishwashers, but also the cooks, and even the managers. You can have a very good employee, a trusted employee, who has been with you for maybe ten months, a year, or two years. One day suddenly he decides that he's tired of it, and wants to move on. And then that person is gone.

So you always have to plan ahead. And this you can do by keeping a current application file of at least 20 or 25 possible hires. Thus, if you lost somebody that morning, you would have numerous applications to go through, and could call these people in for second interviews to try to replace the person who is leaving, or who suddenly quit. The last thing you want to do is run short-handed.

To be specific, let's say, for example, that just before lunch the chef has a bad argument with the manager, and he wants to quit. Well, the thing to do in a case like that is talk to the chef. Though again, I believe that if you get into the kind of an argument where an individual just up and quits with no notice, there must be something wrong someplace. If you have worked well with this employee for any length of time at all, that employee will give you the consideration of at least giving you some notice, and will not just walk off.

On the other hand, there's not much you can do with a spur-of-the-moment termination. That's where I'd fall back on my current applications so as to get somebody in there just as soon as possible. Nevertheless, I think for the rest of the night, or even the rest of the week, you would have to do some juggling with the people you've got. And unless you're in the fortunate situation of being overstaffed—which is normally not the case—whenever somebody leaves, you might as well face the fact that such act will create a gap. And even after you hire someone to replace him, you still have to train him. So you're talking about a week or two of working under crisis management.

To avoid such situations, or at least to decrease the number of restaurant staff who quit on the spur of the moment, without any notice, the manager should emphasize good relationship with his employees. The rule of thumb I've always adhered to is that the employees should always know where they stand. For example, I always figured that if an employee came up to me and asked for a raise, I wasn't doing my job as a manager, because if that person deserved a raise, he or she should have gotten it without asking. And if he didn't deserve a raise, he should have known that, and should not have asked me for it. Conversely, there are managers who wouldn't give a raise to an employee unless the employee asked for it.

Both ways are wrong. If an employee doesn't deserve a raise, or isn't at the point in his development to get a raise, then that employee should know that. He or she should also know why; what he has to do to get the raise, or in what area he needs developing. In that way, employees know their status. And when they know where they stand, they can say to themselves, "O.K. I'm going to work in those areas and improve myself," or, "I don't want to do it. I'm leaving." In any case, you, as the manager should know what the status of that person is, and thus not be caught unexpectedly by somebody saying, 'I'm tired of this,' and then walking out on you.

To keep the communication lines open between you and your staff, I would not advocate formal meetings, because normally you get too many people together at those meetings, and you don't really get to the core of things. Sometimes in smaller groups of perhaps five or six,

$$$-SAVING IDEA

DON'T GET CAUGHT SHORT-HANDED

WHEN THERE IS SPUR-OF-THE-MOMENT TERMINATION

RULE OF THUMB IN EMPLOYEE RELATIONSHIP

EMPLOYEES SHOULD KNOW WHERE THEY STAND WITH RAISES

KEEP COMMUNICATION LINES OPEN BETWEEN YOU AND YOUR STAFF

meetings can be very helpful. The main thing is to communicate with your staff on a continuous basis. Talk to them every time you see them, even if it's just a "How are you?", "What's going on?", "Any problems?" I don't think you can expect to get filled in on one day a week, if you forget about communicating with your staff the rest of the week. Meetings are important. They have their place, but I've never liked general employee meetings where you get everybody together, unless you have a lot of information affecting everybody. I like the one-on-one and smaller group meetings.

EARN YOUR STAFF'S RESPECT

As far as I'm concerned, the most important thing—and it's probably an important thing anytime you're in a supervisory position—is to earn the respect of your staff. Once you've earned their respect, you can be sure of their cooperation. They may not always agree with you, but at least they'll know that the decisions you make, or the directions you give, are based on experience and/or knowledge. This type of respect is very important in dealing with people's problems such as drinking problems.

TWO DIFFERENT KINDS OF DRINKING PROBLEMS

There are probably two different kinds of drinking problems. One of these may not enter into the restaurant itself, and thus doesn't affect an employee's productivity or our team work. If an employee is drinking on the job, however, that's a very serious problem.

Nevertheless, I think in most cases we would not fire that person, at least not immediately. I'm assuming, however, that if the person is working for me, he or she is productive, is a good employee, and is fulfilling the job category, or he or she wouldn't be there anyway. So, assuming these things, I would also have to assume that that person is worth giving a second or even a third chance. Of course, if employees come to the job drunk, I would only let them come to the job drunk once. The second time they'd be gone, because cases like that would require professional counseling.

Again, if it was just a one-time thing, I think probably I would send them home to sober up. And next day I would talk to them and resolve, or at least try to resolve, the problem.

Insofar as "closet cases" are concerned, even when a person hides his or her drinking problem well, and is quite productive on the job, I still think that I should talk to him or her. I would hope that I'm close enough to the employee to be able to talk about something like that. Of course, there is a certain part of people's private life that isn't anybody else's business. But I don't think there's any way that they could hide completely a drinking or a drug problem. In other words, if they really have a serious addiction problem, even if I don't know it, I suspect it would show in their performance. Not that they're drinking, but that they are late, or unreliable, or irrational. I've had incidents where I've let people go when they weren't performing, weren't productive, or were absent too many times. And afterward I'd find out that the cause behind the behavior or acts was a drinking problem. I think an employer sort of owes it to his or her employees to give them counseling, or to help them seek outside help or advice. Of course, you can do only so much.

SHOULD AN EMPLOYER COUNSEL AN EMPLOYEE?

Now in regard to homosexuals: I wouldn't say anything to them. I think that it depends on the individual. Personally, it wouldn't bother me. An individual's sexual orientation is none of my business as long as the job is performed satisfactorily. If the individual doesn't become a problem, then his or her life style is of no concern of mine. However, if a person's conduct is offensive to other employees, then that is a problem, and I would discuss it with him or her. After all, the last thing you want to do is break up the team work on account of one individual.

To us team work is very important. I'm sure there are people of all types of life styles who can get along with anybody, without any problem. But if for some reason an individual is causing some friction amoung the other employees, I would talk to him or her, and if that has no effect, I would terminate the employment. Again, this would become a problem only if the person's life style caused problems with other employees. And this is another instance where proper employer-employee relationship pays off. And by "proper" I mean treating employees in a friendly but not too friendly manner. I don't think you can really treat your employees as part of the family. On the other hand, I would never treat anybody as the hired help. I think that would be a tremendous mistake. The manager can't run the restaurant entirely by himself. He definitely needs other people for various functions. That's why there is kind of a middle ground that you have to reach in your relationship with your employees. You certainly can care for them, and respect them, and provide for them almost as you would for one of the family. But again, there has to be some type of fine line, some specific limitation. Because it is possible to come too close to your employees, and then you can run into all kinds of managerial and disciplinarian problems.

Representing restaurateurs with a diametrically opposite viewpoint is Ismael Venegas, Director of Food Standards for the highly successful multi-state Tia Maria and Red Onion restaurant chains.

We don't *allow* crises to happen in our kitchens. That is, not any staff crises. Our kitchen personnel are trained to operate *with* the chef or *without* the chef. At Tia Maria and the Red Onion restaurants nobody is indispensable. We have in most restaurants one manager, two or three assistant managers, and one kitchen manager/chef. And the assistant managers of each store are trained extensively to take over any kind of a job in the kitchen or in the public area. In fact, we give considerable training to all of our staff, so that in case the chef or cook quits before lunch or dinner, or doesn't show up for the day, there is always another person who can take over the chef's, or the cook's, or even the manager's, responsibilities. Of course, when there's a substitute for a chef, he or she might not be as creative as the regular chef, but the flow of operations in the kitchen does not stop just because somebody quits, or doesn't show up at all.

No. We don't tolerate prima donnas, either in the kitchen or in the public area. Our staff have to be 100 percent professional. And that includes taking criticism. If you are a professional, you have to take criticism like a professional and not fly into a rage. In other words, we believe that a professional person, whether he or she works in an office or in a restaurant—the kitchen or the public area—does not become temperamental. A professional cannot afford to be temperamental.

Of course, that doesn't mean that we don't have any problems. In the restaurant business everybody has problems. But because we have our permanent "back-up" resources, our problems are usually minor.

WHEN AN EMPLOYEE'S LIFE STYLE CAUSES PROBLEMS

PROPER RELATIONSHIP WITH YOUR EMPLOYEES

CASE IN POINT

A PROFESSIONAL CANNOT AFFORD TO BE TEMPERAMENTAL

To us a kitchen crisis is when there's a fire in the kitchen, or if through some technical trouble the sprinkler system in the kitchen goes haywire and floods the kitchen, as happened a few months back in one of our restaurants. That was a crisis, because we had to shut down the kitchen for several hours.

EVERY DRINKING PROBLEM IS DIFFERENT

Insofar as an employee with a drinking problem is concerned, to begin with, every case is different; every case has to be handled differently. But in general, if one of our employees came in drunk, I would send him home. And when he came in the next day, I would talk to him about his problem. That is, if he's willing to talk. Some people are so embarrassed about coming in drunk, or so tightly shut within themselves, that they just don't want to talk about it. In general, we will tolerate an incident like that twice within a certain period of time, such as six months. However, if it happens more than that, the third time is the charmer, and he's fired. Again though, there can be exceptions, mitigating circumstances. For example, last year the wife of one of our good, reliable employees died suddenly, and he tried to drown his sorrow in alcohol. In his case, we made an exception. He came in a few times drunk, and each time we sent him home to sleep it off. But we didn't fire him. We talked to him, and talked to him, and then sent him to a professional for counseling. It worked. He stopped drinking, and now he's once more as efficient and reliable as before.

HOW TO HANDLE CLOSET CASES

As for the closet cases—whether it's alcohol or drugs—we maintain a hands-off policy until or unless something occurs that is bad for the other employees, for him or her, or for the business. If help is needed, I would provide assistance—under strict surveillance. Personal preferences, private lives—just like religion—are none of my business. All I'm interested is that he performs the job for which we hired him in the manner that is according to the high standards of Tia Maria or Red Onion restaurants.

TRY WORKING OUT PROBLEMS WITH EMPLOYEES

All of this doesn't mean that we have a cold, impersonal employer-employee relationships in our restaurants. We pride ourselves on having good relationships with our employees. I, for one, make it a point to get to know the family of every one of our managers and chefs. I think it's very important for an employer to have friendly relationships with his employees—within limits, of course, because you should never treat your employees as if they were members of your family. That wouldn't be fair to them; it wouldn't be fair to you. And most important, it wouldn't be good for your business.

Still another viewpoint is presented by J. Edward Fleishell, the highly visible restaurateur of Le Club:

CASE IN POINT

How to handle kitchen prima donnas or simply temperamental employees depends on the type of restaurant you're running. If I were president of a restaurant chain, I'd give them no leeway. I wouldn't have time, nor could I afford to worry about one chef or one bartender in one particular restaurant among some 20 restaurants. In such a large scale operation, kitchen prima donnas are replaceable.

In a smaller place where you have an owner/operator, as we have in my restaurant, it's just common sense to work out, or at least try to work out, problems that come up with individual employees. Of course, this applies only if the person in question has been valuable to you for a period of time. Here's an example. We have a fellow who's been with us for eight years, since day one, in fact. He's been always a bartender. Suddenly, he decided that he wants to become a waiter, though constitutionally he's not able to be a waiter.

We tried talking to him, but to no avail. We could not dissuade him. He wanted to become a waiter, and nobody could change his mind. It also has to be pointed out that he's a fabulous bartender, but a terrible waiter. Anyway, we wouldn't make him a waiter, so he quit—in a very friendly way though. He went to another leading restaurant. The owner called me and said, "Ed, this guy is over here, and wants a job as a waiter. But I wouldn't hire him until I talked to you." I told the caller, "Hire him! Do anything you can for him. I want him to do what's best for him. I think though, that he'll find out in a matter of weeks that waiting on tables is not good for him. That he can't take that kind of work."

Well, in two weeks he came back to us. But he still wants to be a waiter. So now we're going to try him out as a waiter, even though it's against my best judgment. But because he's been with us a long time, we're bending backwards, jeopardizing the quality of our service in a way, just to convince him that the rigorous work of a waiter is physically too much for him. He's not smart enough to learn by osmosis, so he will have to learn the hard way—by doing it. Our estimate is that within anywhere from three weeks to a month, he'll want to go back to being a bartender. And because he is dynamite as a bartender, we go along with him in what we believe is a folly. Besides, the guy deserves a break. And if anybody is going to give him the break, we have to do it because he's been with us for eight years. And because we're a small family—I hate to use that word, it sounds a little hokey, but in our case it's true—we're going to give him a chance to do what he wants to do, even if we don't agree with him.

WHEN A GUY DESERVES A BREAK

On the other hand, if the chef or that same bartender came in drunk, he would be sent home immediately, and we would "pull" somebody else in. This is part of good management. My manager has a back-up person for every employee in our restaurant. That is, we have a long list of people who are waiting "in the wings," so to speak, anxious to work in our restaurant. So if the chef came in drunk, we would call a back-up chef who then would substitute for the regular chef. And the next day, when the chef came in sober, we'd talk to him, and let him know that if it ever happened again, he'd be through.

GOOD MANAGEMENT IS PREPARED FOR EMPLOYEES

THE HANDY BACK-UP LIST

There are certain things you cannot put up with in a restaurant. To begin with, a chef who comes in inebriated could very well hurt himself and maybe even other people; second, in my restaurant I have to have reliable, consistent people. I have to know that he's going to show up every working day. I have to know that he's going to be in a good mood. I can't make him happy, but sure as hell, I'm going to do everything not to make him unhappy. In other words, I love my staff. And I expect them to be with me until I die. But I'm aware of the frailties of life. Keeping in mind that *everyone* can change, I prepare myself for any eventuality by keeping a viable back-up list.

14

Avoiding the Most Common Pitfalls in Kitchen Staff Management

CHAPTER HIGHLIGHTS

If there is a similar thread running through the fabric of views of successful restaurateurs as to what constitutes "the most common pitfalls in kitchen staff management," it is that the restaurant operator *must* at all times be in complete control of the entire operation. This is true of one-store owners, as well as managers of restaurant chains. Within this matrix, however, the pitfalls range from leaving the control of costs to the chef, to owner-manager not really knowing anything about food (or rather cuisine), to managers who want to do everything themselves (either because they are too insecure or are just not able to delegate responsibilities), and to favoritism.

Mike Walsh of The Holding Company points out two common pitfalls:

> I'd say there are probably two common pitfalls in kitchen staff management, and number one is your cost control. In this day and age, it's extremely difficult to keep up with pricing your items right, on account of prices changing so quickly. Your cost of doing business fluctuates, and you really have to be aware of what you're buying; how much you're buying; and what the price is today, as opposed to what it was yesterday.
>
> It takes a lot of time and effort to keep up with that. A lot of time and concern that your average chef is not aware of. He doesn't see the invoices. He might do the ordering, but he's not in the office taking care of the accounts payable. Often such information is not seen by the people who actually use the ordered products. That's the biggest thing: making everybody in your kitchen aware of your cost of doing business; having somebody watch the prices and relate them to the menu; and making sure that your percentage of profits is built in there. If an item costs itself out of your customers' restaurant budget, that is, if it gets too expensive for your customers, then you need to put in other items that they can afford.

CASE IN POINT

ENSURE THAT YOUR STAFF IS AWARE OF YOUR COST OF DOING BUSINESS

In other words, you tend to look at prices when you set an item and put in on the menu. You cost it out and you watch it for a while. But the price of lettuce underneath the side dish keeps jumping up. The price of peas on top of the side dish keeps jumping up. The prices of all the little things keep jumping up. You have to pay attention to the most minute items. That's where all your costs are.

CHECK OFTEN QUALITY CONTROL IN YOUR KITCHEN

The second most common pitfall is not paying close attention to quality control in the kitchen. As you know, all you have to sell is QUALITY. If you're not watching the items coming out of the kitchen, if you're not doing constant quality control, the people in the kitchen probably aren't doing it either. To put it another way, if your kitchen staff knows how important quality control is to you, and that you have high criteria for items served to the customers, and that you check these things regularly, they too will pay attention to quality control. Moreover, they will be proud of the strict quality control in the kitchen.

THE MANAGER SHOULD SUPERVISE THE WORK, NOT DO THE WORK

Insofar as having a manager who works very hard is concerned—well, he might nearly kill himself doing all the jobs himself, but if he does not delegate any of his responsibilities, he's not doing what you're paying him to do. You are paying him to manage people. You are paying him to supervise and to do quality control, not to do all the work himself. You are not paying him to do physical work.

I went through that experience myself on the very first management job I ever had. The boss came to me and said, "I didn't put you in the manager position to have you do the work. I put you in that position to get the work done." That was a very good lesson for me.

MANAGER MUST COMMUNICATE AND DELEGATE

You have to delegate when you are a manager. That's what management is all about. You have to ensure that other people are doing what needs to get done, even if it is difficult, especially for a young manager. To communicate with employees well enough, to give them a bit of authority, and to make sure they are performing the job is not an easy task. It's a lot easier to do it yourself. You know it's done when you do it yourself. But when you trust other people to do a certain job, you still have to go back and check. A lot of times you have to go back and make them do it over and over again, until they get it the way you want it. It's a difficult thing to do. You have to deal with another person. That is the biggest problem. That's why you have to make sure that your manager delegates. You have to make him understand that he can't do all the work himself.

EFFECTIVE MANAGEMENT IDEAS

His time—his effective management time—is better spent standing in the middle of the restaurant and looking around. Not doing a thing, just looking. Because that's what he is paid to do: to see the problems. Because the customers are going to see them. If your manager doesn't find them, you can guarantee that your customers will find them. So you remind your manager that he's paid just to look, manage, and not do a thing—that is, nothing physically. And if your manager persists in doing things himself, you let him go and get one who is really a manager.

YOUR RESTAURANT IS A REFLECTION OF YOUR PERSONALITY

All of this points to one thing: the restaurant business is a reflection of the people who own it. You will get the types of people in there that you want by the type of restaurant you create. You hire the type of people you want by the type of people you select. You serve the type of food that you want, and it will stay clean the way you want it. Everything is the way you want it. There are no problems in a restaurant. If there's a problem within your restaurant, it's usually one that you have either created, or have not done anything to solve. You are 100% responsible for any problem you have. You created it, and you can solve it. You can do anything you want with it. If your kitchen staff becomes unmanageable, if your restaurant becomes an unprofitable operation, it will die because *you* blew it. There is no excuse for either situation. When you are the owner of a restaurant, everything—good or bad—within that restaurant depends upon you.

IF YOU HAVE A PROBLEM IN YOUR RESTAURANT, YOU ARE RESPONSIBLE FOR IT

J. Edward Fleishell of Le Club has quite different thoughts on this matter.

CASE IN POINT

WHEN MANAGERS DON'T KNOW GOOD FOOD

> One of the most common pitfalls of kitchen management has to do with the fact that a large number of managers know nothing about food. People are not born with taste. The mere fact that you graduate from the best restaurant/cooking school doesn't mean that you know what a dish should taste like. That's a pitfall, because you can buy first class meat, produce and groceries, but if the items are not prepared well, the whole operation is an exercise in futility. In other words, the difference is in the handling of the products.

> Unfortunately, there are too few people in the restaurant business who have decent taste. The history of many restaurant operators, even expensive restaurant operators, is rather bizarre. They will come here on a ship—perhaps jump ship—and get a job as a bus boy. After they are bus boys for a while, they become waiters, and then managers, wearing a shirt and tie. Often one of the patrons will back them financially, and suddenly they own a restaurant, though they really know nothing about cuisine.

> When I went into the restaurant business, I went in sort of backwards, because I like to eat and drink. I started off knowing a little bit about good food. And having been exposed to it here and in Europe, I had an idea of what a dish ought to taste like, and also how it ought to be prepared. So all I did was apply the great taste and style of other professionals to a new restaurant operation, and it seems to have worked.

ONE MAN'S REASON FOR GOING INTO THE RESTAURANT BUSINESS

> I took the same personnel that had been employed in a restaurant that had not been successful, and turned it into a successful business venture. However, since the heart of the restaurant is the chef, and the chef they had was absurd, the first thing I did was to terminate him and hire a new, excellent chef. With this new chef I knew the food would taste good and would be presented with style and elegance. The next thing I had to do was have a menu that made sense; that covered the spectrum of cuisine that the discriminating people I intended to cater to would want. I wanted to cater to people who earn their living with their brains. So my staff did not serve truck driver portions; they served appropriate portions of food that these particular people want to eat. I'm one of those people, so I know what they want to eat. I don't have to hire a menu consultant to tell me what I'd like to have. I know what I'd like to have. And I cater to people who I know have similar taste.

A RESTAURANT IS ONLY AS GOOD AS ITS CHEF

CATERING TO YOUR TARGET CUSTOMERS

> Anyway, my staff and I started running Le Club our way. We didn't care what other restaurants did. We did it in a way that we felt was appropriate. And it worked. We had more than sufficient customers who enjoyed that kind of dinner. We imposed a dress code. We required that

HOW TO KEEP UP HIGH STANDARDS

people wear a coat and tie. And immediately we had many of my friends tell me, "Ed, I can write a check and buy the whole building. Yet you say I can't eat in your restaurant without a coat and tie." And I'd reply, "Absolutely!" As far as I'm concerned that's the only way we can keep out a certain element that will do nothing but detract from the restaurant. I don't care how much money our customers have. All I care is that they are tasteful and civilized people. This is what we've aimed for, and that's how we are maintaining it today. No man comes in unless he's wearing a coat and tie. If men don't have a tie, I have ties there that cost more than the meals. Nevertheless, I just give them a tie, and hope that they'll wear one next time and not ask for another tie each time they come to the restaurant.

HOW TO SOLVE THE "FAVORITISM" PROBLEM

Another widespread pitfall of kitchen staff management is the problem of favoritism. Favoritism is just one tangent of the problem of service. Well, we don't have that kind of problem, because at Le Club there are no tables assigned to a particular waiter. Every waiter is the waiter for all the tables. So there's no question of "I don't want to serve that table because it's not my table." Furthermore, we divide the tips between everyone, including the chef. However, since the chef and manager are paid the highest, they share proportionately less in the tips than the waiters or the bartender. Thus, every one is concerned about every table and every customer. We have two dining rooms, and we assign basically two waiters to one room, and two waiters to the other room. In the latter room the manager/maitre d' acts as a waiter as well, doing the carving and providing the final touches of good club service. Moreover, because the tips are divided equally, the waiters have a tendency to discipline themselves. They don't want to have a waiter working there who's not carrying his fair share; who is not doing a good job; because then his tip would reduce the total amount shared by all.

STAFF DISCIPLINE THEMSELVES

The manager/maitre d' does the buying of everything, except for the kitchen. The chef does the buying for the kitchen. The orders are very simple. For instance, when you have a truffle sauce in our restaurant, you have truffles from France. You don't have ground-up ripe olives pretending to be truffles. When you have pate de foie gras, you're having pate de foie gras and not pig liver, as you have in many restaurants. The difference is pennies, so you may as well do it correctly. Likewise, for a long time we were selling our lobster tails for less than they cost us because very frankly we couldn't charge what the thing was worth. We just hoped that not too many people would order lobster tails, that's all. But you have to do it correctly, no matter what you serve.

QUALITY MAKES A RESTAURANT

Our restaurant is probably a little different than most when it comes to relationships. But that's because it's a small place. Every one is friendly at Le Club. For example, a month ago I had my chef join me in Lyons, France. He and his wife were on vacation in Europe, and they flew down to Lyons to have lunch with me. I personally—and only because of time limitations—don't go out with any of my staff. But it has nothing to do with position; it has to do with time availability. I have too many business engagements; too many committee meetings to attend to join my employees in social activities. But all the people at our restaurant socialize

FRIENDLY RELATIONSHIPS MAKE A KITCHEN OPERATION

with each other on their days off. They go on picnics together; they go to other social functions together; they are friends.

Though we regard the staff as "friends" or "family," let's face it, they work for the money. But they have a job which is from five until midnight, and the waiters earn probably $2,000 a month. Thus the waiters are earning very good money for very few hours, relatively speaking, and no responsibility. They come to work; they put on their uniform; they serve customers' dinners; they make good money; and they're happy. They live good lives. Also, because we're a small restaurant, we've come to the point where we really help each other; where we can count on each other for advice, for counselling. For instance, if an employee is having marital troubles, my manager will talk to the employee's wife, and then talk to him, trying to work out the problem, trying to re-establish good communications.

DON'T EVER FORGET: PEOPLE WORK FOR THE MONEY, BUT THE BIG PLUS IS CONGENIAL JOB ATMOSPHERE

We try to keep people happy. We are aware how difficult it is to leave your home life at home when you come to work. It's easy to say but tough to do. Consequently, we take an interest. If our employees have problems, we help them out. We are also concerned about our staff's morale.

TAKE INTEREST IN EMPLOYEES' PROBLEMS

Specifically, I think one of the worst things for a chef—who is essentially a creative person—is to have to cook dinners all night for anonymous people. So to ensure that our chef's creativeness never dulls because of routine cooking and ennui, I always make it a point—when there is any one of importance at Le Club, any regular customer, or any "name," such as David Rockefeller—to let the chef know. Thus, the man is inspired, and he feels like creating superb dishes. Let's face it, it's really tough to be creative again and again and again without ever knowing for whom you're cooking, and if the audience appreciates your efforts.

STAFF-MOTIVATING IDEA

WAYS TO ENCOURAGE YOUR CHEF'S CREATIVENESS

So we do little things like that to attempt to motivate our employees by other than economic methods. Also, we get write-ups in magazines, and the employees love that. We have *Gourmet* Magazine writing to us, wanting our recipe for mint sauce. This makes our staff very proud, because when they go somewhere, they say "I work at Le Club" and other restaurant people are impressed. Thus our staff knows not only that they have one of the best jobs in the city, but also that the restaurant they work in is quality cuisine. Moreover, we give them bonuses. At the end of the year we divide the net profit with them. And I don't know of any one else in the restaurant business that does that. I'm not talking about a hundred dollars; I'm talking about thousands of dollars. We give our doorman a couple of hundred dollars for Christmas. The people who work in the building there, who also sort of help out, we give them a hundred or two hundred dollars also.

AN EXTRA INCENTIVE: YEAR-END BONUS

NOTE: You can't apply the above employee relationship practices just to any restaurant. When you have, for example, a formula style restaurant, i.e., restaurant chain, you cannot afford to fraternize with your employees. Not usually, anyway. You have to be concerned with your union relationship, or if you're non-union, you don't want to get into the position of influencing your employees for or against the union. You also cannot rely upon the individual judgment of an employee to maintain high standards at any particular location. In fact, you have to specify how many pieces of french fries should be on the side, and that the sandwich should include one piece of lettuce and three strips of bacon. In other words, if you have 500 employees, you cannot allow each of the 500 to set his or her own standard. You would end up with some standards that would be higher than you need, and some that would be lower than you need. Basically, you have to maintain a high degree of general standards, so as not to offend any one.

A COMMON PITFALL: THE FALLACY OF "HARD SELLING"

A common pitfall of many kitchen managements is the way they sell menu items. There are restaurants where they do a lot of "hard selling." Many people resent such practices. If it's subtle, they usually don't mind it. But just imagine: you go to a restaurant and order a cup of soup, an entree, and coffee. If somebody is trying to push other items on you, you resent it. You don't want the waiter or waitress rolling the dessert cart past you and trying to sell you with, "Don't you want this special dessert?", or "Don't you want a salad?", or "Today we have smoked salmon. Why don't you try it?", and so on through the whole menu. You know what you want to eat, and you don't need anybody's forceful suggestions.

Of course, in all fairness, there are a lot of people who do need recommendations as to what to order, what to eat. Most people, however, know what they want to eat, and don't need a waiter or waitress to "hard sell" them on eight other things.

Here, according to Mr. Fleishell, is a classic example. He was a guest of a high-ranking member of the Philippine government. The host had a man with him who did nothing but carry money. They were a party of ten in a well-known and very expensive restaurant in San Francisco. The host asked Mr. Fleishell to order. Subsequently, the restaurant staff placed in front of the party items which Mr. Fleishell had not ordered. When he pointed this out to the waiter, the waiter responded with: "What do you care? You're not paying for it." Later, when the waiters brought the meat course, these customers switched from the white wine they were sipping to the red wine. Yet the captain and one waiter were still pulling corks on two additional bottles of white wine, knowing full well that these customers weren't going to drink them, and that they would either sell the wine to somebody else, or drink it themselves. The restaurant staff did all that because they knew that money was no object. "I absolutely resented that, even though I wasn't paying the bill," says Mr. Fleishell. "To this day I don't go into that restaurant, nor do I take any one there. I don't like their attitude; I don't like their hard-sell technique. When I go to a restaurant, I'm not going there to be sold something; I'm going there to eat dinner."

THE USUAL EFFECT OF "HARD-SELL" TECHNIQUE

TRICK IN SELLING: BE HELPFUL BUT NOT PUSHY IN SELECTING FOOD AND WINE

The trick in selling, according to successful restaurateurs, is for you or your staff to hand the customers the menu and help them *only* if they don't understand the entrees, or if they ask for your assistance. There are a lot of customers who don't know what the entrees really are under the French names. Similarly, on the wine list suggest something *if* you feel the person is not too sure of himself. In other words, you want to be helpful in selecting food and wine, but you don't want to be pushy.

SELLING IS A QUESTION OF DEGREE

Selling in a restaurant is a question of degree. A waiter or waitress can increase profits by being pleasant; by being helpful; by making sure the customer has food and wine; and by providing attentive, good service. For example, the customer may want that second highball or cocktail, but because the waitress is not around when he is ready, he says, "The heck with it. I'll just have wine." On the other hand, how many times have you heard a waitress ask, "Do you care for wine?" and the customer reply, "No. We'll just have cocktails." One has nothing to do with the other. You can have a dozen cocktails, but you'd still want wine with dinner. But as the French say, *chacun à son goût* (each one to his taste).

Another common pitfall in kitchen staff management is the hiring of a chef. Since you are hiring a person to cook, it would be logical for you to taste that person's cooking. While some restaurateurs neglect to attend to this all-important testing, successful restaurant owners adhere to it religiously. Mr. Fleishall says:

> On the three occasions that I've hired chefs, I've always insisted on tasting an item they cooked. Specifically, I would have them cook something familiar to my taste, and see how they prepare it. Basically, in cooking there are only three techniques. I don't care whether it's Italian, French, or whatever. All techniques are the same. You baste it; you roast it; you saute it. What else can you do? Veal scallopini is nothing but beef stroganoff without the sour cream and mushrooms, and using different meat. Very often the difference is only in the use of spices and not technique.

CASE IN POINT

> For a chef you can get a person who is a great artisan in cooking, but doesn't know anything about coordinating a kitchen. The trick is time and motion. Some people are talented in moving with great ease and not getting rattled or falling apart under tension. Most great chefs are quite introverted, though they may be gifted with a great deal of flair. They really are private people. They're thinkers. They're always thinking ahead. Moreover, a chef has to change gears a couple of hundred times a night, every time he makes a different kind of dish. This is especially true in our kind of restaurant where everything is cooked to order. The only thing that's not cooked to order are the ducks. We roast four ducks a day. If you come late, you don't get duck. It takes two hours plus to roast a duck, so we roast them at five o'clock. Thus, they are finished just when the dinner hour starts. And we only have ducks for the first go-around. If you come late, you won't eat duck that day. If we don't sell it, the kitchen staff eats it. We never sell the next day what we cooked the preceding day.

WHEN YOU HIRE A CHEF

Kitchen Staff

Insofar as the kitchen staff is concerned, it should be the chef who selects the people. Since he is going to work with them, he should hire them. You hire the chef, and hope that he will be good in hiring people who will work for him and with him. If he doesn't do a good job of selecting the kitchen staff, however, you will never know. There is no way you are ever going to know, unless the orders aren't coming out of the kitchen correctly. The fact of the matter is that this is the chef's problem. He has to prepare the food at the high standards you have established. He also has to have things ready. He has to see to it that the salad, the dressings, and the sauces, just to mention a few items, are prepared well and on time. In short, it is the chef's responsibility to coordinate all the activities in the kitchen. No easy task by any means.

A CHEF SHOULD PICK HIS OWN STAFF

Manager's Role

The manager has overall responsibility for the restaurant, including personnel for the bar, the dining area, and the lighting and music that create the atmosphere. This is what Mr. Fleishell has to say:

CASE IN POINT

LIGHTING AND MUSIC—
CRITICAL FOR CREATING
APPROPRIATE
ATMOSPHERE

To me, lighting in a restaurant is very important. Most restaurants allow the employee to set the rheostat wherever they want to; wherever they think it's right. This is absurd. You're letting a low-level employee create the atmosphere which is one of the critical things of a restaurant, not to mention the waste of electricity. So in our place I had this top lighting expert come in and set the rheostat where it belongs. And no matter who comes in first, that person has to set it at the specific mark. Not higher, not lower. This saves us money *and* sets the mood; the atmosphere we want. The same philosophy applies to music. You can't have music that's too loud in a restaurant. Music should not be obtrusive. You should *never* be able to make out the tune. Music should be in the background, just enough to break up the silence. There again it's my manager and I who decide where the needle shall be. Having established the mood of the restaurant, the criteria for food and service, I leave my manager to handle totally the acquisition of his staff. However, if he gets a waiter, for example, that I think might be detrimental for our restaurant, I'll tell him. I might say that the man's hair is too long for a waiter, or that he's not neat in his appearance, or that his hands or nails aren't clean enough for Le Club. This occurred once, but only once. Since then I put out the mandate: every night, before the waiters put on their jackets, they wash their hands and nails with a brush. I want clean hands and nails. And if you have a good manager as I have, you just have to say it once, and he follows through. But then, with us it's almost a family relationship.

IMPORTANCE OF STAFF'S
CLEAN HANDS AND
NAILS

In theory, this family-like relationship could make a disciplinary problem. On at least one occasion it did create a problem. A waiter took advantage of his position as a good friend of the manager. But that waiter is no longer with us, because these conditions cure themselves. Either he shapes up, or he's fired. We've had the same core of personnel for eight years. No one has quit. That's because they are all treated as valuable and respected members of a family that has a common goal: pleasing our discriminating customers with the best cuisine and best service possible. After all, a restaurant is in business to sell food, and the kitchen is the critical part of the business. The front part where the waiter puts the dish on the table is all very nice, but if the dish he serves isn't prepared well and of first class materials, you're wasting your time. There are a lot of restaurants in town that are what I call show business places. They're all show and no substance. Their food is inferior because either the manager does not know good cuisine, or they're buying cheap products to save a few pennies, or they just don't have their "act" together.

PROS AND CONS OF THE
FAMILY-LIKE
RELATIONSHIP

QUALITY RESTAURANTS
VS. SHOW PLACES

Ismael Venegas, of the Tia Maria and Red Onion restaurant chain, feels, on the other hand, that the most critical pitfall in kitchen staff management is a manager or chef who runs himself ragged trying to do all the jobs himself, and who does not delegate various tasks to his subordinates. Mr. Venegas states:

CASE IN POINT

If the person is a qualified manager or chef, and valuable to us, then it's worth our effort to solve his problem of not delegating. Actually, we use psychology. We tell him that we will consider him for promotion when and if he learns to delegate. This is not an idle promise, and he knows it. Now, if he or she is ambitious and looking for promotion, then he will learn to delegate work and responsibility to his subordinates. And if he's not ambitious and not looking to climb higher, we don't want him. Our approach is as simple as that. And of course, the main thing is that it works.

Doug Scott of Victoria Station, Inc., uses a different approach to resolve the same problem.

I think first of all you have to build up the particular manager's self-confidence. Then, you can point out to the person that the people who are working under him—be it the assistant manager or hourly employees—aren't being developed, because he's not delegating; he's not giving them additional responsibility. And because he is not directing them or guiding them, they're suffering also. In which case, by the way, I'm sure, the restaurant would be suffering as well. Often, if you point some of these things out, he'll get the message and start to work on it. But delegation is probably one of the hardest things to learn. He has to learn to trust others to do the work right, and do it right the first time. That's very difficult for a manager to learn.

It was certainly difficult for me to learn. There's always the feeling that if you do it yourself, you know it'll get done. And it may be the truth. But then again, if that is the case, you'd better take a look at how well or how badly you have developed the people working for you. You are the only one who can do it.

You might be the most knowledgeable manager, but I don't think that necessarily makes you a good manager. I think a good manager delegates the majority of responsibilities to his staff and he just supervises everything. It is also very important for a manager to develop the potential of the people working for him. As far as Victoria Station is concerned, that's one of the criteria of a truly good manager.

CASE IN POINT

TEACHING A MANAGER
TO DELEGATE

DEVELOP POTENTIAL OF
SUBORDINATES

15

Hot Money-Saving Tool for Restaurant and Commercial Food Operations: Low-Cost, Small Business Computers

CHAPTER HIGHLIGHTS

For a restaurateur to prosper in today's competitive economic climate, he has to know exactly what his cash is used for, i.e., how much, on what, and where his cash is spent. Moreover, since a restaurant's volume of sales must reach and maintain a certain ratio to investment in order to achieve the projected financial goal, the restaurant operator has to be able—at any given time—to compare projected and actual costs, projected and actual results. In other words, to compete with other restaurateurs he or she must have complete control over all finances. This means checking regularly (once or twice a month) how the actual spending compares to the initial budget, and if there is a budget over-run. Because timeliness is crucial in all of these activities, a growing number of one and two unit restaurateurs are becoming dissatisfied with the lengthy manual processing of their accounts receivables, accounts payables, general ledger, inventory, and items-costing applications.

Conversely, because of rising monthly fees and often slow service, many restaurant owners who have turned to data processing are becoming disenchanted with computer service bureaus processing their payroll, tax reports, and financial analysis applications. Thus more and more individual restaurateurs as well as restaurant chains are considering in-house small business computers. This is happening because these minicomputers are proving to be cost justified. And because the prices of the proliferating minicomputers have been lowered so that now they are within the means of small businessmen, you might be missing out on a good dollar-saving tool if you don't look into the possibility of automating your financial transactions on a desk-type small business computer system right in your own office.

CASE IN POINT

Because the service bureau he was using raised the monthly service charges, John Manucio, a New York restaurateur, switched from a data processing service bureau to an in-house minicomputer. The computer system this businessman bought in May 1977, after careful study and evaluation, was the *Data Equipment Corporation's Datasystem 310.* According to Mr. Manucio, the system provides him full accounting applications, plus budget analysis and advertising mailing lists. The accounts receivable programs produce daily sales and payment journals, daily and monthly summaries, monthly aged-trial balance reports by alphabet, and waitress-bartender type of accounts. The accounts payable programs run weekly, and produce a check register and vendor checks. The payables are also compared with the established budget to produce a monthly budget analysis, broken down by category within food, liquor, and overhead expenses. In addition, the sales program produces a daily cash transaction report. Moreover, all required government payroll reports, including W2 and 941 forms, are produced by the payroll program. The system provides totals and averages for the bar and for the dining area daily, by month-to-date, and year-to-date. Mr. Manucio's part-time bookkeeper was trained by the software firm (who supplied the applications package for Datasystem 310) to program the small business computer system in the specially designed "command language." "I'm quite satisfied with this arrangement," says Mr. Manucio, "because I'm getting much more for approximately the same amount I used to pay the service bureau."

ANOTHER CASE IN POINT

When his sales increased, Tom Bell, a restaurant owner in Boston, increased the number of his waitresses, and decided to automate his payroll and sales/costs journals. Subsequently, he contracted a computer service bureau, which then processed those applications. Reluctant to lose control over his accounts receivables and payables, Mr. Bell continued to do those applications himself. However, when typically he had to wait five or six days to receive the previous month's sales/costs reports, he decided that the service bureau was not for him. Besides, the manual chores were taking too much of his time. So he opted for a small, in-house business computer. He wanted one that would give him more and faster information; keep him in control of his accounts receivables and payables; save him money in the long run; and simple enough so that he could operate it between the peak periods of lunch and dinner. He looked at many minicomputers, but none met all of his requirements. Then in September 1977, *Olivetti Corporation* was willing to provide for him a customized small business computer system, and train him in an English-like programming language. "The system sits in my office," says the pleased restaurateur, "right where I used to have the typewriter. It keeps track of all our sales—both food and liquor. And at the end of the day, it produces a summary report in the exact form I want it. It also generates all the pertinent information I need in regard to receivables, payables, and financial statements. And what's more, confidential information doesn't leave my office."

Just What Is a Small Business Computer?

The early minicomputers of the 1960s were inferior to the conventional computers because the machines were painfully slow; the memories were very small; very few peripheral equipment existed; hardly any package software applications were available; and only a handful of people were using them. The current minicomputer resembles the early models only in size. It is still small. In fact, now it is usually housed in a desk, making it just another piece of office equipment. In every other respect, however, the small business computer of today is a complete system with a central processing unit, medium to large main memory, one or more auxiliary storage disks or diskettes, one (or more) video display terminals, and a medium to high speed printer. Many of these minicomputers provide an English-like nonprogrammer language, which the system software then translates into a machine language that the computer can understand. Many more of these small business computer systems, however, still use a high-level programming language, such as COBOL, BASIC, BAL, or ALC.

The only exception, as of this date, is a revolutionary minicomputer called *Adam* (for an overview see page 177), that really runs on plain English verbs and nouns. The reason that this particular small business computer system can understand English (or any other natural language) directly and without any packaged software is that it was designed especially for non-technical persons. More specifically, Adam was built for the small businessman who needs timely information about his business operations; who wants security, i.e., who doesn't want confidential material to leave his office; who has to comply with the constantly growing reporting demands of the federal and state agencies; who cannot afford to add a programmer's salary to his already high labor cost; and who is reluctant to trust all his accounting, payroll, inventory, and sales analysis to an outside service bureau programming staff.

A NEW BREED OF MINICOMPUTER

According to the latest official release on the minicomputer explosion, there are approximately 25,000 small business computers installed in the United States that have cost less than $15,000. And this is just the beginning. When the prices are lowered even further, when all the vendors provide applications programs custom-made to the individual businessman's operations, together with an easy-to-learn "command language" if not the simple English that the above-mentioned small business computer system uses, then the minicomputer will come of age. In sum, when the minicomputers become as easy to handle as today's stereo systems, that's when the small business computers will be as commonplace in offices as typewriters.

MINICOMPUTER COMES OF AGE

When Charles Norman opened his second lobster-and-steak restaurant in Los Angeles, he felt that his business expanded to the point where he needed a more sophisticated recordkeeping method. After careful deliberation, he chose an *IBM System 32* small business system. The system reports on products received, price changes, and other information, enabling Mr. Norman to base all financial and management decisions on complete and recent data. "The most significant feature of the system," says the restaurateur, "is perhaps its ability to give me, in the evening, information I need to assess profits of the same day's operation."

CASE IN POINT

Paul Benson, owner/manager of a Chicago restaurant, for years relied on manually doing his accounting and recordkeeping. In 1976, however, he started looking for a more efficient and faster method. At first he considered a bookeeping type of machine. But when he found out that for not much more he could get a small business computer, he looked into that possibility. After a month of investigation and deliberation, he chose *Wang Laboratories' WCS-20* system.

Within three months Mr. Benson was able to have correct, accurate reports not only on inventory and general accounting activities, but also on sales. Moreover, Mr. Benson, with no previous knowledge of computers, was able to learn in two weeks to operate the system, i.e., to generate reports, and to manipulate correctly the video display terminal.

"To get the kind of in-depth reports that would give us timely inventory control and analyze the sales figures to determine profitability, we decided that we would have to get an in-house computer," says John Anderson, part-owner/manager of a Miami restaurant. "However, we were looking for a small business computer that would adapt to our business, instead of our adapting our business to the computer. In other words, we wanted a minicomputer that didn't need a programmer to operate it and was responsive to our needs and our non-technical abilities."

Anderson and his partner Phil Smith spent over a year looking at various business computer systems. Eventually, they chose *Datapoint's System 1500* which both Anderson and Smith now operate. "Except for inventory control and sales analysis, we are using the system for standard accounting functions," says Mr. Anderson. "But one of the system's major benefits, as far as we are concerned, is the system's ability to spot trends in our selling menu items. Previously it took us a while until we realized which menu items or drinks were selling better than other ones. Now we are aware almost instantly, and can anticipate the surge in certain items."

Available Small Business Computer Systems

Nearly all the well-known large computer manufacturers, such as IBM, NCR, Honeywell, Burroughs Corp., Sperry-Univac, Hewlett-Packard, Control Data Corp., and many others, are bringing out minicomputers. But in addition, many new electronics companies that specialize in the design, development, and marketing of small business computers are springing up across the country.

These minicomputers vie with each other in performance, cost benefits, and size. In fact, most are housed in small office desks, making them blend into most any office decor. The cost for a complete small business computer system ranges from $5,950 to $115,000, with the average around $25,000. All these systems accept either generalized prepackaged programs, or custom programs. This means that when you buy or lease a small business computer, in order to run your applications on it you have to buy "software," i.e., ready-made or customized application programs from a software firm. And then you either learn one of the many special English-like languages, have the vendor train your bookkeeper (or any other of your staff) in the language, or have a programmer run your computer system.

Many non-technical people quickly learn the user-oriented language; process their own accounting, inventory, and sales applications; and what's more, get great satisfaction out of it. But just as many non-technical people have great difficulty in learning a programming language. The latter group usually opts to have their bookkeeper learn the special language through which the business applications can be processed on the computer.

a. What to Do *Before* Buying a Small Business Computer

CAUTION: If you decide to buy an in-house minicomputer, make sure that you thoroughly check out the vendor and his product. Talk with other small businessmen who are using the same computer. Are they satisfied? Is the computer fulfilling their special needs? Is the vendor providing good service? In other words, you go through the same process as with any other vendor who supplies you with produce, meat, grocery items, or kitchen equipment. You check and double-check the vendor and his track record.

Before you automate your manual system and buy a minicomputer, you should prepare in writing a comprehensive profile of your restaurant operations. The profile should detail your business activities, services, and sales, as well as your goals and past and projected growth. Next, you should determine the criteria that the planned-for small business computer system must measure up to, as well as the limit such an in-house computer can cost you.

STEPS TO ENSURE THE RIGHT DECISION

Once you have established your requirements and specifications, you should contact several vendors. As you evaluate vendors, their equipment and services, you should also take time out to visit the customers of the vendors who impressed you the most. The purpose of the visits is to see how the particular system works at various customers' sites. Observe very carefully whether it is easy or difficult for the customers to process their applications. Ask them what in the system is satisfactory; what procedures in the system give them trouble. In short, investigate thoroughly what other customers, who have been working with the particular small business computer system for any length of time, really think of it. Of course, the vendor is going to give you a demonstration on the machine. But don't settle for that alone; a demonstration will only show you what the vendor wants you to see. That's why you should insist on visiting the vendor's customers.

Actually, verifying the reputation of the vendor is not enough. You also should check the expertise of the people who will install your computer system. Very often it isn't the manufacturer who installs the system, but a service company who is under contract to the manufacturer. And they are the ones whom you call if something goes wrong.

CHECK REPUTATION OF ALL PEOPLE INVOLVED

Contract negotiation is another important step when you buy or lease a computer system. The contract should spell out exactly what the vendor is guaranteeing. The contract should also be explicit in regard to what the vendor is going to do for you, if he is supplying the applications software for the system. This section should include how many and what type of reports you're going to get, and other specifications equally important, If, after all of your business applications have been automated, the computer system doesn't perform to your satisfaction, i.e., it doesn't give you in form, legibility, or content what the vendor promised you, the vendor should be contacted. And this is where your contract and your written specifications will save you a lot of arguments and trouble, not to mention money.

SCRUTINIZE CONTRACT

CAUTION: No more than one application at a time should be converted from manual to automated processing. Only when the first application—whether it's payroll, accounts receivables or payables, or sales—is running smoothly and generating satisfactory reports, should the second application be converted and implemented on the computer. Loading a small business computer with several applications at the same time will more than invite trouble; it will guarantee disaster.

b. List of Small Business Computers

Here is a very limited sampling of the multitude of specialized and reasonably priced small business computers on the market. Basically all these computers are the same. They all have a *central processing unit (CPU)*, which contains the main storage, arithmetic unit, and other important parts of the computer system; a *video display terminal* with typewriter-like keyboard through which you type or key in the information you want to file (as in a filing cabinet), or the sums you want to calculate; and a *printer*, which prints the reports you request. The difference among these computers lies in the size of the disk storage (where you file the data for future use); the speed with which the machine responds to your questions and instructions or orders, and retrieves and presents the information you want on the video screen; and the speed of the printer.

Some of the available small business computer systems are:

- *Olivetti Corporation's A5 System* (Photo 1)
  Address: Olivetti Corp. of America
         500 Park Avenue
         New York, NY 10022

- *Datapoint's System 1500* (Photo 2)
  Address: Datapoint Corp.,
         9725 Datapoint Drive
         San Antonio, TX 78284

- *Wang's WCS/20 System* (Photo 3)
  Address: Wang Laboratories, Inc.,
         One Industrial Avenue
         Lowell, MA 01851

- *Digital Equipment's DEC Datasystem 310W* (Photo 4)
  Address: Digital Equipment Corp.
         146 Main Street
         Maynard, MA 01754

- *Logical Machine's Adam System* (Photo 5)
  Address: Logical Machine Corp.
         1294 Hammerwood Ave.
         Sunnyvale, CA 94086

Photographs of these small business computers are shown here.

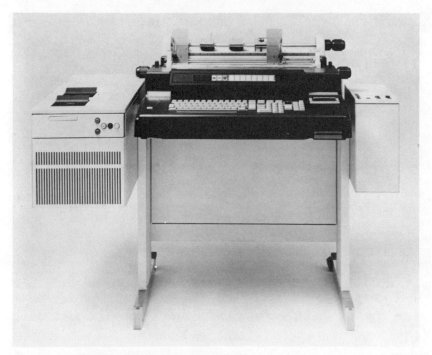

PHOTO 1: Olivetti Corporation's A5 System
Courtesy of Olivetti Corporation of America.

PHOTO 2: Datapoint Corporation's System 1500
Courtesy of Datapoint Corporation.

PHOTO 3: Wang's WCS/20 System
Courtesy of Wang Laboratories, Inc.

PHOTO 4: Digital Equipment Corporation's DEC DATASYSTEM 310W
Courtesy of Digital Equipment Corporation.

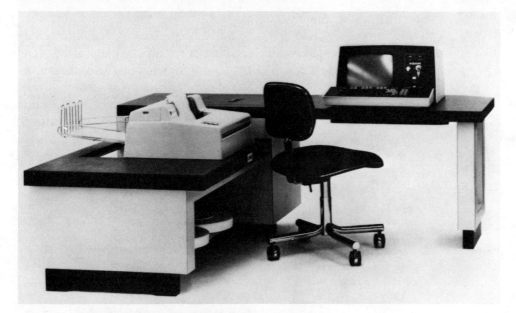

PHOTO 5: Logical Machine's ADAM System
           Courtesy of Logical Machine Corporation.

According to a recent survey most owners of minicomputers are quite pleased with their small business computer systems because of the price/performance benefits, even though some have problems with the software support. And this is the case, whether a full or part-time computer programmer is operating and maintaining the system, or whether the small businessmen (who have learned to program in the special user-oriented language of the prepackaged or customized software) are operating the computer system.

Because the last minicomputer on the above list—Adam—is the only one as of this date that is designed specially for non-technical small business people, because it is a new concept, and because it is the only one that runs without expensive and at times troublesome software package and "programming language," it is worth the restaurateurs' attention.

Overview of Adam

To begin with, you can communicate with Adam in plain English. No mystifying and difficult computer codes are needed for this computer to process your business applications. Many computer experts, in fact, think that Adam is signalling the end of the mystique that has surrounded the computers far too long.

Adam's designers were aware of a couple of things which other computer manufacturers seem to ignore, or at least overlook. Specifically—small businessmen don't have the time or the inclination to study complex programming languages; neither do they have the budget to add a computer programmer to operate a computer system which dictates not only the form and size of data it is willing to process, but the content as well. In the case of Adam, you are the one who dictates in your native tongue the format and content of the data to be processed, and the computer complies.

A MINICOMPUTER THAT
RUNS ON PLAIN
ENGLISH

Adam's basic vocabulary consists of 42 English verbs and nouns which you use and then add to, as you "communicate," or instruct the computer to build an account receivable or payable, a general ledger, an inventory control, a payroll, a sales analysis, or whatever applications you want. (A sample of this computer's basic vocabulary is included here.) Moreover, when you ask Adam to retrieve, for example, the total amount of your payroll three months ago, the machine's response is surprisingly fast. In other words, Adam adjusts to your business procedures, instead of your changing your business practices to suit an uncompromising computer system.

PARTIAL LIST OF ADAM'S* BASIC VOCABULARY

VERB	FILE	FORGET
FIX	RENAME	EXCHANGE
EXCHANGE ALL	LIST VERBS	LIST FILES
LIST NOUNS	LIST REFS	LIST UNDEF
TRACE	STATUS	ALTER
ADD	SUBTRACT	MULTIPLY
DIVIDE	SPLIT	CONTINUE
REPEAT	START	GO TO
LABEL	IF	IF REF
DISPLAY	PRINT	OUTPUT
INPUT	$INPUT	MOVE
CUT	JOIN	SAVE
GET	DELETE	BEGIN
RECAP	RECAP ALL	COMMENT

*ADAM is a registered trademark of Logical Machine Corp.

When Adam is asking you to clarify something, or when it is coaxing you to define the program or the file you are building, or when it is guiding you through job steps, it is communicating with you in lower-case type on the video screen. And when you give Adam an instruction or order, it appears in upper-case type on the screen, adding to your sense of control.

Incidentally, Adam verifies the data you give it *before* it processes it, and if there is an error, it will tell you so on the screen. And finally, because you can use your native language instead of the conventional computer languages, the average time to learn and communicate with this small business computer is only a week, even for the absolutely non-technical person.

Turnkey System: an Alternative

While some people are critical of the "turnkey" system, other businessmen swear by it. There is a lot of confusion about turnkey systems and how they differ from the small, in-house, business computer system. For one thing, the equipment is usually assembled from various manufacturers by the firm that has designed a special software/applications package for a particular industry, or a certain section of a particular industry. In other words, the central processing unit for a turnkey system may be selected from one manufacturer, the video display terminal from another, the auxiliary storage disk from a third, and the printer from a fourth one. The software firm then sells the whole package (equipment, applications programs, and maintenance service), or turnkey system, as it is known in the computer field, to businessmen directly. The turnkey systems firms usually supply programmers to maintain the system for certain monthly fees.

Problems arise, however, when—as critics of turnkey systems point out— any of the equipment malfunctions. If the machine has been assembled from more than one manufacturer, nobody wants to take the responsibility for the breakdown, and the blame is passed around from one manufacturer to another. On the other hand, businessmen who are satisfied with turnkey systems counter that if the firm that sold you the equipment/software/support package is reliable, they will resolve the equipment problem, and you have nothing to worry about.

CASE IN POINT

By converting from computer service bureau to an in-house turnkey system, Bill Brown, a Dallas restaurateur, has been able to have all his inventory control and cash management functions on-line, improve his cash flow, and eliminate the need for an office staff. "The service bureau we had handled only accounts receivables and payables, and inventory," says the Texas restaurateur. "And they were expensive. The bookkeeper, who was manually doing billing and other procedures, was adequate, but still it was another salary I had to pay. Besides, the reports on costs and sales were not timely enough." Mr. Brown, however, admits that he and his key restaurant staff were involved heavily in planning every phase of the in-house turnkey system to ensure its success. "But," says Mr. Brown, "it was worth it. And now I wouldn't have it any other way."

CAUTION: So consider everything, and then make your choice. But when you do decide to automate your manual system, be sure:

a. to define your problems;
b. to list your "musts," "wants," and "service criteria";
c. to establish your "cost limit."

Whether you opt for an in-house small business computer or a turnkey system, do not forget to evaluate the vendor, his product, and his service record, including previous users' experiences. In addition, you should insist on getting an official documentation that clearly states not only how to operate the system, but also how to correct problems that may arise. In other words, don't sign a contract until and unless all of your requirements are met and spelled out in black and white. And lastly, you should consider not only the initial cost but the monthly maintenance cost as well—an important factor in long-range budget planning.

In sum, the main thing when you buy an in-house small business computer system is that you know *before* you call upon vendors, just exactly by what standards you are going to evaluate their merchandise and services. Simply put, an orderly selection route will ensure that you are getting a computer system that suits your particular business practices and saves you money.

APPENDIX

Sampling of a Financial Overview of the Restaurant Business*

Using Restaurant Financial Ratios and Analysis

The following is taken from Chapter 9 of Profitable Restaurant Management, *published by Prentice-Hall, and is reprinted here with minor changes by permission of the publisher. The authors of this chapter are Norman Katz and Kenneth I. Solomon.*

Interpretation of financial statements involves three things:
• An understanding of what each caption represents and its significance.
• Insight into the relationships between items and the manner in which they are interacted within the dynamic pattern of operations.
• A grasp of the significance of changing relationships and patterns as they emerge.

Consequently, a complete analytical study of the financial statements of a business involves, among other things, interpretations of a number of ratios and of trends associated with them. However, each ratio should express a genuine relationship that has particular significance to investors, lenders, or managers. The examples which will be offered in this chapter have been selected for their relevancy to the restaurant business.

Financial statements tell a story. Reading a financial statement is a matter of extracting from it the meaning that lies behind the figures, for every figure reflects a specific fact about the business.

The Balance Sheet, or Statement of Financial Condition, presents a picture of the business at a single point in time. It proclaims "This is how things stood at such-and-such a date. The assets owned by the business were such. And the difference was the ownership equity."

The Profit and Loss Statement, or Income Statement or Statement of Operations, summarizes the results of operations for a stated period — a week, a month, a year. It shows revenues (sales, income) and expenses, classified and grouped to make interpretation easier. It shows profit margins at various levels (after certain expenses, but before others) and net earnings on the bottom line.

The balance sheet

Within each section of the balance sheet, items are grouped into subsections: assets into current and fixed; liabilities into current and long-term. The obvious purpose is to permit evaluation of short-term prospects for meeting obligations as they become due.

Current assets comprise cash and those items that are readily convertible into cash, such as accounts receivable and temporary investments in marketable securities. Inventories are converted into cash in the normal course of business; therefore, inventories are included in current assets. In the restaurant business, inventories tend to be small, implying that their conversion through sales

into receivables or cash is expected to occur quickly. The significance of this characteristic of restaurant inventories should not be overlooked in evaluating current position.

Fixed assets, or capital assets, may include land and building (if they are owned by the restaurant), furniture, fixtures, and equipment. These are reported at original cost less accumulated depreciation (or amortization). This method of evaluation has certain drawbacks: original cost may be quite different from current replacement value, and equipment bought in different years with different dollars is evaluated at a total dollar amount that is difficult to define accurately. Furthermore, accumulated depreciation does not represent a replacement reserve that will automatically become available to purchase new equipment as the old wears out. Obviously, balance sheet valuation of fixed assets can be misleading to the unwary.

From the standpoint of management, it would certainly appear that, within the context of present generally accepted historical cost accounting, the net income figure and the income statement are of far greater value in appraising the worth of an enterprise than the balance sheet.

Sophisticated observers have criticized the balance sheet on other grounds as well. They point, for example, to the assets of a business that go unrecorded either because they are considered to be acquired without payment or because measurement of their value is not agreed on. Thus, human assets, the aggregate skills of the managers and key personnel, are never reported although they contribute substantially to the restaurant's ability to make a profit.

Current liabilities comprise accounts payable, notes payable, accrued expenses and taxes payable or accrued. If a debt is to be paid over a number of years, the portion that becomes due within one year is reported as a current liability. Any other long-term debt is shown in a subsection of its own, separate from current liabilities.

The presentation of net worth reflects the type of business organization: capital accounts for individual proprietorships and partnerships, capital stock for corporations. Accumulated (retained) earnings add to net worth.

The profit and loss statement

The profit and loss statement and its supporting schedules should present both sales and cost of sales by department (dining room, banquets, bar, cigar counter). Controllable expenses should also be reported by department. These include payroll and associated taxes and fringe benefits; such operating expenses as supplies, uniforms, and laundry; and such overhead items as utilities, repairs, and maintenance. Departmental contribution margins are the results of revenues and expenses to this point; the total represents restaurant income before administrative overhead, advertising, depreciation, interest, and income taxes. Net earnings are customarily shown before taxes and after taxes.

*From "Tableservice Restaurant Operations," reprinted with permission of Laventhol & Horwath, Certified Public Accountants, and the National Restaurant Association.

There are several points at which balance sheet and income statement relate to each other. When assets are used up, they become expenses; inventories become part of the cost of sales; fixed assets are depreciated or amortized and expenses are recorded; and prepayments are charged to expense as they expire. On the other hand, assets are built up by revenues: sales generate receivables or bring in cash. And earnings increase net worth.

There are, in fact, many relationships between individual items in financial statements that are worth exploring for the insight they can provide to the workings of the enterprise. Let us describe some of these relationships now.

Financial statement relationships

The geometric axiom that "the whole is equal to the sum of its parts" is extremely inapplicable to financial statements, for restaurants or otherwise. Invariably, financial statement analysis, wherein the component parts are scrutinized in themselves apart from the total picture of financial position and periodic operating results, will yield to the analyst additional useful information for evaluating the enterprise and its operating success or failure. Financial statement analysis is far more than a purely clerical task when properly performed. It is employed as a useful tool by both "insiders" (management) and "outsiders" (creditors, prospective and present investors, representatives of labor, investment bankers, and others).

Financial analysis, which is sometimes labeled as "historical," concerns a comparison of the relevant financial data for the present year with similarly compiled data for the previous year or a large number of prior years. The justification for this type of analysis seems to be the current accountancy craze for "trends" and period comparability, both as indicators of managerial efficiency and as guides to future decision-making.

We have already noted that current assets are set out separately in the balance sheet, and that similar treatment is accorded current liabilities. Relationships between these two groups of items are important because current liabilities will have to be paid in the near term and that means they must be paid out of current assets in the main. Working capital, or net working capital, is the name given to the excess of current assets over current liabilities.

There is a special relationship between equity and debt (between net worth and liabilities). All the assets of a business are acquired in exchange for funds provided by the owners or loaned by banks and other lenders or loaned, in effect, by creditors who are willing to extend terms and wait for payment. What the owners do not put up, they must borrow. Frequently, there is an option. An owner may raise money for his business by making additional contributions of his own, by inviting a partner to join him or by selling stock, thereby increasing the equity in each case. Or he may increase the debt by borrowing.

If the owner chooses to borrow, he increases his lever-age, assuming that the interest rate he pays is lower than the return that his restaurant earns. To illustrate, if a restaurateur borrows to increase his capacity, and the return on this increased volume is sufficient to pay the interest on the loan and leave something over as additional earnings, then the new earnings level, being higher than the old, is also a higher percentage of the owner's equity. This is the principle of leverage, and it results from a differential between the rate of return on assets and the cost of borrowed capital.

While debt financing has a potential for providing leverage, it also increases the owner's risk. Interest must be paid when due and so must instalments on loans. If earnings fall short of expectations, it may be difficult to make these payments. If earnings fall below the rate of interest on borrowings, then leverage operates in reverse, and the owner begins to suffer losses on the borrowed capital. If the owner were to sell stock in his enterprise instead, the exposure to risk would be accepted by the new stockholders. If earnings fall, dividends can be cut, and the restaurant's cash position need not be jeopardized.

These observations make it plain that the relationship between debt and equity is important to the owner because it determines his leverage and it exerts a strong influence on his exposure to risk. But the owner is not alone in his concerns. Prospective lenders will want to satisfy themselves that interest charges on proposed loans, added to interest charges on outstanding loans, will not be so burdensome as to create financial difficulties at the first slackening of business. Fixed charges, charges, including interest payments, can impair the ability of the business to withstand cyclical downturns, stringent competitive conditions, unforeseen emergencies, or other adverse contingencies. In extreme cases, exceptionally sanguine operators with a speculative bent may concentrate their attention so narrowly on the advantages of leverage, ignoring the drawbacks, that they are quite prepared to borrow far beyond the limits of prudence. At some point, excessive borrowing serves to transfer a portion of the owner's risk to the lenders. For, if things go wrong, not only will the owner be wiped out, but the creditors will suffer substantial losses as well. Accordingly, the larger the debt, in proportion to the equity investment, the more difficult it becomes to persuade lenders to provide new money and, of course, the higher the interest they will demand.

Part of our discussion of the relationship between debt and equity turned on another relationship, that between earnings and assets. As we have seen earlier, the total investment in assets is provided by the sum of the owner's investment and borrowings from other sources. The return on invested funds from all sources is a significant measure of the restaurant's ability to meet its obligations to outsiders and provide a fair return to the owners. Both lenders and investors, therefore, are interested in the business's return on investment in the broadest sense. That is to say, the relationship between earnings and total assets has a definite significance of its own, regardless of the source of invested funds.

We have been considering relationships between two individual items or two groups of items: current assets and current liabilities; equity and debt; earnings and investment. Now let us examine a series of sequential relationships known as the cash cycle.

In the ordinary course of business, cash is converted into inventories through the purchase of foods and beverages, the inventories are consumed in preparing meals and drinks that are sold to customers, and these sales produce cash receipts or receivables. Significant relationships exist at several points in this cycle: There is an interesting relationship between inventories and consumption and another between receivables and sales.

Analytical objectives

What do people look for when they analyze financial statements? That will depend on who they are and where their interests lie. Perhaps a better first question would be: What kinds or groups of people are to be found analyzing financial statements? For our purposes, it is sufficient to identify investors, lenders, and managers and to distinguish between two outlooks: the long-term and the short.

Long-term lenders and investors have much in common. They are both interested in the ability of the business to survive as a profitable venture into the future. Therefore, they will want to assess the profitability of the business, the use it makes of its assets as indicated by the adequacy of its return on investment. They will also want to scrutinize the relationship between equity and debt, as an indication of the manner in which risks are spread. Moreover, they will be interested in long-term trends.

Short-term lenders and trade creditors may be forgiven if they take a more limited view. It may be sufficient for them to be satisfied that the current position of the business is adequate to meet current obligations. They will want to look closely at current assets, and particularly at quick assets (those that are immediately convertible into cash and therefore quickly available to pay off debts). But long-term profit potentials are of less interest, except insofar as they may affect continuing relations and renewing credit.

Management has responsibilities to both long-term and short-term creditors, and to the owners as well. Accordingly, its interests include the kinds of analysis that the other groups need. In addition, the management functions of planning and control impose an emphasis on the future, an orientation on where the business is headed and how it proposes to get there and an interest in financial statements as feedback that provides information as to how well the restaurant is keeping on course.

With this background concerning the needs of various groups and the basic concepts for interpreting financial statements, let us proceed to a detailed description of helpful ratios.

Ratio analysis

The ratio of debt to equity may be calculated by divid-

ing net worth into total liabilities. This ratio indicates the strength of the capitalization. It answers such questions as these: Is the owner's stake so small that he is encouraged to speculate with outsiders' money? Will an issue of common stock still permit reasonable leverage? Would obligations to repay debts prove burdensome if the business suffered reverses?

If current liabilities fluctuate, those who prefer a more stable ratio may divide net worth into long-term debt instead of total liabilities. The interpretation of such a ratio will be similar to the ratio described above, except that the numbers will be smaller.

The ratio of earnings to assets requires some explanation. For this calculation, earnings should be taken before deductions for interest and income taxes. These two items are extraneous to the purpose of the ratio, and they can confuse the basic issue. We are looking for a measure of management's effectiveness in employing assets to produce profits. Interest is not a charge against operations, but rather a charge associated with a particular method for raising capital, that is, by borrowing. An evaluation of the effective use of assets should not be confused by charges related to the sources of funds for acquiring the assets. Income taxes need not be considered in evaluating the relationship between earnings and assets because changes in tax rates merely introduce variations that obscure the trends that are sought.

Similarly, total assets are used in the calculation, instead of net worth, because the sources of funds — whether equity or debt — are of no consequence in evaluating the use that is made of the assets themselves. Dividing earnings by assets, as we have now defined both terms, yields a ratio that is capable of measuring return on investment for those who must decide whether to invest in the business or to lend money to it.

The current ratio is obtained by dividing liabilities into current assets. This is a measure of the restaurant's solvency. In the restaurant business, a ratio of 1:1 is considered acceptable in recognition of the fact that inventories are low enough to be of little concern and also low enough to be converted into cash in the normal course in a short time. In other businesses, where inventories are a much larger part of current assets, the 1:1 ratio is held acceptable for the quick ratio rather than the current ratio. The quick ratio, of course, excludes inventories so that only cash, marketable securities and receivables, in total, are divided by current liabilities. The distinction between quick ratio (sometimes the term "acid test" is encountered in pedantic usage) and current ratio is of little consequence to restaurants generally.

The increased emphasis upon the use of the quick-asset ratio has resulted from the frequent clamor for cash or its practical equivalent in our modern monetary economy. In other words, a demand has been created for some device to measure the "liquidity" of an enterprise. By liquidity, financial analysts mean the ease of convertibility of assets into cash, and in a practical context the quick-asset ratio measuring such liquidity serves as a safeguard to detect a current ratio which may hide a condition known as "over-loaded inventories." In effect, a current ratio appearing quite feasible because of excessively high inventories would in reality be a distortion of a seriously impaired current condition and would go unnoticed but for the quick-asset ratio.

Income statements often show a large number of ratios simply by presenting alongside each dollar figure its *percentage to sales.* Thus, individual revenue items are shown as percentages of total revenues; individual expenses and grouped expenses are also related directly to net sales; and margins at various levels are treated similarly. The trends disclosed by these percentages are useful to management in controlling operations and also in planning ahead.

The ratio of prime cost to sales is a key figure for management. Prime cost covers both food (beverages for the bar) and labor, including preparation labor and serving, and it is a principal concept in menu pricing. In any comparison between convenience foods and regular foods, no reasonable basis for decision can fail to include the cost of labor. Hence, prime cost is well established as a figure of fundamental importance. And the ratio of prime cost to sales is watched very carefully.

The ratio of sales to man hours is a useful measure of the productivity of labor. Sales per-man-hour can be calculated for each department to provide information for control. Further analysis into hourly sales per-man-hour can be useful in planning to staff for peak loads and in staggering hours of work.

There are several *turnover ratios* that provide insight into operations. The concept of turnover itself is enlightening, implying as it does a cycle of use and renewal. We have seen that part of the cash cycle involves an inventory cycle: inventories are purchased and consumed alternately. A variation of the cash cycle substitutes working capital for cash, so that working capital is conceived as generating sales by being used over and over. Three turnover ratios will be described next.

Working capital turnover is calculated by dividing working capital (current assets minus current liabilities) into sales. It provides an indication of such things as the adequacy of working capital in consideration of the volume of sales and the possibilities for increasing sales without added investment in working capital.

Inventory turnover for food is calculated by dividing food inventory into the food cost of sales. Since the inventory is valued at cost, a proper turnover ratio can be gotten only by dividing into the cost of sales, rather than sales. A refinement of this ratio calls for dividing by average inventory over the period covered. Inventory turnover for beverages is calculated similarly: by dividing beverage inventory into the beverage cost of sales. The number of times a particular inventory "turns over" in a year can point up overstocking and speculation in inventories when prices look "right" at the moment, two practices that should be avoided for reasons described in another chapter.

Promptness of *collections* is measured by dividing average accounts receivable balances into credit sales. Alternatively, the *number of weeks' sales in open receivables* may be calculated by dividing recent average weekly credit sales into total current accounts receivable. Whichever method is adopted, only credit sales should be used in calculating turnover of receivables, because only credit sales create receivables in the first place. Inclusion of substantial cash sales in such a calculation would only distort the result. Furthermore, since collection patterns differ as between house accounts and accounts on credit cards issued by banks, credit companies, and other outside sources, a restaurant that extends credit in more than one way will find that truly significant ratios can be expressed only by analyzing accounts receivable and sales into homogeneous groups.

What Every Employer Needs To Know About OSHA Recordkeeping

U.S. Department of Labor
Bureau of Labor Statistics
1978
Report 412-3

Preface

The Bureau of Labor Statistics of the U.S. Department of Labor is charged with the responsibility for the recordkeeping system and reporting requirements under the Occupational Safety and Health Act. This pamphlet provides answers to questions employers most frequently ask about recordkeeping and reporting of occupational injuries and illnesses.

This revised edition contains several new sections covering recordkeeping requirements, a brief summary of OSHA recordkeeping guidelines, and the most recent information on other recordkeeping procedures. Also, new questions and answers have been inserted to reflect recent concerns that have arisen since the last edition was published. For questions not covered in this publication, employers may contact the Bureau of Labor Statistics' Regional Offices serving their areas. Addresses and telephone numbers are listed in appendix C.

This pamphlet was prepared in the Office of Occupational Safety and Health Statistics, Theodore J. Golonka, Assistant Commissioner, under the direction of Norman Root, Chief of the Division of Record Requirements and Information.

Material in this publication is in the public domain and may be reproduced without permission of the Federal Government. Please credit the Bureau of Labor Statistics and cite *What Every Employer Needs to Know about OSHA Recordkeeping*, Report 412-3.

Contents

New Recordkeeping Procedures

Since January 1, 1978, OSHA recordkeeping forms have taken on a new look. In accord with recommendations presented in a July 6, 1976, report by the Commission on Federal Paperwork, forms OSHA Nos. 100 and 102, with certain technical changes, have been combined into form OSHA No. 200.

The new form No. 200, the Log and Summary of Occupational Injuries and Illnesses, will help employers maintain records in a much simpler format. Also, the form permits recording of permanent transfers and terminations associated with occupational illnesses (recording of similar information for injuries is no longer required). Illnesses can be identified in separate columns by type. These and other columns can be totaled for running or page totals, at the option of the employer. Yearly totals fulfill the posting requirement formerly done on a separate form (OSHA No. 102). Yearly totals can also be used to complete the annual statistical survey report if an employer is selected to participate.

Employers having 10 or fewer employees are now exempt from recordkeeping unless they are selected to participate in the annual statistical survey. Fewer employers are now selected to participate in the survey.

The recordkeeping and reporting regulations in 29 CFR Part 1904 reflecting the changes in forms and procedures were published on December 30, 1977, in the Federal Register (42 FR.65164).

Forms for ordering additional recordkeeping materials are included at the back of this publication.

Guidelines for Determining Recordability

Basic recordkeeping concepts and guidelines are included with instructions on the back of form OSHA No. 200. This section summarizes the major recordkeeping concepts and provides additional information to aid in keeping records accurately.

1. An injury or illness is considered work related if it occurs in the work environment (defined as any area on the employer's premises, e.g., worksite, company cafeteria, or company parking lot). (See chart 1.) The work environment surrounds the worker wherever he or she goes——in official travel, in dispersed operations, or along regular routes (e.g., sales representative, pipeline worker, vending machine repairer, telephone line worker).

2. All work-related fatalities must be recorded.

3. All diagnosed work-related illnesses must be recorded.

4. All work-related injuries requiring medical treatment or involving loss of consciousness, restriction of work or motion, or transfer to another job must be recorded.

Recordable and nonrecordable injuries are distinguished by the treatment provided; i.e., if the injury required medical treatment, it is recordable; if *only* first aid was required, it is *not* recordable. However, medical treatment is only one of several criteria for determining recordability. Regardless of treatment, if the injury involved loss of consciousness, restriction of work or motion, transfer to another job, or termination of employment, the injury is recordable.

Medical treatment. The following are considered to involve medical treatment and must be recorded for a work-related injury.

— Antiseptics applied on second or subsequent visit to a doctor or nurse.
— Burns of second or third degree.
— Butterfly sutures.
— Compresses, hot or cold, on second or subsequent visit to a doctor or nurse.
— Cutting away dead skin (surgical debridement).

— Diathermy treatment.
— Foreign bodies, removal if embedded in eye.
— Foreign bodies, if removal from wound requires a physician because of depth of embedment, size or shape of object(s) or location of wound.
— Infection, treatment for.
— Prescription medications used.
— Soaking, hot or cold, on second or subsequent visit.
— Sutures (stitches).
— Whirlpool treatment.
— X-ray which is positive.

First-aid treatment. The following are considered to involve only first-aid treatment and need not be recorded if the work-related injury does not involve loss of consciousness, restriction of work or motion, or transfer to another job.

— Antiseptics, application of, on first visit to a doctor or nurse.
— Bandaging on any visit to a doctor or nurse.
— Burns of first degree.
— Compresses, hot or cold, on first visit to a doctor or nurse only.
— Elastic bandage, use of, on first visit to a doctor or nurse only.
— Foreign bodies, not embedded, irrigation of eye for removal.
— Foreign bodies, removal from wound by tweezers or other simple techniques.
— Nonprescription medications, use of.
— Observation of injury on second or subsequent visit.
— Ointments applied to abrasions to prevent drying or cracking.

Other procedures not considered medical treatment. The following are not considered medical treatment.

— Tetanus shots, initial or boosters alone.
— Hospitalization for observation (no treatment other than first aid).
— X-ray which is negative.

2

Guide to Recordability of Cases Under the Occupational Safety and Health Act

**(In addition, any accident which results in a death or hospitalization of
5 or more employees must be reported by telephone or telegraph within 48
hours to the Area Director of the Occupational Safety and Health Administration.)**

If a case

Note: A case must involve a death, or an illness, or an injury to an employee.

Results from a work accident or from an exposure in the work environment and is

Does not result from a work accident or from an exposure in the work environment

A death

An illness

An injury which involves

Medical treatment (other than first aid)

Loss of consciousness

Restriction of work or motion

Transfer to another job

None of these

Then case must be recorded

Then case is not to be recorded

Recordkeeping Forms

Log and Summary of Occupational Injuries and Illnesses, OSHA No. 200. (In the following discussion this is referred to as the log.) Each employer subject to the recordkeeping requirements of the Occupational Safety and Health Act of 1970 must maintain for each establishment a log of all recordable occupational injuries and illnesses. A substitute for the log, such as a computer-generated form, is acceptable if it is as detailed, easily readable, and understandable as form OSHA No. 200. Employers' logs should contain entries for all recordable cases no later than 6 working days after receipt of information that a recordable injury or illness has occurred. Employers who maintain centralized recordkeeping systems (e.g., computer-generated at a central location for several establishments) must have available at each establishment a log which is complete and current to a date within 45 calendar days.

Supplementary Record of Occupational Injuries and Illnesses, OSHA No. 101. This form supplements the log and must be available at the establishment within 6 working days after the employer has been notified of the injury or illness. Workers' compensation, insurance, or other reports may substitute if they contain all the necessary information or have been supplemented to do so.

The Occupational Injuries and Illnesses Annual Survey Form 200S. The form will be mailed to each employer selected to participate in the Bureau of Labor Statistics' Annual Survey of Occupational Injuries and Illnesses. Upon receipt, the employer shall promptly complete and return the form in accordance with the instructions.

Posting Requirements

From February 1 to March 1, each establishment must post in areas where notices to employees are customarily posted a copy of the year's totals and information following the fold line of the last page of form OSHA No. 200. An OSHA No. 200 with only the yearly totals, establishment identification, and certification may be used for this purpose.

Establishments having no injuries or illnesses during the year must enter zeros on the total line and post the form.

The person responsible for the annual summary totals shall certify that the totals are true and sign the form.

Record Maintenance, Retention, and Access

Recordkeeping forms must be retained for 5 years after the end of the calendar year to which they relate. Additionally, logs (OSHA No. 200) must be maintained for the same period; i.e., changes in extent of and outcome of cases must be made directly to the original case entries, even though the entries were dated in prior years.

All recordkeeping forms (current and retained) must be available at the establishment for inspection and copying by representatives of the Department of Labor; the Department of Health, Education, and Welfare; or States accorded jurisdiction under the act.

The log, form OSHA No. 200, shall, upon request, be made available by the employer to any employee, former employee, and to their representatives for examination and copying in a reasonable manner and at reasonable times. Access to the log shall be for any establishment in which the employee is or has been employed and covers all logs required to be maintained or retained by the employer.

5

Questions and Answers on OSHA Recordkeeping

AGGRAVATION OF PRE-EXISTING PHYSICAL DEFICIENCY

1. Q. What are the reporting requirements of pre-existing physical deficiencies so far as the OSH Act is concerned?

A. None. However, each case which involves aggravation of pre-existing physical deficiency must be examined to determine whether or not the employee's work was a contributing factor. If a work accident or exposure in the work environment contributed to the aggravation, the case is work related. It must be recorded if it meets the other requirements of recordability.

2. Q. In December of last year one of my employees injured his back and the injury was recorded on the log. In February of this year the employee has again lost time because of his back. Should I record the case on this year's log?

A. If the latest period of disability resulted from an incident, such as slip, trip, fall, or blow to the back, the case should be recorded as a new injury on this year's log. If there was no such incident, there was no new injury and no new entry should be made. The number of lost workdays should be added to any lost workdays shown on last year's log when the injury was originally recorded.

AGRICULTURE

3. Q. Describe how the farmer is covered, since coverage relates only to interstate commerce.

A. Farmers are covered because they "affect commerce." They are required to keep records in the same manner as other employers.

However Congress may provide otherwise in the Appropriations Acts for the Departments of Labor and Health, Education, and Welfare. The 1977 and 1978 Appropriations Acts contained provisions which exempted farmers with 10 or fewer employees from *all* provisions of the OSH Act. (See answer No. 21, and also see New Recordkeeping Procedures.)

ALLEGED INJURY OR ILLNESS

4. Q. What about occupational injuries and illnesses that can be disputed? When should they be recorded or reported?

A. Within 6 working days after receiving information that an injury or illness has occurred, the employer must determine whether the case is recordable. Any entry in the log, OSHA No. 200, may be lined out if it is determined later that the case did not result from a work accident or from an exposure in the work environment. (See also answer No. 6.)

5. Q. If an employer decides that an injury is not work related and the victim at a later date establishes—— by legal action or other means——that the injury *is* work related, how is this recorded?

A. The question seems to refer to a workers' compensation determination. Although such determinations have no direct bearing on recordability under OSHA, if the facts indicate that the case resulted from a work accident or from an exposure in the work environment, the case should be recorded, with the actual date of injury entered in column B of the OSHA No. 200.

6. Q. When an employee claims an occupational illness and the company disagrees, what will the Occupational Safety and Health Administration do if the employee makes a complaint?

A. The complaint probably would be investigated. The employer should be prepared to defend the decision. Perhaps the best advice to an employer is to record a doubtful case in the OSHA No. 200, and if it is later determined not be to work related, line it out.

7. Q. Suppose a worker says she hurt her back 2 weeks ago, but there was no record or report of it at that time. Is it subsequently recordable?

A. Yes. If it is established that the back injury was recordable, it must be included in the OSHA No. 200, even though the determination was made subsequently. The actual date of injury should be entered in column B.

8. Q. If an employee alleges inability to work because of conditions in the plant——an oil mess or a similar situation——who determines whether the absence is recordable?

A. The employer has to make the determination. The question does not mention an injury or illness. If there is none, there is nothing to record.

9. Q. What entries, if any, need to be made in instances of employer-employee disputes involving State workers' compensation measures to determine the facts related to alleged injuries or deaths?

A. Workers' compensation determinations have no direct bearing on recordability under OSHA. Some cases may be covered by workers' compensation but are not recordable; others may be recordable but are not covered by workers' compensation. (See answer No. 5.)

AMPUTATION

10. Q. Is there a provision involving amputation of part of a finger or toe that does not result in lost workdays?

A. There is no specific provision, but any work-related amputation would certainly be recordable because it would involve medical treatment other than first aid.

ATHLETIC EVENTS

11. Q. Our employees participate in many sports activities such as impromptu softball games at noon, bowling leagues at night, and a football team which plays its games on weekends. If any of our employees are injured in those activities and require medical treatment, should the injuries be recorded?

A. If these injuries occur on the employer's premises, they must be recorded. On the other hand, if the activities take place off the premises and the employees are not being paid (even though the employer is providing uniforms and/or equipment), injuries which occur are not recordable. Of course, if the employees are paid for these activities, injuries that result must be recorded no matter whether they occur on or off the premises.

BACK INJURY

12. Q. Are there specific requirements for back or hernia cases?

A. No.

13. Q. Suppose a person says he hurt his back 2 weeks ago, but there was no record or report of it at that time. Is it subsequently recordable?

A. (See answer No. 7.)

CALENDAR-YEAR RECORDS

14. Q. Must OSHA records be kept on a calendar-year basis, or can they be kept on a fiscal-year basis?

A. OSHA records must be kept on a calendar-year basis (January 1 to December 31).

CHANGE OF OWNERSHIP

15. Q. An employer with a number of establishments is dissolving her business. Some establishments are being transferred to another firm; some are being closed. What should be done with the OSHA records?

A. For those establishments in which there is change of ownership, the occupational injury and illness records must be transferred to the new owner. The owner must preserve those records for 5 years following the end of the year to which they relate, but is not responsible for maintaining them, e.g., updating log entries. The new owner will, of course, be responsible for work injury and illness records subsequent to the takeover date.

For those establishments, which are discontinued as part of a general dissolution, the obligation to preserve or maintain the injury and illness records for those establishments is ended. Of course, if the employer's business was continuing, the injury and illness records of the discontinued establishments should be transferred to a central office (or another establishment if there is no central office) and maintained for 5 years following the end of the year to which they relate.

CONSISTENCY

16. Q. We have plants in Iowa and Illinois. It appears that the various area directors will have different interpretations of the standards, and so forth. What will you do to have uniformity so we can plan corporate program standards for all of our plants?

A. BLS cannot speak for the standards, only for the recordkeeping system. We endeavor to assure uniform interpretations by our regional offices and State agencies which are cooperating in the program with the Bureau of Labor Statistics.

CONSTRUCTION INDUSTRY

17. Q. **Will a construction contractor have to maintain records at each individual jobsite, or can the records be maintained at the regional or central office?**

A. If employees report each day to a given place and the employer is able to maintain records for it, we would assume that such a site constitutes an establishment. Certainly, if someone has a plumbing shop with five trucks operating out of it and going to different sites every day, the establishment is the shop. Also, records for employees who do not report to any fixed establishment on a regular basis but are subject to common supervision may be maintained at a central location.

18. Q. **If a general contractor with 10 offices and perhaps 70 to 80 projects underway keeps records on the individual location basis, can reports be made the same way or must these records be consolidated at the home office into a single report?**

A. (See answer No. 17 above and No. 43.)

CONTRACT LABOR

19. Q. **I sometimes secure help from a temporary-help supply service. Do I record injuries to these temporary workers, or does the service?**

A. Generally temporary-help supply services will keep the records because the personnel concerned are their employees. There are some situations, however, in which personnel are being supplied for indefinite periods of time, and the "temporary-help supply service" is acting merely as a personnel department for the using firm. Under those circumstances, the Occupational Safety and Health Review Commission has held that the using firm must keep the records for personnel supplied by the service.

20. Q. **If an employee who is working in a plant on a contract basis is injured, is the injury recorded on the plant records or on the records of the contractor?**

A. The contractor is responsible for his employee's safety, so the contractor would record this injury on his records. There is, however, an exception in certain circumstances for personnel supplied by a temporary-help supply service. See the answer to the previous question.

COVERAGE UNDER RECORDKEEPING REGULATIONS

21. Q. **Since the OSH Act governs all establishments engaged in interstate commerce, how do you identify such an establishment? For example, would a local grain elevator or farm feed and seed retail store be covered?**

A. The question contains some incorrect wording. The law says "affecting commerce," which is far broader than "engaged in interstate commerce." Because of the phrase "affecting commerce," this law covers virtually everybody.

22. Q. **Will municipal government agencies be required to participate in the recordkeeping and reporting provisions of the act? If such a requirement exists, what directive or reference source established the requirement?**

A. Local government agencies are required to participate in recordkeeping and reporting activities if the State has an approved plan for carrying out the provisions of the act. (See section 18 (c) (6) of the act.) However, non-plan States may require recordkeeping on their own.

23. Q. **Are the working family members of farmers or ranchers considered employees? Must the farmer maintain records to cover them?**

A. No. Immediate family members of farm employers are not regarded as employees.

24. Q. **Are OSHA records maintained for "exchange labor?"**

A. No. "Exchange labor" is usually just an informal arrangement among neighborhood farmers to help one another out. No formal employer-employee relationships exist.

25. Q. **When does coverage begin for an employee in travel status? When he or she leaves home? At terminal? At airport, train station, etc.?**

A. When the employee leaves home.

26. Q. **During what periods of time is the employee covered while in travel status?**

A. An employee in travel status is covered the entire period, i.e., 24 hours a day.

27. Q. **Do records have to be maintained for employees traveling overseas on business?**

A. If an employee becomes ill or injured while on a temporary assignment in a foreign country, such occurrences must be recorded at the establishment which is considered his or her home base or at the point from which the employee is paid in the United States.

If an employee is permanently assigned to an overseas position, recordkeeping requirements no longer apply.

28. Q. Does the act cover persons employed by charitable and nonprofit organizations?

A. Yes. Economic tests such as whether the organization is operated at a profit may not be used to exclude an employer.

29. Q. Are churches or religious organizations considered employers under the act if they employ persons in secular activities?

A. The act covers hospitals, schools, commercial establishments, and administrative or office personnel employed by religious organizations. Excluded from coverage are clergy and other participants in religious services.

30. Q. Do injury and illness records have to be kept for domestics?

A. No. Employers of domestics in the employer's private residence for the usual purposes of housekeeping or child care, or both, are not required to keep records.

31. Q. Are employers of employees on American flag vessels required to keep injury and illness records?

A. Yes. Employers of employees working on American flag vessels, including commercial fishing ships, are required to maintain OSHA records of occupational injuries and illnesses which occur aboard the vessel, regardless of the geographical location of their occurrence.

Hours of exposure for employees on such vessels will include all hours while aboard vessels, since employees are on call at all times, plus any time off vessel while performing duties for the employer.

DECISION AUTHORITY

32. Q. Every time a question comes up about who decides what is recordable, the answer is the employer. Why the employer? Why can't it be the company doctor? The doctor or the medical department decides whether an employee is capable of working after an injury.

A. The act says that the employer is responsible for keeping the records. The employer may delegate the responsibility to someone else, or may place great reliance on the determination of a doctor, but the decision is ultimately the employer's.

However, the decision cannot be an arbitrary one. Information from medical, hospital, or supervisor reports about the worker's medical condition and the ability of the worker to do his or her regular job cannot be ignored in the final determination. (See also answers Nos. 6 and 33.)

33. Q. Will the company doctor, the employee's doctor, or a third doctor decide if an illness is recordable?

A. A diagnosis of an occupational illness by any licensed medical doctor which becomes known to the employer, is sufficient for recording an occupational illness. Instructions for column B on the back of form OSHA No. 200 state that "For occupational illnesses, enter the date of initial diagnosis of illness or . . . which was later diagnosed or recognized."

34. Q. What authority decides if the injured is capable of working?

A. This decision must be the employer's. There will be a few cases in which the employer and the employer's physician are certain that an employee was perfectly able to work, but the employee disagrees. If the employer is absolutely certain about the case, it should not be entered in the log, OSHA No. 200. However, if the employer has any doubt about the case, it should be entered on the log; if it later turns out that the employee was able to perform his or her job, it must be lined out. (See also Nos. 32 and 33.)

DELAYED REPORTS

35. Q. If an employee does not report an injury at once, is there a time limit within which an employee may claim occupational injury?

A. There is no personal advantage to the employee in "claiming" an injury for these records, as there is in workers' compensation records. If, for any reason, the injury is not recorded when it happens, it should be recorded as soon as it comes to the employer's attention. As in any other case, the employer must determine whether there was an injury or illness, whether it resulted from a work accident or from an exposure in the work environment, and whether it was of recordable extent or outcome. If the answers are yes, the injury should be entered in the log, OSHA No. 200, with the data of occurrence in column B.

DEPARTMENT OF TRANSPORTATION

36. Q. Fatal accidents involving motor carriers must be reported to the U.S. Department of Transportation (DOT) within 24 hours. They must also be reported to BLS. Wil this duplication continue?

A. No. Immediate reports of death are never made to BLS. Usually, reports of work-related fatalities are made to OSHA. However, if the death results from a *working* condition *regulated* by the Department of Transportation, an immediate report is made to DOT as required by regulations. Nevertheless, as the fatality was work-related, it should be included in the OSHA recordkeeping system. (See also answer No. 95.)

DOMESTIC EMPLOYEES

37. Q. Do injury and illness records have to be kept for domestics?

A. No. (See answer No. 30.)

EMPLOYEES

38. Q. If an employee who is working in a plant on a contract basis is injured, is the injury recorded on the plant records or on the records of the contractor?

A. (See answers Nos. 19 and 20.)

39. Q. Are students under grants-in-aid or scholarships covered?

A. If they have an employee status, they are covered.

EMPLOYER

40. Q. Are stockholders in a corporation employers?

A. No. The corporation is the employer. On the other hand, stockholders employed in the corporation are employees; these include managers.

41. Q. Two partners operate a small electrical contracting firm. They have no employees. Are they covered by the OSH Act?

A. No. This firm has no employees, because partners are not considered employees. A firm which has no employees is not covered by the act, and does not have to maintain any OSHA records.

42. Q. Two partners operate a drycleaning business. They have nine employees. Does the small employer exemption apply to them?

A. Yes. The partners themselves are employers; therefore, this firm has only nine employees. As long as the firm has no more than 10 employees at any one time

during the previous year, and is not selected in the statistical sample of small employers, no OSHA records need be maintained. A firm selected in the statistical sample will be notified by mail in advance and provided with the necessary recordkeeping materials. Some States with approved State plans require that employers in their States keep OSHA records, regardless of the number of employees.

ESTABLISHMENT

43. Q. Can the summary at the end of a year be on a total company basis, or does it have to be broken down into the individual reporting locations involving perhaps some 80 locations?

A. One purpose of the summary is to provide the employees and management with information on the experience at the local establishment level. The answer, then, is that a summary is to be prepared and posted for each establishment.

44. Q. Even though individual establishments must maintain records at their sites, can a company file a consolidated summary, and if so, is the summary submitted to Washington or to the regional offices?

A. Neither. A consolidated summary is never prepared for different establishments. A summary is prepared only for the establishment to which it refers.

The summary is never sent to Washington or to the regional offices. The summary is used only for year-end totaling and informing employees of the injury and illness experience for that establishment during the previous calendar year. If they are selected to participate in the annual survey, employers will receive an occupational injuries and illnesses survey reporting form at the end of the recordkeeping period. The completed reporting form is then mailed to a participating State agency or to the Bureau of Labor Statistics, as indicated on the form. The form will identify which reporting unit is to be included in the report. Sometimes all establishments in a specified area, such as a county, are included.

45. Q. If a location has more than one operational facility, each having its own management but all facilities utilizing one medical department and one personnel office, are separate records required for each facility, or can one set of records be kept for all facilities at one geographic location?

A. This gets back to the definition of "establishment." BLS wants individual records maintained for each establishment, such as these facilities seem to be. (See answer No. 43.)

46. Q. Will a construction contractor have to maintain records at each individual jobsite, or can the records be maintained at the regional or central office?

A. (See answer No. 17.)

47. Q. How many sets of records must be kept in this case: At one location, Division A makes metal tools, while Division B makes wooden chairs?

A. If they are separate establishments, each division should keep its own records. Two divisions making such dissimilar products are probably separate establishments.

48. Q. Would a manufacturing operation with a warehouse attached need to keep separate records?

A. Yes, if the warehouse is a distinctly separate activity.

49. Q. Do fleet records have to be maintained separately? If several manufacturing facilities have separate trucking operations do separate records have to be maintained by each fleet?

A. If a fleet is a separate establishment, it requires separate records. There are, of course, operations having a limited number of trucks under the same supervision as other operations, in which case you cannot tell truckdrivers from other employees in the employment records. In these cases, separate records for the trucks would not be kept.

50. Q. Please define "on premises" for the trucking industry. Is the cab of a truck the premises? What about loading and unloading? Is the driver or helper on the premises?

A. For completing the supplementary record (OSHA No. 101), a truck on the road or loading and unloading away from its home base would be "off the employer's premises."

51. Q. How is "establishment" as it pertains to gas facilities defined?

A. The regulations state that in firms engaged in physically dispersed operations such as gas services, records may be maintained at the place to which employees report each day. This is the point at which the records should be kept.

FATALITIES

52. Q. An employee has an occupational illness which keeps him away from work for 6 months. At the end of that time he dies. How do you record the case?

A. Any entries in columns 9 through 12 should be lined out and the date of death entered in column 8.

53. Q. How can fatalities resulting from heart attacks or like causes be reported within 48 hours when in most cases the employer cannot determine in that period whether or not it is occupationally related?

A. When in doubt of the occupational origin of a fatality, report it. The report can be canceled or withdrawn later if it is determined that the case was not occupational in origin.

54. Q. How does an employer cancel a report of fatality to the OSHA area director if the death proves to be not work related?

A. This question should be referred to the Occupational Safety and Health Administration Area Office. (See appendix A.)

FIRST AID

55. Q. If there is more than one followup visit to the registered nurse for cuts or burns, is such an injury to be recorded under the new system?

A. If the second visit is simply for observation, or to change an adhesive or small bandage, the injury would not be recorded.

56. Q. By themselves are the following considered "medical treatment" or "first aid?"

1. Microthermy treatments if offered only minimum times.

2. Two heat treatments or more.

3. Prescriptions, when no other form of treatment is offered.

4. Whirlpool treatments.

5. Second visit for observation of small puncture.

6. Nonprescription medication for pain.

7. Simple removal of foreign body from eye with no complications.

A. Because BLS is committed to simple definitions interpreted by the employer, generalizations cannot be made which could be used in a variety of circumstances. As with tetanus shots and diagnostic X-rays, these procedures may not be the only criteria for recordability and are covered under Guidelines for Determining Recordability earlier in this report.

Medical treatment is only one criterion for determining recordability. An injury which required only first-aid treatment but involved loss of consciousness, restriction of work or motion, or transfer to another job is recordable.

57. Q. Our plant does not have a nurse available on the second and third shifts. Injuries on these shifts are sent to the hospital. If this is the only time the injury is treated, does it have to be recorded?

A. If medical treatment is administered, the case is recordable. If only first-aid treatment is administered, then the case is not recordable. See the definition on the back of the OSHA No. 200. The kind of treatment is the determining factor, not the place.

58. Q. If an employee is treated in the medical department but does not need a doctor's care, such as for cuts, burns, etc., does a report need to be made of the injury?

A. If the case comes under the definition of "medical care" rather than "first aid," a record would have to be maintained. On the other hand, even first-aid treatment given by a doctor would not be recorded. (See also answer No. 57.)

FLAG VESSELS AND OTHER TRANSPORT

59. Q. Are employers of employees on American flag vessels required to keep injury and illness records?

A. (See answer No. 31. For questions and answers to other transport areas, see Nos. 36, 95, and 110.)

FORMS

60. Q. What forms do I need to keep injury and illness records?

A. The OSHA recordkeeping forms consist of the Log and Summary (OSHA No. 200) and the Supplementary Record (OSHA No. 101).

Employers can use an equivalent of the OSHA No. 200 if it is completed according to the instructions contained in the form and if the information is as readable and comprehensible as the OSHA form. A substitute supplementary record form must include or be supplemented to include all items covered on OSHA No. 101. (See Introduction, Recordkeeping Forms.)

HEARING LOSS

61. Q. How should long-term hearing loss be reported? Does the employer, under the law, have any responsibility for testing employees' hearing and for dispensing hearing aids? What compliance recommendations do you have?

A. BLS cannot comment on the standards and compliance aspects of this question. To distinguish between injuries and illnesses, it is necessary to determine the extent of exposure to the hazardous environment. For recordkeeping purposes, hearing loss from prolonged exposure to noise is classified as an occupational illness, whereas hearing loss from a single incident is classified as an occupational injury.

HEART ATTACK

62. Q. Under OSHA regulations, do we record and report an employee's dying of a heart attack while phoning the office from a phone booth while having his car washed? The workers' compensation carrier set up a reserve for this case.

A. Although it is prudent for the insurance carrier to set up a reserve for any possibility of a work connection, additional information is needed to make a decision in this particular case. If the heart attack had nothing to do with the employee's work, it would not be recorded.

HERNIA

63. Q. Are there any specific requirements for hernia or back cases?

A. No.

HOSPITAL EMPLOYEES

64. Q. If an employee in a hospital contracts an illness from a patient and all employees in the unit are inoculated to prevent spread of the illness, is each person so treated considered a recordable case?

A. No. Such cases would not be recordable because the employees are not injured or ill. Of course, the case of the person who contracted the disease should be recorded.

HOSPITAL TREATMENT

65. Q. Our plant does not have a nurse available on the second and third shifts. Injuries on these shifts are sent to the hospital. If this is the only time this injury is treated, does it have to be recorded?

A. (See answer No. 57.)

HOURS WORKED

66. Q. How and on what form would hours worked, be reported?

A. Hours worked are compiled only for the survey report forms which are mailed to a sample of employers.

The employer is asked to enter the total number of hours worked by all employees during the reporting period, but to exclude all nonwork time even though paid (vacation, sick leave, holiday, etc.). For those employees for whom actual hours worked are not available, the report form contains instructions for estimating hours worked.

INFORMATION SERVICES

67. Q. Where can I get answers to additional questions on reporting?

A. Call or write the State agency which is cooperating in the program with the Bureau of Labor Statistics or the Bureau's regional office. (See appendixes B and C for telephone numbers and addresses.)

INJURIES vs ILLNESSES

68. Q. How do you distinguish an injury from an illness? For example, it appears that a burn can be one or the other.

A. The basic definition of an occupational injury is any injury which results from a work accident or from an exposure involving a single incident in the work environment. Contact with a hot surface or a caustic chemical, which produces a burn in that single moment of contact, is an injury. Sunburn, or welding flash burns which result from prolonged exposure to sunrays or welding flashes are considered illnesses. Similarly, a one time blow which damages the tendons of the hand is considered an injury, while repeated trauma (or repetitious movement) over a period of time which produces tenosynovitis is considered an illness.

The basic determinant is the single-incident concept. If the incident resulted from something that happened in one instant, it is an injury. If the case resulted from prolonged exposure to a hazardous substance or environmental factor, it is an illness.

INOCULATION

69. Q. If an employee in a hospital contracts an illness from a patient, and all employees in the unit are inoculated to prevent spread of the illness, is each person so treated considered a recordable case?

A. (See answer No. 64.)

70. Q. If an employee has a minor scratch but the doctor gives him a tetanus shot anyway, is that a recordable case?

A. Such tetanus shots should not be regarded as medical treatment.

Frequently, however, a wound severe enough to warrant a tetanus shot requires medical treatment, such as suturing, which would make the case recordable. If no medical treatment was given, a tetanus shot for a minor wound would not be a recordable case.

INSURANCE CARRIER AND WORKERS' COMPENSATION

71. Q. Does a workers' compensation carrier have any responsibility or liability under OSHA?

A. Section 4(b) (4) of the act says that "nothing in this Act shall be construed to supersede or in any manner affect any workmen's compensation law or to enlarge or diminish or affect in any other manner the common law or statutory rights, duties, or liabilities of employers and employees under any law with respect to injuries, diseases, or death of employees arising out of, or in the course of, employment."

LIABILITY

72. Q. If the employer makes the determination on recording on other than a physician's evaluation, what is the employer's legal liability regarding possible unintentional reporting errors? Who has the legal liability—person who signs forms, local manager, or a company executive officer?

A. An honest error in evaluating the injury will not constitute a violation. However, if the employer is in doubt he or she should record the case. The liability applies to the person responsible for reporting—if the employer is a corporation, this person would have to be identified. (See answer No. 34.)

73. Q. The act states that whoever supplies false information is subject to penalty. Does this cover the employee and the employer, if either knowingly supplies false information?

A. Most of the penalty provisions in section 17 of the act apply to "any employer," but the penalty for false statements applies to "whoever knowingly makes any false statement. . ." BLS believes this would apply to employers and employees alike.

LOG AND SUMMARY

74. Q. Can we use our own version of the log and summary (OSHA No. 200) with modifications to include information we would like to gather?

A. Yes. An equivalent to the log and summary may be used if it is completed according to the instructions in the OSHA No. 200. However, such information must be as readable and comprehensible to a person not familiar with the substitute as information in the log and summary. (See Recordkeeping Forms.)

75. Q. Why can't we keep the OSHA No. 200 in our central office rather than in each individual establishment?

A. For centralized recordkeeping, the OSHA No. 200 may be kept in some place other than the establishment, such as a central office. If that is done, a copy of the OSHA No. 200 which is current to within 45 calendar days must be available in the establishment.

76. Q. If an establishment has more than one operational facility, each having its own management, but all facilities utilize one medical department and one personnel office, are separate records required for each facility; or, can one set of records be kept for all facilities at one geographic location?

A. (See answers Nos. 43 and 45.)

77. Q. We understand that the OSHA No. 200 must be maintained for 5 years. Does this mean that entries on past years' logs would have to be changed if there were changes in the outcome of a recorded case?

A. Yes, logs must be kept current and retained for 5 years following the end of the calendar year to which they relate. Directions on the reverse of the OSHA No. 200 form describe how to record changes in extent of or outcome of the injury or illness.

78. Q. Can I keep OSHA records on microfiche or magnetic tape?

A. As a practical matter, it would be almost impossible to keep current OSHA records on microfiche or magnetic tape because of the requirements for updating the log for providing ready accessibility to compliance officers and other authorized persons at each establishment. Although it is conceivable that past years' records might be retained on microfiche or tape, the requirements to update and provide accessibility would deter using such methods. If an employer can overcome these difficulties, however, each establishment should have the necessary equipment, such as a microfiche reader, for ready access to the records.

LOST WORKDAY CASES

79. Q. In a three-person combined operation each employee is expected to perform each of the three tasks, but at any particular time each employee works on only one of the tasks. The three employees have identical job titles and pay scales and the three tasks require the same level of skill. For a period of 1 week after an employee was injured she was unable to perform one of the three tasks, but could perform the other two. She switched tasks with another employee in the combined operation and worked at that task throughout the week. Should this be regarded as a lost workday case?

A. Yes. This should be recorded as a lost workday case involving days of restricted activity. (Check in column 2 and the number of days entered in column 5 of the OSHA No. 200.)

If we regard these jobs as three identical jobs each of which involves three tasks, lost workdays (of restricted activity) should be counted for any day following the day of injury on which the injured employee could not perform all three tasks.

If we regard these jobs as three different jobs, each of which involves only one task, the switch of tasks is a temporary assignment to another job and lost workdays (of restricted activity) should be counted for any day following the day of injury on which this temporary assignment was in effect.

80. Q. An employee is injured on a Wednesday and has lost time due to the injury Thursday and Friday of that week. The next 2 weeks the plant closes and all employees are on vacation. The employee is still injured and would not have been able to work if the plant had been in operation. Should the paid vacation time be counted as lost workdays for this employee?

A. Lost workdays include days during which the employee would have worked but could not do so. In this case the employee was not scheduled to work during the period of plant close down for vacation. The employee lost 2 workdays before the plant closed plus any workdays lost due to the injury after the 2 weeks ended.

81. Q. If an employee receives a minor injury—a fall, burn, or cut, requiring first aid only—but the injury is such that the person cannot perform normal duties for 1 to 2 days, is the case recordable?

A. Yes, and the case should be classified as a lost workday case with days of restricted activity.

82. Q. A regular employee experiences a bona fide lost-time injury on a construction job. Before the employee is able to return to work, the project is completed and the employer leaves the area. How is this recorded on the OSHA No. 200?

A. If we assume that this job was in an establishment which maintained separate records, the establishment ceased to exist at the time the job was closed. The case is recorded but the count of lost workdays stops when the project is completed.

However, if the job was not a separate establishment and the employee was neither transferred nor terminated, the actual number of days the employee would have worked but could not because of injury or illness should be entered in the OSHA No. 200.

83. Q. If an ill employee is terminated or transferred for a reason not related to the illness, how is the illness recorded? Lost workdays case or nonfatal without lost workdays?

A. Two situations are involved here. First, if the ill employee lost workdays before a permanent transfer or termination, the lost workday count would cease on the day the employee was permanently transferred or terminated. If no lost workdays occurred before the permanent transfer or termination, the case would be recorded as a "nonfatal case without lost workdays." In either case, an asterisk should be placed to the right of the entry in the illness column. Second, if the question refers to a temporary transfer, the lost workday count continues until the ill employee can perform all duties of his regular job.

84. Q. When do lost workdays cease to accumulate for injured employees who have long-term (1 year) medical restrictions (no lifting over 30 pounds) and who have returned to work?

A. If such restrictions prevent them from performing any duties normally assigned to their jobs, then count each day that they cannot perform all their regular duties. Some long-term restrictions may be regarded as assignments to modified jobs.

85. Q. If an employee is permanently transferred from his or her regular job because of a systemic effect of toxic material (i.e., elevated blood-lead) is this recorded as permanent time loss?

A. There is no such category as permanent time loss. If workdays were lost the case would be recorded as a lost workday case and identified as a permanent transfer case, and the number of workdays lost before the transfer would be recorded. If no workdays were lost, it would be recorded as a nonfatal case without lost workdays and identified as a permanent transfer case. (See answer No. 83.)

86. Q. If total disability would end the count of lost workdays for a case, would retirement likewise end the count?

A. Yes, separation because of total disability and separation by retirement would be treated in the same manner.

87. Q. In December of last year one of my employees injured his back and the injury was recorded on the log. In February of this year the employee has again lost time because of his back. Should I record the case on this year's log?

A. If the latest period of disability resulted from an incident such as a slip, trip, fall, or blow to the back, the injury should be recorded on this year's log. If there was no such incident, no new entry should be made and the number of lost workdays should be added to last year's log.

88. Q. Why aren't lost workdays listed as criteria for recording injuries?

A. It is not necessary because any work-related injury that involves lost workdays falls under the criterion of restriction of work or motion.

89. Q. If normal work schedules encompass overtime (6 days), are the overtime days counted as lost workdays?

A. Yes. If the employee would have worked the overtime days had he or she not been injured, then the days should be counted.

90. Q. How does the employer count lost workdays for employees who are off the job due to "work stoppage" or strikes?

A. Lost workdays are only those days the injured or ill employee would have worked but could not. Thus, no lost workdays are counted if he or she would not normally have worked because of a work stoppage.

91. Q. How do I handle a lost workday case that carries over into the next year? For example, an employee is injured in December 1978 and is still out on January 31, 1979.

A. Two important points are involved. First, the same case should not appear in the records for 2 years;

second, it is important not to lose the count of the number of lost workdays, which is a measure of the severity of the case.

On the 1978 log, estimate the number of workdays the employee is expected to lose in 1979 and add that to the count of workdays lost up to the time of making that estimate. Enter that number in column 4 or column 11, as appropriate for this case. When the employee returns to work and is able to perform all the duties of his or her regular job or the count of lost workdays is otherwise ended, verify the actual count of lost workdays (days away and any days of restricted activity) and correct the entry on the 1978 log as necessary.

MEDICAL TREATMENT

92. Q. Is this a recordable injury? An employee receives a small laceration which the doctor or nurse dresses. A day or two later, the nurse sees the cut is healing satisfactorily, applies antiseptic, and dismisses patient, who is told to report back if there is any trouble. Nothing develops. What if the nurse examines and replaces a small bandage two or more times?

A. If the laceration would not ordinarily require medical care, this would be a first-aid case and not recordable.

See Guidelines for Determining Recordability and also see questions and answers in the section under "First Aid."

MIGRANT LABOR

93. Q. How does the recordkeeping requirement apply to migrant labor camps? Is it the same as for other areas?

A. Yes. Migrant labor camps are covered the same as any other segment of the economy.

MINING

94. Q. Does the mining industry which comes under the inspection jurisdiction of another Federal agency, participate in the OSHA recordkeeping program?

A. Mining employers are not required to keep records or report under OSHA, since they must maintain a program of recordkeeping and reporting, developed in cooperation with the Bureau of Labor Statistics, which produces similar information.

In March 1978, jurisdiction over mine safety and health was transferred by Congress from the Interior Department to the Labor Department under the new Mine Safety and Health Administration. At the time of writing this booklet, recordkeeping for mines remained as before, under the direction of the new agency.

This does not mean that all mining company employees are excluded from coverage under OSHA. If a mining company has a company store, and the Mine Safety and Health Administration does not require a record for the company store, then the company store would fall under OSHA.

MOTOR VEHICLE FLEETS

95. Q. To what extent are motor carriers covered under OSHA recordkeeping regulations since they are under Department of Transportation regulations?

A. They are under U.S. Department of Transportation regulations for certain kinds of accidents, but they are covered by the Occupational Safety and Health Act for injuries and illnesses that are required to be recorded under the OSHA system. (See also answer No. 36.)

96. Q. Do fleet records have to be maintained separately? If several manufacturing facilities each have separate trucking operations, do separate records have to be maintained by each fleet?

A. (See answer No. 49.)

NONOCCUPATIONAL CASES

97. Q. An employee is sent to the doctor for a definite diagnosis. The doctor decides the employee's condition is not related to his work. Where do you put this one in the OSHA No. 200?

A. If the employer is in agreement with the doctor, the case is not recorded in the log since it is not connected with the employee's work.

OCCUPATIONAL ILLNESS

98. Q. Are occupational illnesses recorded only if they require treatment beyond the initial day reported?

A. Any diagnosed occupational illness reported to the employer is recordable, whether or not medical treatment is given or lost workdays are involved. The instructions to the OSHA No. 200 say that an illness shall be recorded as of the date of diagnosis; or, if the diagnosis follows a period during which a person has been unable to perform for unknown reasons, the date entered should be the first day of absence under that spell of illness.

Also, see questions and answers given under "Alleged Injury or Illness," "Fatalities," "Hearing Loss," and No. 118.

99. Q. How do you distinguish an injury from an illness? For example, it appears that a burn can be one or the other.

A. (See answer No. 68.)

ORDERING ADDITIONAL FORMS AND MATERIALS

100. Q. Where can forms OSHA No. 200, and No. 101 be obtained?

A. These forms and other recordkeeping materials can be obtained through the State agency which is cooperating in the program with the Bureau of Labor Statistics or the Bureau's regional offices. (See appendixes B and C for telephone numbers and addresses.)

PHYSICIAN

101. Q. Is it mandatory for an injured party to go to the company doctor, or can she go to her own family doctor?

A. The recordkeeping regulations do not speak to this question at all.

102. Q. Every time a question comes up about who decides what is reportable, the answer is the employer. Why the employer? Why can't it be the company doctor? The doctor or the medical department decides whether an employee is capable of working after an injury.

A. (See answer No. 32.)

POSTING AN ANNUAL SUMMARY

103. Q. What is supposed to be accomplished by posting an annual summary in the workplace?

A. Posting the annual summary (1) provides employees with their establishment's record of injuries and illnesses, (2) makes employers and employees more safety conscious, and (3) promotes joint labor-management safety and health efforts.

104. Q. Must the employer post the annual summary at the jobsite of a seasonal operation if the site is shut down throughout the posting period?

A. Posting informs the employees of the past year's injury and illness experience for that establishment. Since posting in a deserted establishment would not do that, posting will not be required.

105. Q. How do traveling sales representatives or other workers with no permanent worksite get informed about the annual summary?

A. Employers must mail a copy of the annual summary during the posting period to employees with no permanent worksite.

106. Q. How long must the summary be posted at each establishment?

A. The annual summary portion of the OSHA No. 200 is to be posted by February 1 of each year and is to remain in place until March 1.

107. Q. Must you post a copy of the annual summary on every bulletin board, or will the posting of only one copy comply with the law?

A. The regulations say that the annual summary is to be posted "at each establishment in a conspicuous place where notices to its employees are posted customarily."

PREMISES

108. Q. An injury occurred on property where an employer conducts business operations. He neither owns nor leases the property. Under OSHA would the property be considered the employer's premises?

A. The reference is to items 10 and 11 of OSHA No. 101. The key to the question is the degree to which the employer controls the accident site, not whether he owns or leases it. As a general rule, if the site is in an establishment of the employer, it is on his premises. Highway injuries and those to employees engaged in, for instance, installation or repair functions in a customer's home or establishment are off the premises. In intermediate situations, such as a contractor's activities on a construction site, the answer should be "yes" if the employer had any substantial control over working conditions and hazards on the site. (See also No. 115.)

109. Q. Are the rights-of-way used by public utility companies considered to be the "employer's premises?"

A. Yes. The utilities have sufficient control over the rights-of-way to be considered the "Employer's premises."

RAILROADS

110. Q. Are railroad employers required to keep records of injuries and illnesses of their employees?

A. Yes. In recent years the Federal Railroad Administration has adopted the definitions of the OSHA recordkeeping system. Railroad employers report occupational injury and illness data annually to the Federal Railroad Administration, which in turn provides the data to BLS for statistical purposes.

RATES

111.   Q.   **What is the basis of the injury and illness rates?**

A.   We calculate an incidence rate based on the number of recordable injuries and illnesses per 200,000 employee hours.   This is 100 full-time employees working 50 weeks, 40 hours per week.   Although hours and weeks may vary somewhat from industry to industry, use of rates based on the standard formula will permit cross-industry comparisons.

112.   Q.   **Do we include nonfatal cases without lost workdays in determining the rate of an establishment?**

A.   Yes, The total incidence rate will include fatalities, lost workday cases, and nonfatal cases without lost workdays.

113.   Q.   **Is there just one injury rate?**

A.   No. Incidence rates may be computed for each of the following categories:

(a.)   Total injuries (or illnesses).

(b.)   Injuries (or illnesses) involving lost workdays.

(c.)   Injuries (or illnesses) without lost workdays.

In addition, rates may be computed for the number of lost workdays.   These rates may be computed on the same basis as described in No. 111.

RECORDABILITY

114.   Q.   **Is the case recordable if an injury to an employee occurs while the employee is walking to work on a public sidewalk from a company-owned or -leased parking lot?**

Could an injury be recordable which takes place after a person checks into work but while he or she is off the company premises on a public sidewalk enroute to a restaurant for a cup of coffee?

A.   The first case does not appear to be recordable. An occupational injury is an injury to an employee which either results from an accident while at work or from exposure in the work environment.   In the first case, the employee is "walking to work" and, therefore, is not yet at work.   Furthermore, public places are not a part of the employee's work environment unless he or she is engaged in performing some of the duties of the job in those places.

For example, the work environment for a route salesman may include public sidewalks, streets, and highways.

The second case might be recordable if the employee was performing duties (such as going at the direction of the foreman to get coffee for the crew) or if the work environment includes public places (example, a route sales representative).   More information is needed to make a determination of this case.

115.   Q.   **If an employee is hurt during lunch break on the employer's premises, is the injury recordable?**

A.   Yes. The broad concept is that any injury or illness occurring in the work environment is recordable. The work environment is construed to include the total establishment. (See also Nos. 116 and 117.)

116.   Q.   **An employee is injured in an accident on the company parking lot.   The accident occurs before the employee's scheduled reporting time.   Is it a recordable case?**

A.   Yes. (See No. 115.)

117.   Q.   **Do I have to record an injury that occurs to an employee as the result of horseplay?   Would I have to record the case if it occurred as the result of a robbery?**

A.   Yes.   Many events such as the results of a robbery, horseplay, or fight among the employees are considered to be work related.   The basis for determining work relationship for OSHA recordkeeping purposes at least, is that the event occurred on the employer's premises or in the work environment which surrounds workers with no fixed place of employment.

118.   Q.   **What are the reporting requirements for test results which indicate elevated blood lead level?**

A.   The reference is to the growing practice by employers to conduct surveillance and monitoring tests for employees working with hazardous substances, such as lead.   Records and statistics of test results could increase understanding and avoid hazards.   However, such tests do not now cover all exposed workers, so including their results would give a partial and confusing addition to present records.   Therefore, cases identified only by test results should not now be included in the records. If testing becomes universal, possibly because of new regulations, it may be necessary to modify recordkeeping rules to include specified test results.

On the other hand, other recordkeeping criteria are still applicable.   Employers are still required to record cases where the worker (1) has symptoms, such as colic, nerve or renal damage, anemia, and gum problems, which have been diagnosed as resulting from poisoning; (2) receives medical treatment for lead poisoning or to lower blood lead levels.

119. Q. If a driver involved in an auto accident is sent for a physical examination without lost time and without any specific injury, should this case be recorded?

A. This would be in the nature of preventive medicine and would not be recordable under the regulations, unless the examination reveals a recordable injury from the accident.

REPORTING

120. Q. Will we have to submit our occupational injury and illness records to the Occupational Safety and Health Administration?

A. No. The records at the individual establishment level must be available for inspection by Federal or State compliance officers and Federal or State representatives involved with statistical acitivities.

The employers who fall into the statistical sample, however, will be required to report to the Bureau of Labor Statistics, or to the State agency which is cooperating in the program with BLS. (See Nos. 121 and 122.)

121. Q. Are forms OSHA Nos. 200 or 101 mailed to any agency representative? Are these forms considered as survey collection documents?

A. No. Each establishment must retain these forms for 5 years after the end of the year to which they relate. Only employers selected for the annual survey will receive a survey form, which they will be required to complete and return.

122. Q. What is form OSHA No. 200S? Is completion of this form mandatory?

A. OSHA No. 200S is the report form. Completion of the form is mandatory for those employers who have been selected to be in the survey.

123. Q. Even though individual establishments must maintain records at their sites, can a company file a consolidated summary, and if so, is the summary submitted to Washington or to the regional offices?

A. (See answer No. 44.)

124. Q. I recently read about an employer being cited and fined for failing to report an employee who had been hospitalized due to an injury. Where is the requirement stated in the regulations?

A. The regulations do not require a report of a single hospitalization. Section 1904.8 of the Code of Federal Regulations, requires that every accident which results in one death or more or in hospitalization of five employees or more must be reported to the Occupational Safety and Health Administration area director within 48 hours. The report may be made orally or in writing. (See appendix A for addresses of area offices.) Some States have approved plans and reports are made to them. (See appendix B for addresses of State agencies.)

RESPONSIBILITY FOR ACCIDENT

125. Q. If an employee, e.g., a subcontractor's employee, is injured on the job as the result of an outside agency, is the injury recordable?

A. Yes, responsibility or fault for an accident does not affect recordability.

RESTRICTION OF MOTION

126. Q. What constitutes restriction of motion? A bandage, sling, sore muscle, anatomical percentage loss, bruise?

A. All of these may or may not involve restriction of motion. Each case must be evaluated separately.

127. Q. Is a small bandage for a cut on the finger joint a restriction of motion and recordable under the regulations?

A. It would be considered a restriction and the case recordable if it restricts the employee's ability to perform his or her work. (See No. 81.)

RETENTION OF RECORDS

128. Q. Can I keep OSHA records on microfiche or magnetic tape?

A. (See answer No. 78.)

SCHOOLS

129. Q. Does the act require universities and colleges to keep records?

A. Private universities and colleges must keep records of injuries and illnesses for their employees, but students are not included unless they are employed on a full- or part-time basis. Graduate students with paid teaching assignments are covered.

State and local government colleges and universities keep such records only if their State has a plan approved for implementing the provisions of the act.

130. Q. Are employees of local school districts covered in the act?

A A. No, but those employed in States which have an approved plan for implementing the provisions of the act are covered by State laws and regulations.

131. Q. Are students under grants-in-aid or scholarships covered?

A. If they have an employee status, they are covered.

SMALL EMPLOYERS

132. Q. Must small businesses keep records?

A. We define small employers as those who never at any time during a calendar year had more than ten (10) employees. They will not have to keep injury and illness records during the following calendar year. However, some small employers will be notified in writing that they have been selected for a statistical survey of occupational injuries and illnesses. They will be supplied with record-keeping instructions and materials. Even though an employer is exempted from the recordkeeping requirements, he must report to the Occupational Safety and Health Administration area director within 48 hours each accident that results in one death or more or in hopitalization of five employees or more. Some States require all employers, regardless of size, to keep injury and illness records.

133. Q. Two partners operate a small electrical contracting firm. They have no employees. Are they covered by the act?

A. No. (See answer No. 41.)

134. Q. Two partners operate a drycleaning business. They have nine employees. Does the small-employer exemption apply to them?

A. Yes. (See answer No. 42.)

STATE PLAN

135. Q. When State plans are approved, will such States be required to adopt the same reporting forms as now are required by BLS?

A. Yes. Basic reporting would be identical, but States could add additional items to the BLS requirements.

136. Q. Assuming approval of a State plan, will reporting be to State agencies instead of to BLS, and if so, when?

A. Yes, in States with approved plans completed annual survey forms will be mailed to their State agencies.

SUMMARY, ANNUAL

137. Q. When will an establishment have to send its annual summary to the Bureau of Labor Statistics?

A. Never. The establishment must retain recordkeeping forms, OSHA No. 200 and No. 101, for 5 years after the year of reference. Only establishments selected to participate in the statistical survey will receive a reporting form in the mail. If your establishment does not receive a form, you need only maintain and retain your records according to the regulations.

138. Q. Can the summary at the end of the year be on a total company basis, or does it have to be broken down into the individual reporting locations involving perhaps some 80 locations?

A. (See answer No. 43.)

139. Q. If no recordable cases occurred during a report period, must a summary be prepared?

A. Yes. Even though there were no recordable cases during the previous year, the summary portion of the form OSHA No. 200 must be completed and posted in each establishment no later than February 1, and remain in place until March 1. Zeros must be entered in all cells of the "totals" line.

140. Q. Who is responsible for the preparation of the annual summary?

A. The employer, who may direct an employee to prepare and certify the annual summary. The form must be signed by the person responsible for its preparation as certification that the information contained on the form is correct.

141. Q. How do I handle a lost workday case that carries over into the next year? For example, an employee is injured in December 1978 and is still out on January 31, 1979.

A. Two important points are involved. First, the same case should not appear in the records for 2 years; second, it is important not to lose the count of the number of lost workdays which is a measure of the severity of the case.

On the 1978 log, estimate the number of work-days the employee is expected to lose in 1979 and add that to the count of workdays lost up to the time of making that estimate. Enter that number in column 4 or column 11, as appropriate for this case. When the employee returns to work and is able to perform all the duties of his or her regular job or the count of lost workdays is otherwise ended, verify the actual count of lost workdays (days away and any days of restricted activity) and correct the entry on the 1978 log as necessary.

SUPPLEMENTARY RECORD

142. Q. If our company injury form, which is generally similar to OSHA No. 101, does not include information such as social security number, sex, etc., is it mandatory that we apply for a variance?

A. No. There is nothing mandatory about the form used as the supplementary record and any other form may be used if it contains all of the OSHA No. 101 items or is supplemented to do so. In this case a longhand entry of the sex of the individual and the social security number would satisfy the need.

143. Q. Do we need to complete OSHA No. 101 if we presently use the State workers' compensation form?

A. Workers' compensation first report of injury forms are acceptable if the information which must be entered includes all the items on the OSHA No. 101 or is supplemented to do so. Employers should be sure that all OSHA No. 101 items are on the first report forms. Employers may enter missing items somewhere on the State form or provide the missing items on a separate attachment. They may consult the State agency which is cooperating in the program with the Bureau of Labor Statistics or the Bureau's regional office for information about which items are missing from any State form. (See appendixes B and C for telephone numbers and addresses.)

144. Q. Our State workers' compensation forms list only disabling injuries. How can we use this in place of OSHA No. 101?

A. Some States require all injuries to be reported on their forms; others require only disabling injuries. If a State requires reports of disabling injuries only, the employer will have to complete some forms just for OSHA requirements, and use OSHA No. 101 or some acceptable substitute such as an insurance form or internal accident report from for the nondisabling injuries.

145. Q. Is there activity under way, or contemplated, to have various State workers' compensation forms conform to OSHA No. 101 to avoid duplication of reporting?

A. Yes. Many States have revised their forms to include all of the items on OSHA No. 101. The State agency which is cooperating in the program with the Bureau of Labor Statistics or the Bureau's regional office will be able to tell which items are missing from any State form. (See appendixes B and C for telephone numbers and addresses.)

146. Q. Does information on the supplementary record (OSHA No. 101) need to be in one file? Our information is split up between our mailing department, safety department, and workers' compensation department.

A. Yes, it must be in one file, on either form OSHA No. 101 or a satisfactory substitute.

TEMPORARY JOB

147. Q. Please define "temporary job."

A. A temporary job is one to which an injured or ill employee is assigned temporarily, eventually returning to his or her regular job.

TERMINATION OF EMPLOYMENT

148. Q. In casual day-to-day employment a worker is injured and does not return. How is the lost time determined?

A. First, the employer may not always be as uninformed as that question suggests. If this injury is going to be compensable for medical costs, the employer does know something about it. Sometimes the employer never hears from the person again. You cannot continue to count lost workdays in these cases, so these should be considered as termination of employment.

If the employer wants to keep a record of terminations because of injuries he or she may do so. This requirement is optional for occupational injuries but is required for occupational illnesses. See the back of form OSHA No. 200, under instructions for recording terminations and permanent transfers.

TRANSFER

149. Q. Why must lost workdays be recorded for an injured person transferred to another job due to injury, when the employer still gets a day's work out of the employee?

A. The workdays that are counted are those on which the employee cannot contribute a full day's work on all parts of his or her permanent job. The definition was chosen to be simple and uniform, and to preclude concealment of significant injuries or illnesses by temporary assignment to nonproductive jobs. To evaluate the seriousness of lost workdays, they are separated into two classes: Days away from work and days of restricted activity.

150. Q. Many of our employees shift from job to job within their occupational job classification. If a person moves to another job within his or her occupation due to an accident, may we consider this not recordable?

A. If the switch or transfer is caused by an injury or illness, it is recordable.

151. Q. What about an employee who is not working at his or her regular job when injured, and after receiving treatment from a doctor returns to the regular job, without limitations; should this case be counted?

A. Regardless of what the worker was doing at the time of injury, if the injury required medical treatment (other than first aid) and was work connected, it would be counted.

The capability of doing his or her regular job determines whether or not the case will be counted as a lost workday case.

152. Q. If a person is injured to the degree that he or she transferred to light duty, is the time spent on such duty recordable as lost workdays?

A. Yes, a check would be made in column 2 of OSHA No. 200 and the number of lost workdays would be entered in column 5 (days of restricted activity.)

153. Q. If an employee is permanently transferred from his or her regular job because of a systemic effect of toxic material (elevated blood lead), is this recorded as permanent time loss?

A. (See answer No. 85.)

154. Q. In casual day-to-day employment, a worker is injured and does not return. How is the lost determined?

A. (See answer No. 148.)

WORK RESTRICTIONS

155. Q. When do lost workdays cease to accumulate for injured employees who have long-term (1 year) medical restriction (no lifting over 30 pounds) and who have returned to work?

A. (See answer No. 84.)

WORKERS' COMPENSATION

156. Q. Why can't the Department of Labor gather the information it needs from existing workers' compensation records?

A. In cooperation with many States, BLS is utilizing information from workers' compensation records. These State data provide detailed information about individual cases. However, statistics on National incidence rates cannot be produced from these State data, because workers' compensation records are not uniform, and do not cover some OSHA recordable cases.

157. Q. What is the connection between OSHA records and reports and the reporting requirements of State workers' compensation acts?

A. There is no direct connection between workers' compensation laws and recordkeeping requirements under the Occupational Safety and Health Act. Nevertheless, it would be advantageous to employers, State workers' compensation agencies, and the Federal agencies to have greater uniformity in recordkeeping and reporting. A number of State workers' compensation agencies have revised their first report forms to make them fully acceptable in place of OSHA No. 101. This is a start; BLS hopes that more can be done in the future.

158. Q. Do we need to complete OSHA No. 101 if we presently use the State workers' compensation form?

A. (See answer No. 143.)

159. Q. Our State workers' compensation forms list only disabling injuries. How can we use this place of OSHA NO. 101?

A. (See answer No. 144.)

160. Q. Is there activity under way, or contemplated, to have various State workers' compensation forms conform to OSHA No. 101 to avoid duplication of reporting?

A. (See answer No. 145.)

161. Q. Does a workers' compensation carrier have any responsibility or liability under OSHA?

A. (See answer No. 71.)

162. Q. What entries, if any, need to be made in those instances of employer-employee disputes involving State workers' compensation measures to determine the facts related to alleged injuries or deaths?

A. (See answer No. 9.)

X-RAY

163.   Q.   During the course of employment, an employee is involved in an accident while driving on the highway and is taken to a hospital for X-rays. The X-rays indicate no fracture. Is this a recordable case?

A.   Diagnostic X-rays are not considered medical treatment. In fact, such an X-ray may indicate that no treatment is needed. If this employee received no medical treatment and was able to continue working at his or her permanent job, this case is not recordable under the regulations.

Appendix A. OSHA Field Locations

The list below gives addresses and telephone numbers for OSHA Regional Offices and cities in which other offices are located. Complete information on field locations may be obtained from any OSHA Regional Office.

Region I: Connecticut, Maine, Massachusetts, New Hampshire, Rhode Island, Vermont
JFK Federal Building
Room 1804–Government Center
Boston, Massachusetts 02203
Phone: 617-223-6712

Area Offices:

Hartford, Connecticut
Springfield, Massachusetts
Waltham, Massachusetts
Concord, New Hampshire

District Offices:

Providence, Rhode Island

Region II: New York, New Jersey, Puerto Rico, Virgin Islands, Canal Zone
1515 Broadway–Room 3445
New York, New York 10036
Phone: 212-399-5754

Area Offices:

Belle Mead, New Jersey
Camden, New Jersey
Dover, New Jersey
Hasbrouck Heights, New Jersey
Newark, New Jersey
Albany, New York
Brooklyn, New York
Buffalo, New York
Flushing, New York
New York, New York
Rochester, New York
Syracuse, New York
Westbury, New York
White Plains, New York
Hato Rey, Puerto Rico

Region III: Delaware, District of Columbia, Maryland, Pennsylvania, Virginia, West Virginia
Gateway Building–Suite 2100
3535 Market Street
Philadelphia, Pennsylvania 19104
Phone: 215-596-1201

Area Offices:

Washington, D.C.
Baltimore, Maryland
Harrisburg, Pennsylvania
Philadelphia, Pennsylvania
Pittsburgh, Pennsylvania
Wilkes Barre, Pennsylvania
Richmond, Virginia
Charleston, West Virginia

District Offices:

Wilmington, Delaware
Norfolk, Virginia

Field Stations:

Allentown, Pennsylvania
Johnstown, Pennsylvania
Lancaster, Pennsylvania
Meadville, Pennsylvania
State College, Pennsylvania
Falls Church, Virginia
Roanoke, Virginia
Elkins, West Virginia
Wheeling, West Virginia

Region IV: Alabama, Florida, Georgia, Kentucky, Mississippi, North Carolina, South Carolina, Tennessee
1375 Peachtree Street, NE.–Suite 587
Atlanta, Georgia 30309
Phone: 404-881-3573

Area Offices:

Birmingham, Alabama
Mobile, Alabama
Fort Lauderdale, Florida
Jacksonville, Florida
Tampa, Florida
Macon, Georgia
Savannah, Georgia
Tucker, Georgia
Louisville, Kentucky
Jackson, Mississippi
Raleigh, North Carolina
Columbia, South Carolina
Nashville, Tennessee

Field Stations:

Anniston, Alabama
Huntsville, Alabama
Montgomery, Alabama
Sheffield, Alabama
Pensacola, Florida
Tallahassee, Florida
Gulfport, Mississippi
Charleston, South Carolina

Region V: Illinois, Indiana, Michigan, Minnesota, Ohio, Wisconsin
230 South Dearborn Street–Room 3263
Chicago, Illinois 60604
Phone: 312-353-2220

Area Offices:

Calumet City, Illinois
Niles, Illinois

North Aurora, Illinois
Peoria, Illinois
Indianapolis, Indiana
Detroit, Michigan
Minneapolis, Minnesota
Cincinnati, Ohio
Cleveland, Ohio
Columbus, Ohio
Toledo, Ohio
Appleton, Wisconsin
Milwaukee, Wisconsin

District Offices:

Belleville, Illinois
Eau Claire, Wisconsin
Madison, Wisconsin

Region VI: Arkansas, Louisiana, New Mexico, Oklahoma, Texas
555 Griffin Square Building–Room 602
Dallas, Texas 75202
Phone: 214-767-4731

Area Offices:

Little Rock, Arkansas
Baton Rouge, Louisiana
New Orleans, Louisiana
Albuquerque, New Mexico
Oklahoma City, Oklahoma
Tulsa, Oklahoma
Austin, Texas
Fort Worth, Texas
Harlingen, Texas
Houston, Texas
Irving, Texas
Lubbock, Texas
San Antonio, Texas
Tyler, Texas

District Office:

Corpus Christi, Texas

Field Stations:

Shreveport, Louisiana
Beaumont, Texas
El Paso, Texas

Region VII: Iowa, Kansas, Missouri, Nebraska
911 Walnut Street–Room 3000
Kansas City, Missouri 64106
Phone: 816-374-5861

Area Offices:

Des Moines, Iowa
Wichita, Kansas

Region VII—Continued
  Area Offices—Continued

   Kansas City, Missouri
   St. Louis, Missouri
   North Platte, Nebraska
   Omaha, Nebraska

Region VIII: Colorado, Montana, North
Dakota, South Dakota, Utah, Wyoming
1961 Stout Street—Room 15042
Denver, Colorado 80294
   Phone: 303-837-3883

Area Offices:

   Lakewood, Colorado
   Billings, Montana
   Bismarck, North Dakota
   Sioux Falls, South Dakota
   Salt Lake City, Utah

Region IX: Arizona, California, Hawaii,
Nevada, Guam, American Samoa, Trust
Territory of the Pacific Islands
450 Golden Gate Avenue—Room 9470
Box 36017
San Francisco, California 94102
   Phone: 415-556-0584

Area Offices:

   Phoenix, Arizona
   Long Beach, California
   San Francisco, California
   Honolulu, Hawaii
   Carson City, Nevada

Field Stations:

   Tucson, Arizona
   Fresno, California
   Sacramento, California
   Las Vegas, Nevada

Region X: Alaska, Idaho, Oregon,
Washington
Federal Office Building—Room 6048
909 First Avenue
Seattle, Washington 98174
   Phone: 206-442-5930

Area Offices:

   Anchorage, Alaska
   Boise, Idaho
   Portland, Oregon
   Bellevue, Washington

Field Stations:

   Coeur D'Alene, Idaho
   Lewiston, Idaho
   Pocatello, Idaho

Appendix B. Participating State Statistical Agencies

Agencies preceded by an asterisk (*) are those in which, as of Janaury 1, 1978, a State safety and health plan under section 18 (b) of the act was in operation. This agency may be contacted directly for specific information regarding regulations in the State.

Alabama Department of Labor
600 Administrative Building
Montgomery, Alabama 36130
Phone: 205-832-6270

* Alaska Department of Labor
Research and Analysis Section
Post Office Box 1149
Juneau, Alaska 99802
Phone: 907- 465- 4520

American Samoa Department of Manpower
Resources
Office of Retirement
Government of American Samoa 96799
Phone: 633-5851

* Arizona Industrial Commission
Post Office Box 19070
Phoenix, Arizona 85007
Phone: 602-271-3739

Arkansas Department of Labor
OSH Statistics—Room 412
1515 West Seventh Street
Little Rock, Arkansas 72202
Phone: 501-371-2770

* California Department of Industrial Relations
Labor Statistics and Research
Post Office Box 603
San Francisco, California 94901
Phone: 415-557-1466

* Colorado Department of Labor and Employment
Division of Labor
1313 Sherman, Room 323
Denver, Colorado 80203
Phone: 303-839-3740

* Connecticut Department of Labor
200 Folly Brook Boulevard
Wethersfield, Connecticut 06109
Phone: 203-566-4380

Delaware Department of Labor
Division of Industrial Affairs
820 No. French Street 6th Fl.
Wilmington, Delaware 19805
Phone: 302-571-2879

District of Columbia Department of
Labor
Division of Occupational Safety and Health
2900 Newton Street, N.E.—1st Flr.
Washington, D.C. 20018
Phone: 202-832-1572

Florida Department of Labor
Division of Labor—Room 208
1321 Executive Center Drive, East
Tallahassee, Florida 32301
Phone: 904-488-5837

Guam Department of Labor
Government of Guam
Post Office Box 2950
Agana, Guam 96910
Phone: 477-9667

* Hawaii Department of Labor
and Industrial Relations
Room 612
1164 Bishop Street
Honolulu, Hawaii 96813
Phone: 808-548-6398

Idaho Industrial Commission
317 Main Street
Boise, Idaho 83707
Phone: 208-384-2529

*Indiana Division of Labor
100 No. Senate Avenue—Room 1013
Indianapolis, Indiana 46204
Phone: 317-633-5845

*Iowa Bureau of Labor
307 East 7th Street
Des Moines, Iowa 50319
Phone: 515-281-5151

Kansas Department of Health and
Environment
Division of Environment
Occupational Safety and Health
Topeka, Kansas 66620
Phone: 913-862-9360 Ext. 209

* Kentucky Department of Labor
Occupational Safety and Health Program
U.S. 127 South
Frankfort, Kentucky 40601
Phone: 502-564-3100

Louisiana Department of Labor
Office of Employment Security—OSH
1001 North 23rd and Fuqua
Baton Rouge, Louisiana 70804
Phone: 504-342- 3126

Maine Department of Manpower Affairs
Bureau of Labor and Industry
Division of Research Statistics
State Office Building—6th Flr.
Augusta, Maine 04333
Phone: 207-289-3331

* Maryland Department of Licensing
and Regulation
Division of Labor and Industry
203 E. Baltimore Street
Baltimore, Maryland 21202
Phone: 301-383-2264

Massachusetts Department of Labor
and Industries
Division of Statistics
100 Cambridge Street
Boston, Massachusetts 02202
Phone: 617-727-3593

* Michigan Department of Labor
7150 Harris Drive, Secondary Complex
Box 30015
Lansing, Michigan 48909
Phone: 517-322- 1851

* Minnesota Department of Labor and
Industry
444 Lafayette Road
Saint Paul, Minnesota 55101
Phone: 612-296-3947

Mississippi State Board of Health
Occupational Safety and Health
Post Office Box 1700
Jackson, Mississippi 39205
Phone: 601-354-7233

Missouri Department of Labor and
Industrial Relations
Division of Workers' Compensation
Post Office Box 58
Jefferson City, Missouri 65102
Phone: 314-751- 4231

Montana Department of Labor and
Industry
Workers' Compensation Division
815 Front Street
Helena, Montana 59601
Phone: 406-449-2994

Nebraska Worker's Compensation Court
State Capitol
Lincoln, Nebraska 68509
Phone: 402-471-2568

* Nevada Department of Industrial Safety
Industrial Commission
515 E. Musser Street
Carson City, Nevada 89714
   Phone: 702-885-5240

New Jersey Department of Labor
   and Industry
Division of Planning and Research
Post Office Box 359
Trenton, New Jersey 08625
   Phone: 609-292-8997

* New Mexico Health and Environment Department
Environmental Improvement Division
Occupational Health and Safety
Post Office Box 968—Crown Building
Santa Fe, New Mexico 87503
   Phone: 505-827-5271 Ext. 230

New York Department of Labor
Division of Research and Statistics
2 World Trade Center
New York, New York 10047
   Phone : 212-488-4661

* North Carolina Department of Labor
Division of Statisitcs
4 West Edenton Street
Raleigh, North Carolina 27601
   Phone: 919-733-4940

Ohio Department of Industrial Relations
OSHA Survey Operations
Post Office Box 12355
Columbus, Ohio 43212
   Phone: 614-466-7520

* Oregon Workers' Compensation Department
Research and Statistical Section
Labor and Industries Building
Salem, Oregon 97310
   Phone: 503-378-8254

Pennsylvania Department of Labor
   and Industry
OSH Statistics
Room 1551
Labor and Industry Building
Harrisburg, Pennsylvania 17120
   Phone: 717-787-1918

* Puerto Rico Department of Labor
   and Human Resources
Bureau of Labor Statistics
414 Barbosa Avenue
Hato Rey, Puerto Rico 00917
   Phone: 809-751-0655

Rhode Island Department of Labor
Division of Statistics
220 Elmwood Avenue
Providence, Rhode Island 02907
   Phone: 401-277-2731

* South Carolina Department of Labor
Division of Research and Statisitcs
Post Office Drawer 11329
Columbia, South Carolina 29211
   Phone: 803-758-8507

South Dakota Department of Health
Public Health Statistics
Foss Building
Pierre, South Dakota 57501
   Phone: 605-773-3355

* Tennessee Department of Labor
Research and Statistics
501 Union Building, 2nd Floor
Nashville, Tennessee 37219
   Phone: 615-741-1748

Texas Department of Health
Division of Occupational Safety
1100 West 49th Street
Austin, Texas 78756
   Phone: 512-454-3781

* Utah Industrial Commission
OSH Statistical Section
448 South 4th East
Salt Lake City, Utah 84111
   Phone: 801-533-5688

* Vermont Department of Labor and
   Industry
State Office Building
Montpelier, Vermont 05602
   Phone: 802-828-2286

* Virgin Islands Department of Labor
Post Office Box 148
St. Thomas, Virgin Islands 00801
   Phone: 809-774-3650

* Virginia Department of Labor and
   Industry
Marketing Research and Services
205 North 4th Street
Post Office Box 12064
Richmond, Virginia 23241
   Phone: 804-786-2384

* Washington Department of Labor
   and Industries
Industrial Safety and Health
308 East 4th Avenue
Post Office Box 207
Olympia, Washington 98504
   Phone: 206-753- 4013

West Virginia Department of Labor
Division of Labor Statistics
Room B437
Building Six, Capitol Complex
1900 Washington Street, East
Charleston, West Virginia 25305
   Phone: 304-348-7890

Wisconsin Department of Industry,
   Labor, and Human Relations
201 E. Washington Avenue
Madison, Wisconsin 53702
   Phone: 608-266-7850

* Wyoming Department of Labor and
   Statistics
Barrett Building, 4th Floor
Cheyenne, Wyoming 82002
   Phone: 307-777-7261

Appendix C. Bureau of Labor Statistical Regional Offices

Region I—Boston
  1603–A Federal Office Building
  Boston, Massachusetts 02203
    Phone: 617-223-4533
      Connecticut
      Maine
      Massachusetts
      New Hampshire
      Rhode Island
      Vermont

Region II—New York
  1515 Broadway
  New York, New York 10036
    Phone: 212-399-5915
      New Jersey
      New York
      Puerto Rico
      Virgin Islands

Region III—Philadelphia
  Post Office Box 13309
  Philadelphia, Pennsylvania 19101
    Phone: 215-596-1162
      Delaware
      District of Columbia
      Maryland
      Pennsylvania
      Virginia
      West Virginia

Region IV—Atlanta
  1371 Peachtree Street, NE.
  Atlanta, Georgia 30309
    Phone: 404-881-3660
      Alabama   Mississippi
      Florida   North Carolina
      Georgia   South Carolina
      Kentucky   Tennessee

Region V—Chicago
  9th Floor Federal Office Building
  230 South Dearborn Street
  Chicago, Illinois 60604
    Phone: 312-353-7253
      Illinois
      Indiana
      Michigan
      Minnesota
      Ohio
      Wisconsin

Region VI—Dallas
  555 Griffin Square Building
  2nd Floor
  Dallas, Texas 75202
    Phone: 214-767-6954
      Arkansas
      Louisiana
      New Mexico
      Oklahoma
      Texas

Regions VII and VIII—Kansas City
  and Denver
  Federal Office Building
  911 Walnut Street
  Kansas City, Missouri 64106
    Phone: 816-374-3685
      Colorado Nebraska
      Iowa   North Dakota
      Kansas   South Dakota
      Missouri Utah
      Montana Wyoming

Regions IX and X—San Francisco
  and Seattle
  450 Golden Gate Avenue
  Box 36017
  San Francisco, California 94102
    Phone: 415-556-8980
      Alaska   Hawaii
      American Samoa Idaho
      Arizona   Nevada
      California   Oregon
      Guam   Washington

ORDER FORM

From: **Name**_____

         Firm_____

         Street Address_____

         City and State_____**ZIP**_____

——Please send me the following items at no charge:
——Recordkeeping Booklets
——Log and Summary of Occupational Injuries and Illnesses (OSHA No. 200)
——Supplementary Record of Occupational Injuries and Illnesses (OSHA No. 101)
——Poster: Job Safety and Health Protection
——Booklet: What Every Employer Needs to Know About OSHA Recordkeeping

ADDRESS LABEL

Please Type or Print

Name_____

Firm_____

Street Address_____

City and State_____**ZIP**_____

ORDER FORM

From: **Name**_____

         Firm_____

         Street Address_____

         City and State_____**ZIP**_____

——Please send me the following items at no charge:
——Recordkeeping Booklets
——Log and Summary of Occupational Injuries and Illnesses (OSHA No. 200)
——Supplementary Record of Occupational Injuries and Illnesses (OSHA No. 101)
——Poster: Job Safety and Health Protection
——Booklet: What Every Employer Needs to Know About OSHA Recordkeeping

ADDRESS LABEL

Please Type or Print

Name_____

Firm_____

Street Address_____

City and State_____**ZIP**_____

29

Bureau of Labor Statistics
Log and Summary of Occupational
Injuries and Illnesses

NOTE:	This form is required by Public Law 91-596 and must be kept in the establishment for *5 years*. Failure to maintain and post can result in the issuance of citations and assessment of penalties. *(See posting requirements on the other side of form.)*

RECORDABLE CASES: You are required to record information about every occupational **death**; every nonfatal occupational **illness**; and those nonfatal occupational **injuries** which involve one or more of the following: loss of consciousness, restriction of work or motion, transfer to another job, or medical treatment (other than first aid). *(See definitions on the other side of form.)*

Case or File Number	Date of Injury or Onset of Illness	Employee's Name	Occupation	Department	Description of Injury or Illness
Enter a nonduplicating number which will facilitate comparisons with supplementary records.	Enter Mo./day.	Enter first name or initial, middle initial, last name.	Enter regular job title, not activity employee was performing when injured or at onset of illness. In the absence of a formal title, enter a brief description of the employee's duties.	Enter department in which the employee is regularly employed or a description of normal workplace to which employee is assigned, even though temporarily working in another department at the time of injury or illness.	Enter a brief description of the injury or illness and indicate the part or parts of body affected. Typical entries for this column might be: Amputation of 1st joint right forefinger; Strain of lower back; Contact dermatitis on both hands; Electrocution—body.
(A)	(B)	(C)	(D)	(E)	(F)
					PREVIOUS PAGE TOTALS →
					TOTALS (Instructions on other side of form.) →

OSHA No. 200

☆ U.S. GOVERNMENT PRINTING OFFICE: 1978—261-018:653

FOLD

U.S. Department of Labor

For Calendar Year 19 _____   Page ____ of ____

Company Name

Establishment Name

Establishment Address

Form Approved
O.M.B. No. 44R 1453

Extent of and Outcome of INJURY						Type, Extent of, and Outcome of ILLNESS												
Fatalities	Nonfatal Injuries					Type of Illness							Fatalities	Nonfatal Illnesses				
Injury Related	Injuries With Lost Workdays				Injuries Without Lost Workdays	CHECK Only One Column for Each Illness *(See other side of form for terminations or permanent transfers.)*							Illness Related	Illnesses With Lost Workdays				Illnesses Without Lost Workdays
Enter DATE of death. Mo./day/yr.	Enter a CHECK if injury involves days away from work, or days of restricted work activity, or both.	Enter a CHECK if injury involves days away from work.	Enter number of DAYS *away from work.*	Enter number of DAYS of *restricted work activity.*	Enter a CHECK if no entry was made in columns 1 or 2 but the injury is recordable as defined above.	Occupational skin diseases or disorders	Dust diseases of the lungs	Respiratory conditions due to toxic agents	Poisoning (systemic effects of toxic materials)	Disorders due to physical agents	Disorders associated with repeated trauma	All other occupational illnesses	Enter DATE of death. Mo./day/yr.	Enter a CHECK if illness involves days away from work, or days of restricted work activity, or both.	Enter a CHECK if illness involves days away from work.	Enter number of DAYS *away from work.*	Enter number of DAYS of *restricted work activity.*	Enter a CHECK if no entry was made in columns 8 or 9.
(1)	(2)	(3)	(4)	(5)	(6)	(7)							(8)	(9)	(10)	(11)	(12)	(13)
						(a)	(b)	(c)	(d)	(e)	(f)	(g)						

Certification of Annual Summary Totals By _____ Title _____ Date _____

OSHA No. 200   **POST ONLY THIS PORTION OF THE LAST PAGE NO LATER THAN FEBRUARY 1.**

Instructions for OSHA No. 200

I.   Log and Summary of Occupational Injuries and Illnesses

Each employer who is subject to the recordkeeping requirements of the Occupational Safety and Health Act of 1970 must maintain for each establishment a log of all recordable occupational injuries and illnesses. This form (OSHA No. 200) may be used for that purpose. A substitute for the OSHA No. 200 is acceptable if it is as detailed, easily readable, and understandable as the OSHA No. 200.

Enter each recordable case on the log within six (6) workdays after learning of its occurrence. Although other records must be maintained at the establishment to which they refer, it is possible to prepare and maintain the log at another location, using data processing equipment if desired. If the log is prepared elsewhere, a copy updated to within 45 calendar days must be present at all times in the establishment.

Logs must be maintained and retained for five (5) years following the end of the calendar year to which they relate. Logs must be available (normally at the establishment) for inspection and copying by representatives of the Department of Labor, or the Department of Health, Education and Welfare, or States accorded jurisdiction under the Act.

II. Changes in Extent of or Outcome of Injury or Illness

If, during the 5-year period the log must be retained, there is a change in an extent and outcome of an injury or illness which affects entries in columns 1, 2, 6, 8, 9, or 13, the first entry should be lined out and a new entry made. For example, if an injured employee at first required only medical treatment but later lost workdays away from work, the check in column 6 should be lined out, and checks entered in columns 2 and 3 and the number of lost workdays entered in column 4.

In another example, if an employee with an occupational illness lost workdays, returned to work, and then died of the illness, any entries in columns 9 through 12 should be lined out and the date of death entered in column 8.

The entire entry for an injury or illness should be lined out if later found to be nonrecordable. For example: an injury which is later determined not to be work related, or which was initially thought to involve medical treatment but later was determined to have involved only first aid.

III. Posting Requirements

A copy of the totals and information following the fold line of the last page for the year must be posted at each establishment in the place or places where notices to employees are customarily posted. This copy must be posted no later than *February 1 and must remain in place until March 1.*

Even though there were no injuries or illnesses during the year, zeros must be entered on the totals line, and the form posted.

The person responsible for the *annual summary totals* shall certify that the totals are true and complete by signing at the bottom of the form.

IV. Instructions for Completing Log and Summary of Occupational Injuries and Illnesses

Column A — CASE OR FILE NUMBER. Self-explanatory.

Column B — DATE OF INJURY OR ONSET OF ILLNESS. For occupational injuries, enter the date of the work accident which resulted in injury. For occupational illnesses, enter the date of initial diagnosis of illness, or, if absence from work occurred before diagnosis, enter the first day of the absence attributable to the illness which was later diagnosed or recognized.

Columns
C through F— Self-explanatory.

Columns
1 and 8 — INJURY OR ILLNESS-RELATED DEATHS. Self-explanatory.

Columns
2 and 9 — INJURIES OR ILLNESSES WITH LOST WORKDAYS. Self-explanatory.

Any injury which involves days away from work, or days of restricted work activity, or both must be recorded since it always involves one or more of the criteria for recordability.

Columns
3 and 10 — INJURIES OR ILLNESSES INVOLVING DAYS AWAY FROM WORK. Self-explanatory.

Columns
4 and 11 — LOST WORKDAYS––DAYS AWAY FROM WORK. Enter the number of workdays (consecutive or not) on which the employee would have worked but could not because of occupational injury or illness. The number of lost workdays should not include the day of injury or onset of illness or any days on which the employee would not have worked even though able to work.
NOTE: For employees not having a regularly scheduled shift, such as certain truck drivers, construction workers, farm labor, casual labor, part-time employees, etc., it may be necessary to estimate the number of lost workdays. Estimates of lost workdays shall be based on prior work history of the employee AND days worked by employees, not ill or injured, working in the department and/or occupation of the ill or injured employee.

Columns
5 and 12 — LOST WORKDAYS––DAYS OF RESTRICTED WORK ACTIVITY. Enter the number of workdays (consecutive or not) on which because of injury or illness:
(1)   the employee was assigned to another job on a temporary basis, or
(2)   the employee worked at a permanent job less than full time, or
(3)   the employee worked at a permanently assigned job but could not perform all duties normally connected with it.

The number of lost workdays should not include the day of injury or onset of illness or any days on which the employee would not have worked even though able to work.

Columns
6 and 13 — INJURIES OR ILLNESSES WITHOUT LOST WORKDAYS. Self-explanatory.

Columns 7a
through 7g — TYPE OF ILLNESS.
Enter a check in only *one* column for each illness.

TERMINATION OR PERMANENT TRANSFER—Place an asterisk to the right of the entry in columns 7a through 7g (type of illness) which represented a termination of employment or permanent transfer.

V. Totals

Add number of entries in columns 1 and 8.
Add number of checks in columns 2, 3, 6, 7, 9, 10, and 13.
Add number of days in columns 4, 5, 11, and 12.
Yearly totals for each column (1-13) are required for posting. Running or page totals may be generated at the discretion of the employer.

If an employee's loss of workdays is continuing at the time the totals are summarized, estimate the number of future workdays the employee will lose and add that estimate to the workdays already lost and include this figure in the annual totals. No further entries are to be made with respect to such cases in the next year's log.

VI. Definitions

OCCUPATIONAL INJURY is any injury such as a cut, fracture, sprain, amputation, etc., which results from a work accident or from an exposure involving a single incident in the work environment.
NOTE: Conditions resulting from animal bites, such as insect or snake bites or from one-time exposure to chemicals, are considered to be injuries.

OCCUPATIONAL ILLNESS of an employee is any abnormal condition or disorder, other than one resulting from an occupational injury, caused by exposure to environmental factors associated with employment. It includes acute and chronic illnesses or diseases which may be caused by inhalation, absorption, ingestion, or direct contact.

The following listing gives the categories of occupational illnesses and disorders that will be utilized for the purpose of classifying recordable illnesses. For purposes of information, examples of each category are given. These are typical examples, however, and are not to be considered the complete listing of the types of illnesses and disorders that are to be counted under each category.

7a. **Occupational Skin Diseases or Disorders**
Examples: Contact dermatitis, eczema, or rash caused by primary irritants and sensitizers or poisonous plants; oil acne; chrome ulcers; chemical burns or inflammations; etc.

7b. **Dust Diseases of the Lungs (Pneumoconioses)**
Examples: Silicosis, asbestosis, coal worker's pneumoconiosis, byssinosis, siderosis, and other pneumoconioses.

7c. **Respiratory Conditions Due to Toxic Agents**
Examples: Pneumonitis, pharyngitis, rhinitis or acute congestion due to chemicals, dusts, gases, or fumes; farmer's lung; etc.

7d. **Poisoning (Systemic Effect of Toxic Materials)**
Examples: Poisoning by lead, mercury, cadmium, arsenic, or other metals; poisoning by carbon monoxide, hydrogen sulfide, or other gases; poisoning by benzol, carbon tetrachloride, or other organic solvents; poisoning by insecticide sprays such as parathion, lead arsenate; poisoning by other chemicals such as formaldehyde, plastics, and resins; etc.

7e. **Disorders Due to Physical Agents (Other than Toxic Materials)**
Examples: Heatstroke, sunstroke, heat exhaustion, and other effects of environmental heat; freezing, frostbite, and effects of exposure to low temperatures; caisson disease; effects of ionizing radiation (isotopes, X-rays, radium); effects of nonionizing radiation (welding flash, ultraviolet rays, microwaves, sunburn); etc.

7f. **Disorders Associated With Repeated Trauma**
Examples: Noise-induced hearing loss; synovitis, tenosynovitis, and bursitis; Raynaud's phenomena; and other conditions due to repeated motion, vibration, or pressure.

7g. **All Other Occupational Illnesses**
Examples: Anthrax, brucellosis, infectious hepatitis, malignant and benign tumors, food poisoning, histoplasmosis, coccidioidomycosis, etc.

MEDICAL TREATMENT includes treatment (other than first aid) administered by a physician or by registered professional personnel under the standing orders of a physician. Medical treatment does NOT include first-aid treatment (one-time treatment and subsequent observation of minor scratches, cuts, burns, splinters, and so forth, which do not ordinarily require medical care) even though provided by a physician or registered professional personnel.

ESTABLISHMENT: A single physical location where business is conducted or where services or industrial operations are performed (for example: a factory, mill, store, hotel, restaurant, movie theater, farm, ranch, bank, sales office, warehouse, or central administrative office). Where distinctly separate activities are performed at a single physical location, such as construction activities operated from the same physical location as a lumber yard, each activity shall be treated as a separate establishment.

For firms engaged in activities which may be physically dispersed, such as agriculture; construction; transportation; communications; and electric, gas, and sanitary services, records may be maintained at a place to which employees report each day.

Records for personnel who do not primarily report or work at a single establishment, such as traveling salesmen, technicians, engineers, etc., shall be maintained at the location from which they are paid or the base from which personnel operate to carry out their activities.

WORK ENVIRONMENT is comprised of the physical location, equipment, materials processed or used, and the kinds of operations performed in the course of an employee's work, whether on or off the employer's premises.

OSHA No. 101   Form approved
Case or File No. ------------   OMB No. 44R 1453

Supplementary Record of Occupational Injuries and Illnesses

EMPLOYER

    1. Name --

    2. Mail address --
          (No. and street)   (City or town)   (State)

    3. Location, if different from mail address --

INJURED OR ILL EMPLOYEE

    4. Name -- Social Security No. ------------------
          (First name)   (Middle name)   (Last name)

    5. Home address --
          (No. and street)   (City or town)   (State)

    6. Age --------------   7. Sex: Male------------ Female------------ (Check one)

    8. Occupation --
          (Enter regular job title, *not* the specific activity he was performing at time of injury.)

    9. Department --
          (Enter name of department or division in which the injured person is regularly employed, even
          though he may have been temporarily working in another department at the time of injury.)

THE ACCIDENT OR EXPOSURE TO OCCUPATIONAL ILLNESS

    10. Place of accident or exposure --
           (No. and street)   (City or town)   (State)
        If accident or exposure occurred on employer's premises, give address of plant or establishment in which
        it occurred. Do not indicate department or division within the plant or establishment. If accident oc-
        curred outside employer's premises at an identifiable address, give that address. If it occurred on a pub-
        lic highway or at any other place which cannot be identified by number and street, please provide place
        references locating the place of injury as accurately as possible.

    11. Was place of accident or exposure on employer's premises? -------------- (Yes or No)

    12. What was the employee doing when injured? ---
                      (Be specific. If he was using tools or equipment or handling material,
----
          name them and tell what he was doing with them.)
----

    13. How did the accident occur? ---
                  (Describe fully the events which resulted in the injury or occupational illness. Tell **what**
----
happened and how it happened. Name any objects or substances involved and tell how they were involved. Give
----
full details on all factors which led or contributed to the accident. Use separate sheet for additional space.)

OCCUPATIONAL INJURY OR OCCUPATIONAL ILLNESS

    14. Describe the injury or illness in detail and indicate the part of body affected. --------------------
                                      (e.g.: amputation of right index finger
----
          at second joint; fracture of ribs; lead poisoning; dermatitis of left hand, etc.)

    15. Name the object or substance which directly injured the employee. (For example, the machine or thing
        he struck against or which struck him; the vapor or poison he inhaled or swallowed; the chemical or ra-
        diation which irritated his skin; or in cases of strains, hernias, etc., the thing he was lifting, pulling, etc.)

----

    16. Date of injury or initial diagnosis of occupational illness -----------------------------------
                                       (Date)

    17. Did employee die? ------------ (Yes or No)

OTHER

    18. Name and address of physician ---

    19. If hospitalized, name and address of hospital ---

    Date of report ---------------- Prepared by --

    Official position ----------------------------

SUPPLEMENTARY RECORD OF
OCCUPATIONAL INJURIES
AND ILLNESSES

To supplement the Log and Summary of Occupational Injuries and Illnesses (OSHA No. 200), each establishment must maintain a record of each recordable occupational injury or illness. Worker's compensation, insurance, or other reports are acceptable as records if they contain all facts listed below or are supplemented to do so. If no suitable report is made for other purposes, this form (OSHA No. 101) may be used or the necessary facts can be listed on a separate plain sheet of paper. These records must also be available in the establishment without delay and at reasonable times for examination by representatives of the Department of Labor and the Department of Health, Education and Welfare, and States accorded jurisdiction under the Act. The records must be maintained for a period of not less than five years following the end of the calendar year to which they relate.

Such records must contain at least the following facts:

1) *About the employer*—name. mail address, and location if different from mail address.

2) *About the injured or ill employee*—name, social security number, home address, age, sex, occupation, and department.

3) *About the accident or exposure to occupational illness*—place of accident or exposure, whether it was on employer's premises, what the employee was doing when injured, and how the accident occurred.

4) *About the occupational injury or illness*—description of the injury or illness, including part of body affected; name of the object or substance which directly injured the employee; and date of injury or diagnosis of illness.

5) *Other*—name and address of physician; if hospitalized, name and address of hospital; date of report; and name and position of person preparing the report.

SEE *DEFINITIONS* ON THE BACK OF OSHA FORM 200.

Bibliography of Selected References

Amendola, Joseph, and Berrini, James, *Practical Cooking and Baking for Schools and Institutions,* Ahrens Publishing Co., Inc., N.Y., 1971.

Boutell, Wayne S., *Computer-Oriented Business Systems,* Prentice-Hall, Inc., Englewood Cliffs, N.J., 1968.

Brodner, Joseph, Maschal, Henry T., Carlson, Howard M., *Profitable Food and Beverage Operation,* Rev. 4th Ed., Hayden Books Co., Inc., Rochelle Park, N.J., 1962.

Coltman, Michael M., *Food and Beverage Cost Control,* Prentice-Hall, Inc., Englewood Cliffs, N.J., 1977 (Prentice-Hall Series in Foodservice Management).

Culinary Institute of America, The, and the Editors of *Institutions* Magazine, 4th Ed., "The Professional Chef," Institutions/Volume Feeding Mag., Distributed by Cahners Books, Boston, Mass., 1974.

Dukas, Peter, *How to Plan and Operate a Restaurant,* Rev. 2nd Ed., Ahrens Series, Hayden Books Co. Inc., Rochelle Park, N.J., 1973.

Haines, Robert G., 2nd Ed., *Food Preparation for Hotels, Restaurants, and Cafeterias,* American Technology Society, Chicago, 1973.

Kahrl, *Introduction to Modern Food and Beverage Service,* Prentice-Hall, Inc., Englewood Cliffs, N.J., 1977.

Kahrl, *Advanced Modern Food and Beverage Service,* Prentice-Hall, Inc., Englewood Cliffs, N.J., 1977.

Levitt, Theodore, "Marketing Myopia," *Modern Marketing Strategy,* Editors: Edward C. Bursk and John F. Chapman, Harvard University Press, Cambridge, Mass., 1964.

Solomon, Kenneth I., and Katz, Norman, *Profitable Restaurant Management,* Prentice-Hall, Inc., Englewood Cliffs, N.J., 1974.

Olney, Richard, *The French Menu Cookbook,* Simon & Schuster, N.Y., 1970.

Wilkinson, Jule, *The Complete Book of Cooking Equipment,* Rev. Ed., Cahners Books, Inc., Boston, Mass., 1975.

Wolfe, Kenneth C., *Cooking for the Professional Chef,* Van Nostrand-Reinhold Co., N.Y., 1976.

INDEX